KINSKI
UNCUT

Also by Klaus Kinski

Kinski Paganini

KINSKI

THE AUTOBIOGRAPHY OF KLAUS KINSKI

UNCUT

TRANSLATED FROM GERMAN BY
JOACHIM NEUGRÖSCHEL

VIKING

VIKING
Published by the Penguin Group
Penguin Books USA Inc., 375 Hudson Street, New York, New York 10014, U.S.A.
Penguin Books Ltd, 27 Wrights Lane, London W8 5TZ, England
Penguin Books Australia Ltd, Ringwood, Victoria, Australia
Penguin Books Canada Ltd, 10 Alcorn Avenue, Toronto, Ontario, Canada M4V 3B2
Penguin Books (N.Z.) Ltd, 182–190 Wairau Road, Auckland 10, New Zealand

Penguin Books Ltd, Registered Offices:
Harmondsworth, Middlesex, England

This edition first published in 1996 by
Viking Penguin, a division of Penguin Books USA Inc.

10   9   8   7   6   5   4   3   2   1

Previously published in German as *Kinski: Ich Brauche Liebe*
by Wilhelm Heyne Verlag, 1991.

Photographs courtesy of the Estate of Klaus Kinski unless otherwise indicated.

LIBRARY OF CONGRESS CATALOGING-IN-PUBLICATION DATA
Kinski, Klaus.
    [Ich brauche Liebe.   English]
    Kinski uncut : the autobiography of Klaus Kinski / translated from German by
Joachim Neugröschel.
        p.   cm.
    Includes index.
    ISBN 0-670-86744-6
    1. Kinski, Klaus.   2. Actors—Germany—Biography.   I. Title.
PN2658.K52A3   1996
791.43'028'092—dc20
    [B]   96-4921

This book is printed on acid-free paper.

Printed in the United States of America
Set in Bulmer
Designed by Junie Lee

We are cripples, we artists. Our art is nothing, because our tools are too dull to get at the essence and express it. Christ alone has that ability. He affects us directly without writing, without painting; at every moment he transforms his entire life into an artwork.
—*Vincent van Gogh*

For my son, Nanhoï, whom I love more than anything in the world.

KINSKI
UNCUT

"Wanted: Jesus Christ. Occupation: worker. Address: unknown. He has no religion. He belongs to no party. He is never seen at public assemblies. He is accused of larceny, contributing to the delinquency of minors, blasphemy, desecrating churches, insulting authority, flouting laws, consorting with whores and criminals—"

Now some jerk in the audience heckles me. I can't see him. I'm blinded by powerful spotlights, all focusing on me. The auditorium of Berlin's Deutschlandhalle (capacity: about twenty thousand people) is a pitch-black wall.

Why is that idiot harassing me? I'm wired. I've been on my feet for over seventy hours, I haven't slept a wink for several nights. Endless TV and radio interviews, newspapers. Plus I've eaten nothing and smoked at least eighty cigarettes since yesterday morning. And now I'm standing on this high scaffold as if it were a gallows.

"Come up here if you've got something to say," I shout into the darkness. "Otherwise stay on your butt and keep your trap shut!"

What does he want? Is he trying to sound important? The only important thing now is what I have to recite. I've come here to tell the most exciting story in the history of mankind: the life of Jesus Christ.

I'm not talking about the Jesus in those horribly gaudy pictures. Not the Jesus with the jaundice-yellow skin—whom a crazy human society has turned into the biggest whore of all time. Whose corpse they perversely drag around on disgraceful crosses. I don't mean the jabbering about God or the blubbering hymns. I don't mean the Jesus whose moldy kiss frightens little girls out of horny dreams before their First Communion and then makes them die of shame and disgust when they foam in the latrines.

I'm talking about the man: *the restless man who says we have to turn over a new leaf all the time, now! I'm talking about the adventurer, the freest, most fearless, most modern of all men, the one who preferred being massacred to rotting with others. I'm talking about the man who is like what all of us want to be. You and I.*

Meanwhile, the shithead who interrupted me has arrived on the scaffold. I hand him the mike because I haven't the foggiest clue what he's after.

"Christ was a saint," the bastard howls, "he never consorted with whores and criminals. . . . He wasn't as violent as Kinski. . . ."

What do you call "violent," you blabbermouth? Yeah, I've got violence in me, but no negative violence. My violence is the violence of the free man who refuses to knuckle under. Creation is violent. Life is violent. Birth is a violent process. Tempests and earthquakes are violent movements of nature. My violence is the violence of life. It is not violence against nature, like the violence of the state, which sends your kids to the slaughterhouse, deadens your minds, and drives out your souls!

I grab the mike from that moron's hand because he refuses to give it back to me. The bouncers take care of the rest. When he tries to fight them, they simply throw him down the stairs. Other brawlers, who have only come to raise a rumpus, join in. When the first punches start smashing away, a huge police contingent fans out to prevent a free-for-all. The cops whack away with clubs in their hands and protective helmets on their faces.

Oh well, I think, it's just like two thousand years ago.

I hurl out the mike and the tripod, which is attached to a long cable hanging from the ceiling, from the scaffold. Then I go backstage and wait to see what happens, while the tripod zooms back and forth like an empty trapeze over the heads of the spectators.

Flash bulbs flashing all over the place. Movie cameras whirring. Reporters asking idiotic questions. It's all turning my stomach. I yell at the vultures who circle me nonstop—I can't get rid of them, they sneak behind me even when I take a piss.

Spectators come dashing backstage, hugging and kissing me. People who've seen me at thousands of performances when I tore my heart from my body and held it out to them. Minhoï clings to my neck and cries. She's scared and worried about me; she's never seen me on stage. People beg me to get back on the scaffold. Yes! The show'll go on. But only when these rowdies stop smashing faces and, above all, keep their traps shut! This riffraff is even more fucked up than the Pharisees. At least they let Jesus finish talking before they nailed him to the cross.

The spectators are still out in force; none of them wants to go home. They're all waiting for me to come back.

Midnight. The place slowly calms down. No one coughs. No one clears his throat. Now there's total silence.

A lot of spectators have left their back rows and are thronging the empty space in front of the scaffold. Camping on the floor. It's Woodstock.

I jump down from the scaffold and join them. My exhaustion has vanished. I no longer feel my body. I see them very clearly in front of me: their faces; the finest reaction in each individual face. Thousands of eyes gazing at me. Yearning eyes, ablaze with passion. I go from one spectator to the next. Stand in front of them. Sit down with them. Hug them. Girls and boys, women and men of all ages.

I once asked a Gypsy girlfriend whether she ever went to the theater or the movies, and she replied: "When I was fourteen, two men fought with knives over me. One stabbed the other to death. I touched the dead man; he was really dead. The other was really alive."

That's the difference between make-believe life and real life. Mine is real.

"Don't move," says my father, bowing to me.

I usually don't obey him. But he begs so urgently that I halt out of curiosity.

What's he up to? Why shouldn't I go in with him? Does he even have the money to enter a place like that? I don't have time to verbalize my thoughts. My father has already stepped inside the crowded boutique.

I don't move. I only shift occasionally from one leg to the other because my feet are burning in my tight shoes.

I've often wondered why my father bows to small children. This is what I think: My father, who claims he used to be an opera singer, got into the habit of bowing when he was doing a guest performance in Japan. Once I watched my father at a mirror. He didn't realize he was being watched. He was making faces, breathtaking grimaces with the hypnotic power of Kabuki masks. He gestured and yanked open his mouth as if he were about to sing. His chest rose and sank intensely; even the vein in his neck swelled. But, weirdly enough, not a sound emerged from his throat.

"There you are!" I thought. "You saw for yourself that he can't sing!"

I believe that his story is a hoax. None of us has ever heard my father sing. In any case, my father is a pharmacist and not an opera singer.

Nobody knows where my father comes from or what he's done. Gossip has it that he had no parents. Maybe that's why he bows to little children. That's all we know. He never confides in anyone.

We street kids call my father "Baldie," "Turnip," "Bulli," or simply "Bulb." And his bald pate really does shine like a light bulb. He's nicknamed Turnip because when he shaves his head, it sounds as if he were scraping a turnip. He really shouldn't be using the rusty razor, which is covered with nicks like an old weeder. Even my mother, who's normally quite deft, has hacked out whole pieces of his skin.

Only very seldom does he go to a real barber. The barber applies his perilously sharp blade like a Jewish slaughterer, and he has never injured my father. My mother spied on him. She pressed her face up against the barbershop window and breathlessly watched the slaughterer nimbly pirouetting around my father's baldness. When the shaving was done, my father deliberately and snottily flung sixty cents on the table even though the shave cost only fifty.

My father always tries to look chic in order to camouflage his poverty. It's not so easy, for his so-called wardrobe, which consists exclusively of whatever he's wearing, can peel off him at any moment, the way rotten flesh peels off a leper. I believe that's why he moves so gingerly, never leans on anything, never crooks his knees or elbows, never bends down, never sits, always stands. In short, his movements are spare because he doesn't want to put a strain on his clothes. I suspect that he never dares to take a deep breath except when he's naked.

The worn, greasy ass of his trousers, the puffed-out knees and elbows are so threadbare that you can see his skin shimmering through the weave.

His shoes, as glossy as mirrors, are so brittle that they could disintegrate any moment now. He constantly seems to guard against bumping into anything. I feel as if he floats rather than walks. He barely grazes the ground. He probably moves like that chiefly because of his shoe soles, which are detached from the leather uppers all the way to the trouser strap. Normally, with each forward step of a foot, such a sole would clap shut like a crocodile's maw and then bang loudly on the ground. But my father has devised a method to prevent anyone from discovering the catastrophic state of his shoes. He doesn't bend his knees while walking; instead, he lifts his entire leg directly from the hip as if it were on a rubber band, gently raising it from the ground and forward; by this means the shoe sole snuggles against the upper leather. Then he places his foot back on the ground, as smoothly as a yo-yo.

But everyone first gapes at my father's monocle anyway. It's not really a monocle, it's a loose, cloudy eyeglass lens. However, my father has the nerve to wedge this shard into his left socket. This eye can't see without the monocle. His right eye is totally blind. In any case, because of the mock-up monocle his hair-raising clothes are out of danger, and no one makes fun of them.

It's been ages since he went inside the boutique. I look all around for a place to take a leak. I'm slowly losing patience.

He's nicknamed Bulli not only because of his thick dick and his big balls. "Bulli" is also short for "bulldog." Not because he's bald (English bulldogs always look bald), but because of his entire face. Everything on it droops as if he had too much skin. On his neck and forehead, the creases, which are as deep as scars, end abruptly at his bald head.

I once heard him say, "The jaws of bulldogs and sharks can't be pried apart once their double rows of teeth sink into something. That's why those animals are so dangerous."

While I don't believe that my father would try to bite anyone, I did hope for a while that people would be scared of him. Not only because of his bulldog face. His muscles are unusually strong, and he's as broad as an athlete.

But I was mistaken. A stranger can't see my father's muscles, and so he cynically thinks, Jerk. Or, Baldie. When dressed my father looks slender. His bulldog face makes no impact; people just poke fun at it. I had to learn that bulldogs are considered freaks by amateurs, which is what most people are. They are said to be totally harmless, and they are so rare in Germany that they tend to be unknown. In fact, I once heard a little boy say to his mother when a bulldog waddled by, "Look, Mom, a pig."

So I know my father is regarded at best as a harmless pig. That pains me. For I love my father, and I wish other people were scared of him. If you're poor your only weapon is to instill fear.

I'm so dizzy from strenuous thinking and from hunger that I'm in something like a state of intoxication. . . . Suddenly my father comes scooting out of the boutique and I hear a voice shrieking, "Stop, thief! Bang him on his bald head! Grab him, hold him!"

It's the shopkeeper, who's stumbling over me and yanking me around so that I crash into the fruit stands outside his store. The apples zoom in all directions. I quickly gather some into my apron and get the hell out of there without knowing where to turn.

Panting, weighed down by the apples in my apron, cursing our poverty, the robbing, the store owner, and my father, who started this goddamn mess in the first place.

I bang one fist into my spleen, while the other fist clutches the apron with the apples, which keep swinging into my legs, interfering with my running.

The slamming of my soles on the hard asphalt echoes in my skull like a carpet beater. My huffing and puffing stab into my lungs like a knife. The world goes black before my eyes . . . and I notice that I'm pissing in my pants. Too late to open my fly. I feel the hot liquid streaming down the insides of my thighs. I didn't want to embarrass my father by pissing against a building wall.

"Where the hell is he?"

Swearing like a trooper I kick away all the stones in my path. Even though my mother warned me not to do that because this is my only pair of shoes.

All at once a gigantic hand grabs my collar and pulls me into a building entrance. Whirling around, I see it's my father. Thick drops of sweat cover his baldness.

"Papa, what's wrong?"

Instead of replying, he sobs like a little boy and hugs me so violently that he squeezes all the air out of me. He squashes a bar of chocolate in his cramped fist.

Aside from the mayhem he triggered, is chocolate all he bagged? And only one bar? And for that one bar he made me spend over an hour standing in the street in tight shoes and with a full bladder? I start frisking him so far as I can while I'm caught in his paws. Nothing! He's really got nothing else! And why is he crying? My eyes are glued to the chocolate; I'm worried he's gonna wreck it totally.

"Why are you crying, Papa?"

I try to wriggle out of his sweat box. He's so absorbed in his emotions that he doesn't realize he's almost choking me. He tries to say something but his voice dissolves into further sobs.

Is he embarrassed because his little expedition was a wild goose chase? Is he still terrified through and through? That's no reason to cry. And what if it's not the reason? What if he's ashamed that he stole something, and decides to blab first chance he gets? Shit! He'll just put everyone in danger if he can't get hold of himself.

My father never has money because he doesn't have a job. Even though he's been wearing his heels flat looking for work, it never pans out. Either no one wants him or else he gets kicked out within four weeks. I don't know why, but it always turns into a fight.

Is that why you sacrificed the best years of your youth, burning the midnight oil cramming Greek and Latin? To become a common laborer, to steal a bar of chocolate when you're sixty, to run away from some clown, and to cry because you're ashamed? What are you surprised at? Isn't it quite in order that each pharmacy owner can toss you out on your ear if he feels like it? "What nerve!" you say. "Knowledge is worth more than money," you claim. Don't make me laugh! You're a laborer. You can never even dream of comparing yourself to a pharmacy owner! You'd have to toil for years, for decades—for centuries—to pay for your own drugstore, unless you robbed a bank! No, no! You're gonna remain a laborer. A well-educated man, but a laborer all the same. In any event, you're unimportant; otherwise they'd give you a job.

I feel a desire to do something for him, help him, protect him. I yank insanely on the fists that he bores into his eyes.

"Please stop crying, Papa. Papa! Dear Papa!"

One thing is certain: We can never allow him to go shoplifting again. And definitely not by himself. And besides, I can't take all that waiting in front of the store and then that running.

He clings to me so beseechingly, as if he were begging, "Let me try it just one more time."

I know—it's not easy to stop stealing once you've tasted blood. But goddammit, you shouldn't let it get out of hand. He has to see that he's not much of a shoplifter. He's simply not tough enough. And his face and bald head make him stand out. He's just not the type.

This is an especially awful day. We haven't eaten in forty-eight hours.

A week ago I was groping through the pitch-black hallway and I bumped into one of those repulsive pieces of furniture with which the landlord has blocked up the entire house. They all look like enameled coffins. I hurt my ankle, which has swollen badly. It's put an end to my thieving. The tiny emergency reserve of money was used up days ago, and I feel so sick that I have to sit on the stoop for a long time until I feel strong enough to limp to my grocery store. Today I'm going to get there no matter what, even if I have to crawl on all fours. My mother sits down next to me.

"Don't you have sharp pains?"

"It's all right."

"My poor dear has to put up with so much now."

"I'm no sissy!"

"Sorry. At least come inside."

"I don't wanna."

"You shouldn't go outdoors with your bad ankle. Besides, this just isn't the right place for my little darling."

She is promptly taken aback by her own nonsense.

"Where is the right place for me, Mom?"

My mother is terribly embarrassed; she lovingly tugs at my hair, purring like a cat, hemming and hawing, trying to come up with something meaningful.

"Is your ankle very hot? Do you want me to put another compress on it?"

"No, thanks. It's not very hot."

"We'll all get something to eat today—you can count on it."

Like the rest of us, she clings to that obsessive notion, which keeps us going from hour to hour.

"Yes, Mom."

What I really want to say is: You can count on the fact that I won't give up. That nothing and no one will force me to my knees. That some day I will pay you back for your courageous love. That I will make sure you don't have to drudge like a convict. That someday I will earn so much money that I'll be able to buy you a winter coat, mittens, and warm shoes for your chilblains. That you will drink as much real coffee as you like, and eat rolls and butter and real honey.

Yes, that's what I'd like to say. But I don't, because I want to surprise her someday.

"It'll never again get as bad as today, don't worry, my little dump—"

"No, Mom."

Her throat is dry from lying.

"Everything'll work out," she whispers very close to my face.

I slowly swallow the lump in my throat to keep from bursting into tears. I mustn't wimp out. I need all my strength for what I'm about to do.

"Yes, Mom."

Her mouth twists into a weak, cautious smile; she avoids exposing her ruined teeth.

"Aren't you scared of your toothless mom?"

"Don't keep saying 'toothless mom'!"

"But it's true. Anyone can I see that I have almost no teeth left, even though I'm still so young. Sometimes I worry that you're ashamed of me."

"That's not true! I want you to kiss me all my life, even without teeth!"

She takes my head into her strong worker's hands and presses it into her open lap, so that I inhale her arousing smell. I keep my face very close to her firm abdomen, and my lips graze her hot belly and her small, impudent tits, until my mouth is on hers. She spreads her damp lip flesh out over me, and her gigantic, beautiful eyes shine like glass marbles in her starving face.

As soon as I'm alone I struggle to my feet, hobble as fast as I can along the street, and crawl into my place under the wooden shelves outside the grocery store, where the merchandise is piled up in mounds or pyramids.

I mustn't make a false move, lose my nerve, or shiver. For delicate work like this you have to have a calm hand, sensitive fingers. As if you were playing tiddlywinks.

The free space under the wooden shelves is very low. I have to stay crouched to avoid banging into the racks and making them wobble. I have to twist my spine like spaghetti, forcing my head facedown, low and forward. I wrench my head on my left or right ear—it all depends—and press my knees against my tense throat. Right on the Adam's apple. My butt has to stay down without bumping on the cobblestones; otherwise I'll tumble backward. My stomach, liver, and gallbladder squeeze so tight against my heart and chest that the blood dams up in my veins and I can only breathe in short gasps. My apron hangs from my knees, lying on the cobblestones. Its big pocket is where I'll stash the goods.

Once I've gotten into this position, I can't risk changing it, except maybe by lifting either foot like a chicken. But I can't draw my feet in like a chicken.

My swollen ankle really hurts when I squat like this. Whenever I can, I'll shift my whole body weight to my healthy foot. Maybe the pain will let up a bit, and I won't have to yell. But if I can't help yelling, I'll stuff a potato or something into my mouth.

The shopkeeper, whom I recognize by the cheesy stench of his feet, keeps coming outside to build up all sorts of wares or remove something from the stands. What a pedant! He keeps feeling everything up, and his stinky feet stay right in front of my nose for an eternity. I can escape the stench very briefly by simply not breathing—until my head almost bursts and I have to inhale a little of the stench to avoid writhing. Otherwise I can't do a thing while Cheesy-Feet hangs around.

If Cheesy-Feet comes out unexpectedly, I have to freeze in mid-motion. That's like playing *tableaux vivants,* where you split your sides over the craziest petrified gestures. Except that in my tight squeeze I don't feel like laughing.

The pain in my ankle gets so unbearable that I shove a cabbage leaf into my mouth so as not to shriek. . . .

I must have fainted temporarily, but then I come to, with the cabbage leaf in my mouth. Panicking like a cornered rat, I try to free myself from my agonizing position. No use. My body is dead all the way down to my tippy-toes. My ears are burning. I feel a stabbing pain in my chest. My nose is dripping blood on my shoes.

It's dark out by now. What time is it, for God's sake? What if the store's about to close? The goods on display may be taken inside any moment! And I've got nothing in my apron! Grabbing anything I can get my numb fingers on, I nearly tear the stands apart.

When I'm fully loaded—I don't even know with what—I wedge my way out, bit by bit. Straightening up centimeter by centimeter, I finally scream in pain.

Luckily no one's in front of the store, nor is anyone walking by.

I'm nearly across the street when a passing motorbike catches me and drags me along for some thirty yards, with my head bumping on the asphalt.

The accident is all the more idiotic because the traffic is usually very light in this neighborhood and I always watch like a hawk when I cross the street. It probably happened because I'm so feeble and I can only limp.

By the time the biker finally stops, the contents of my apron have catapulted every which way. Lemons, cucumbers, carrots, potatoes, monkey bread have ricocheted through the air like bullets. A small jar of jam has shattered on the sidewalk.

Pedestrians yell at the biker as if they're about to lynch him. Pale as a ghost, he cringes like a kicked puppy, shielding his head with his elbows. I myself have a hole in my skull.

Bleeding profusely, I try to regather the food in my apron. The pedestrians are so touched that they unhand the biker and carry me home along with whatever loot's still edible.

Rainy days are bad for stealing. Snowy days are even worse. When it's freezing out, the stands are moved inside the store. Besides, you can't possibly squat under the racks if the street is icy.

When a store is empty—of customers, that is—we need a gang so that the shoplifting won't be noticed. I don't like working in groups. If there's a bunch of you, the loot has to be divvied up among too many people, and there's always a fight. Of course, you can barge into a store, just grab something, and then split. This method sounds very crude, but a surprise attack usually works. By the time they catch on, you're already at the other end of town. Naturally, you've gotta scoot like a rabbit. There's one disadvantage, though: You can never set foot in that store again.

Yes—getting something to eat depends partly on the weather. Often we sit on the cold floor in our room until late at night, with empty stomachs and no toys. For if it's a harsh winter day, we can't even go outdoors. We have no warm clothing. No coat, no mittens, no boots.

Aside from our frostbite, we're inured to the cold, but my mother is worried about all of us because Arne has asthma. Achim has never even had the sniffles. Inge is a solid rock. My father has never been sick a day his life, and my mother has never worn a winter coat. I myself may land on my nose if I run too fast, but I've never been ill.

I stand at the window like a zoo animal standing on its hind legs at the bars of its cage.

If only this miserable building didn't stink so horribly. A stench of decay oozes from every nook and cranny so that I seriously wonder where the landlord has hidden his dead mother's body to avoid coughing up for a funeral. He's such a shithead that he even counts the apples on his two scrawny apple trees, the strawberries in their lousy patches, and the gooseberries on their stunted bushes.

As soon as he realizes that we've begun stealing, he rages like a wild boar in scrub. He's so scared of not completing the harvest in one day that he simply gulps down everything, whole handfuls, without chewing as he walks. Meanwhile he curses like a woman, in a quavery voice, lamenting that he's been taken in.

The apples he picks are stone hard. No one could eat them without developing jaundice.

But the bastard is also a pawnbroker, extortionist, and bloodsucker. He pulls my mother's wedding band off her finger! What can we do? We don't have a choice. We can't pay the rent. We have no food and no fuel. He knows we don't. He also knows that I steal. All he has to do is blab what he knows, and we're done for. It's a vicious circle. If my mother accepts his loans, she'll be his for life. If she refuses, we'll starve and freeze to death because he'll throw us out into the street. Or turn us in. Or both. How will it end? Will my mother have to go to bed with him? I believe that her fear of becoming a whore enables her to endure any humiliation. First she begs him to at least leave her wedding band on her finger. She says she's willing to sign an IOU. He tells her not to worry, he's going to pull the ring off her finger anyway. That's what happens when you pawn something. So the fucker pulls the ring off her finger. A notched band, somewhat lighter than the rest of her tanned skin, remains on my mother's ring finger.

Every morning we're chewed up by bedbugs. Our faces are puffed up, too. I tell myself these are mosquito bites—they're not as disgusting. The bedbugs are everywhere. In the old mattress we got from the rag dealer, in the fart-soaked couch, and especially behind the decaying wallpaper. Gigantic breeding grounds. Our bed and the walls are thoroughly bloodstained, as if we'd killed one another. After all, it's our blood they're covered with, and it squirts and smears whenever we lean against the wall, making them burst, or when we squoosh them with our fingers.

As for the cockroaches, when they're fully grown they're the size of baby turtles. We burn them alive. Otherwise they scoot away so incredibly fast that we usually just manage to scorch their asses. We stamp on the silverfish, but it's no use. There are too many of them.

We have no bathroom. We wash at the kitchen faucet or under the street pump, with soft soap or sand. On some winter days there's an icicle hanging from the faucet. We break it off and wash with it. There's no such thing as hot water. If my mother boils water, it's usually for our chilblains. The winters are so murderously cold that we sleep in our clothes. To treat our frostbite we have to stick our hands and feet into boiling water. This makes the chilblains so painful that all we can do is shriek. But the treatment doesn't help. Our chilblains keep breaking open, filling with pus, and itching, even through the entire summer.

Our toilet is a hole with a lid. If you raise the lid, you nearly pass out from the stench of piss and shit. Pissing outdoors is a lot more hygienic anyway. And I'd much rather take a dump in the bushes. Once when I was asleep I pissed on my sister because I dreamed she was a tree.

We have no electric light. Either the current's been turned off or there's no line. In any case, I've never seen a light bulb burning. We've gotten used to it by now, and we're developing radar sense, like bats.

We're always starving. Even if I could shoplift every day, we still wouldn't have enough.

The leech has locked up all his food, not to mention his money and other valuables. All the doors and skylights are heavily padlocked, and, like a guard in a prison, he carries a clutch of keys around day and night, always remaining within range of vision and never spending much time away even when he goes shopping.

If we have briquettes and can start a fire, we huddle at the Dutch stove, pressing our frostbitten hands and feet—and sometimes our mouths as well—against the tiles.

My mother drudges for us from dawn till dusk, and she's grateful if she can earn a few meager pennies by washing other people's filthy laundry. Her despair explodes in wild outbursts:

"I'm totally useless in this world! I'm not even capable of feeding my own kids! And what about you? Why don't you have a job? Why can't you keep your trap shut when someone finally hires you? Why did I have to meet you, of all men? We move from one bedbug-infested hole to the next and we live like pigs! Why?!"

Sometimes I think it won't be long before my mother collapses altogether. If she does any work, she trembles so hard that she drops everything. What'll happen if she gets worse?

My father never says a word during my mother's fits. He lets all the insults and accusations wash over him. It's only when she calms down a little and stops berating him that he picks up my desperate mother, who's collapsed.

When we toss and turn at night because we can't stretch out and our bones ache, my father sneaks out of the room to leave us his part of the bed. He then often sits in a chair all night or wanders forlornly through the streets. He never sets foot in a bar or spends money on himself, even for a beer.

Christmas Eve. The festival of peace and joy. Our room is icy and so dark that we can't even see one another. Nobody says a word. We can barely hear each other breathing. But I know we're all here.

During the past few weeks I've watched people lugging packages and Christmas trees from dawn till dusk. Now, from our window, I can seen the burning candles on the Christmas trees behind the curtains in the buildings across the way, I can see the multicolored balls and the flickering tinsel, the wreaths of gold and silver paper and the transparent stars glued to the windowpanes.

I've stolen a crippled Christmas tree, but we have no candles or any of the other glittery stuff to decorate it. We don't even have a cast-iron stand for holding it upright. It leans wearily in a corner like a hunchbacked child being punished.

The only adornments on our window are the glimmering frost flowers—millions of the finest crystals, an inexhaustible wealth of patterns lavishly spread across the glass and far more beautiful than the most expensive curtain.

I imagine how warm it now must be in the other apartments, where people may even be walking on carpets. I picture the food stewing in the pots or baking in the ovens. I conjure up the fragrances. The countless packages of gifts that have already been opened, and the countless others still sheathed in shiny, magical paper, mysteriously lying under the heavily laden branches. Suddenly I unwrap the packages myself. I marvel at the board games, the Erector sets, the steam engines. . . . I attach the skates, the ice skates, to my bare feet. . . . I sit bare-assed on the brand-new sled and let myself be pulled across the Persian rug. . . . I press the wool sweater to my cheek and it's as soft as the down of fledglings. . . . I try on the mittens, I deeply inhale the aroma of the box calfskin of my new boots, I kiss their genuine leather soles and take them along to bed. . . . I weep over the little girl with the sulfur matches and laugh at the Katzenjammer Kids and the other cartoon characters. . . . And I'm so deeply engrossed in the volume of fairy tales that I come to only when the children's post office falls on my toes. With the rubber stamps I stamp everything that's stampable and I paste a tiny children's postage stamp to my father's bald head. I kiss my teddy bear on the mouth and eyes, beat the tin drum, and shoot the air gun. . . . I play the accordion, play the harmonica, and blast the jazz trumpet. . . . I lay the curving tracks of the toy train around the bed and table legs and the straight tracks through the whole bright, warm apartment. . . . I rock on the gaudy hobbyhorse until my head whirls. . . . I crack nuts, I endlessly stuff gingerbread, *lebkuchen,* and marzipan into my mouth and I munch nougat, almond cookies, stollen, dates, figs, and all the candy on the tree. . . . I let the soft dough of the butter biscuits and sugar pastries slowly melt on my tongue before I swallow it. . . . Wait! The roast goose! How could I forget it?! The drumstick belongs to me! Why just one? I want both drumsticks. . . . I tear apart both wings and the breast flesh underneath and shove everything together with mountains of red cabbage and steamed apples down my gullet. I drink the sauce straight out of the ladle. . . . I also have to push down a couple of dry boiled potatoes, nothing on them. . . . Maybe I've overdone it, guzzling the rich sauce down by the ladle. In any event, I'm bursting at the seams. My teeth are aching from the sweets and the nuts, which I always crack with my teeth. After a belch and a fart, I fall asleep in this Never-Never Land—while roast pigeons try to flutter into my snoring mouth, and sausages and entire hams drop from the trees like ripe fruit. . . .

It's still dark when I wake up on the cold floor and hear my mother weeping. I smack my face to see if I'm dreaming. It hurts. So this is reality. My eyes instantly adjust to the darkness. My mother can't be too far from me. Right. She sits at the table with her face buried in her hands. I crawl over to caress her. When I grope in her direction, I find both my brothers clinging to her thighs. My sister is asleep on her feet, her head sideways on the tabletop. At the window my father's silhouette peels out of the night; he seems to be staring immobile into the snow.

The pawnbroker has told my mother to go to bed with him if she wants to get her wedding ring back and to keep him from denouncing us to the police. My father, who has the loving-kindness of Jesus Christ, goes over, and his gigantic fists crack the bastard's face open like an ax.

Now we're sitting in the street with our rags tied up in cartons. Thank goodness it's spring. I pump the new air into my lungs as if I'd been buried alive.

Four A.M. We've been on the move since we got thrown out of the room and we're making the rounds of third-class hotels. Nobody wants us. They get turned off the instant they see our "baggage." Nor does anyone want kids. And four at that. And imagine what we look like!

My father now tries to do it alone. The rest of us hide when he rings for the night clerk. My father wedges his "monocle" into his eye, convinced it makes an impression. But that's bullshit. He has no hat, and his face and head haven't been shaved in days. He looks like an escaped convict. The night clerks are suspicious anyway if someone shows up at dawn without a suitcase, and all of them, without exception, want to be paid in advance. So it's fucked up. We're totally wiped out and so tired and hungry that we stagger like drunkards.

At seven A.M. we're finally taken in by a flophouse near the railroad terminal. Once again six of us in one room and in one bed. My mother has her period and starts hemorrhaging. No doubt because of the terrible stress. Her legs have to be propped up. She occupies half the bed. We can't sleep anyway—we're too hungry. We keep bumping into one another and it hurts like hell.

My brothers and sisters don't go to school. Not till we have an apartment. This is a new neighborhood for me to steal in; I have to get my bearings. Besides, the traffic is murderous, and I can't go out into the street. When we can't stand our hunger anymore, Arne is sent out to beg for cake crumbs in a bakery. But he returns without a single crumb.

The racket in the street is unbearable. So is the smoke from the station. And then the struggle for every crust of bread. Money! Money! Where should it come from?

My mother stays on her feet as if struggling to reach some decision. Then she resolutely goes to a bakery and spends her last dime on two cookies for me. Now we have to walk instead of riding the trolley. She stubbornly refuses to have a bite of one of the cookies.

It's raining cats and dogs. Outside the hotel we run into my father. He hasn't eaten for days. My mother takes off her shoes and sells them to a secondhand dealer not far from the hotel. He pays her two marks. We buy a "Warsaw" and a family-size bottle of chocolate milk and take everything back to the hotel.

A Warsaw consists of repeatedly charred cutoffs of yeast cakes and anything else that breaks off breads and pastries and whatever the bakers sweep up from their counters and floors. The whole thing is pasted into a mass and shoved back in the oven so it holds together. When you buy it, you have to watch out for broom straws, wooden splinters, metal, bits of paper, and even shards of glass. A real Warsaw, which is the size of a loaf of rye bread, costs about twenty pennies.

My father's got a job! So we lose no time getting out of the hotel! Pallasstrasse. Third rear court. The apartment is a fluke. The previous tenant committed suicide. For us it's paradise. One room. Three feet of corridor. It's got a kitchen, and we share a latrine with the other tenants on the landing. We also have a Dutch stove and a gas range. The range works through a coin meter. You insert a dime and you can start cooking on the spot. The sealed meters are opened every month by the gas man, the coins are removed, and the apparatus is resealed. Our predecessor took over the gas man's work. He broke the meter open himself, confiscated the coins, and reinserted them. Then he gassed himself. Now he's lying in the morgue, and we're in his apartment.

It's also a nest of bedbugs. We tear down the wallpaper, wipe out the breeding ground with Flit, and repaint the surface. At first we sleep on the bare floor. Then we buy an old iron bedstead and an old mattress from a junk dealer. The mattress is likewise teeming with bedbugs. We squirt so much Flit into it that we drop like bedbugs ourselves when we approach the mattress during the day. The stench of poison is indescribable. We lay our folded clothing on the floorboards in the corner. Our window directly faces the backyard of an elementary school, P.S. 22, where Inge, Achim, and Arne are enrolled.

Arne's asthma is so serious now that he turns as blue as ink when he climbs the stairs to our apartment. He needs very expensive medicine, and my father steals it from the drugstore. It's a large pouch of yellow powder, which Arne has to eat spoonfuls of every day. The rest of us envy him for his powder, because it's something to eat. My mother has to hide it so we don't gobble it up.

I'm sent to a children's home because I don't attend school yet.

This way, the others have more to eat and more room to sleep in. Mainly, however, my mother believes that I'll get enough to eat in the home and have toys and my own bed. But in reality this so-called children's home is something like a penitentiary, and I call it a children's hell.

The torturers who "take care" of us slap us little kids and cane us on our hands, thighs, and heads if we can't choke down the swill. I can't understand what impels these slave drivers to force us to swallow disgusting pieces of fat the mere stench or sight of which makes me retch.

Some pig puts a brimming bowl of soup in front of me on the table. Clumps of white, bloated fat are floating in the liquid like drowned bodies, and the gruesome brew overflows because that prison slut stuck her thumb in it, all the way up to her wrist. I feel like puking.

We have to stay at the table until we've eaten up, even if it takes us all day. One child had to sit outdoors at the table all last night. This morning he's dead. We don't find out why.

I can't get the lumps of fat down. I just can't. I keep them in my cheek pouches for hours, like a squirrel. I don't even swallow the saliva that gathers in my mouth—otherwise I'd taste the fat and vomit. I breathe only through my mouth in order to tune out my taste buds. I barely stir. The least puff of air caused by a movement might jog my nausea, making me disgorge the swill.

"Well, is the little devil tamed? Have we broken his resistance?"

I can't even answer that I wish this prison slut a slow, agonizing death: I can't talk because my cheek pouches are full of fat.

"You're not saying anything. Could it be you haven't swallowed? Let me see. Open your mouth!"

That's too much for me. I puke right in her goddamn face. I puke up everything, including what's in my belly. All that shit shoots up spasmodically from my gaping gullet like from a manure pump, practically ripping my guts apart, until I can't pump up anymore.

I writhe in cramps and dash off, shrieking, while the beast nearly chokes on my vomit, yelling curses at me until her voice goes.

Now these bloodhounds fan out, trying to catch me. I scream and scream. . . . What do they get out of torturing us? Nothing but torture. Never a smile when we're bewildered. Never comfort when we're sad. Never a kind word when we cry for our moms. I scream until they're all scared of me. They probably think I've lost my mind. The head torturer sends for my mother. I scream and scream, I just don't stop screaming. . . .

When my mother comes, I nearly go insane. I dig my nails into her. I want to return to her womb. We hold one another so tight that we become a single body, and it hurts when our bodies come apart, and I walk out of the children's hell, clutching her hand.

My mother's got a job. Homework. Sewing toiletry pouches. For every pouch she gets between fifteen and twenty pennies. In a store the same pouch goes for twenty marks. A markup of ten thousand percent.

First she has to get a sewing machine. A new one is out of the question. My mother decides on an old Singer. We pay the thirty-five marks in eighteen monthly installments. Naturally it's not an electric machine. My mother has to keep treading down nonstop. But the big problem is the machine itself. It's so noisy that the other tenants, right and left, above and below, protest because they can't get a wink of sleep. Because they can't hear their radios. Because they can't have a quiet breakfast, lunch, or supper—they can't even find peace in the latrine. They bang on the walls, they whack on the ceiling, they stamp on the floor, they yell from the windows, they ring up a storm on our buzzer, they write threatening letters, and they complain to the landlord. All because of the sewing machine, for my mother won't stop sewing until her legs have swollen up, and she collapses in exhaustion at the machine. In this position she wakes up again and promptly resumes treading. When a delivery deadline approaches, she never leaves her place at the sewing machine except to go to the toilet. She even eats at the sewing machine. My sister does the cooking.

Rat-a-tat-tat-tat . . . Rat-a-tat-tat-tat . . . The sewing machine becomes a nightmare not only for the other tenants but for us too. At night the racket wakes us up, even if we do manage to fall asleep. The only music that rattles toward us in the staircase when we come home: the sewing machine.

We spread sheaves of old newspapers on the floor to muffle the agony. But that doesn't help much, and soon we're going to have to move out of this apartment too. For aside from my father's meager wages, the sewing machine is our only provider.

We live in constant hostility with the other tenants. You can understand them. They're all workers who need their sleep because they have to get up early. They even look daggers at us kids, as if it were our fault that we have to help our mother sew at night instead of sleeping. We never get a night's sleep, we merely doze at intervals of one or two hours. In between we work in shifts. Two kids get into bed with our father and two sit on the floor next to the rattling machine, passing the individual sewn and stitched parts from hand to hand after snipping away the extra rubber lining close to the seams or biting off the dangling threads. This is a real assembly line, and no one must get out of the work rhythm, much less fall asleep in exhaustion, so long as the sewing machine rattles.

Once the pouches are finished—fifty, one hundred, five hundred, depending on the order—they are tied into gigantic bales and lugged to the delivery place. It's usually far away and can be reached only by subway or trolley. One of us always accompanies my mother because she can't tote the bales alone.

On every delivery day she and her escort then go to Woolworth's or the KDW department store. In the food section we eat hot Vienna sausages with potato salad and lots of mustard and slippery green, red, and yellow Jell-O.

Delivery day for the pouches is also the day on which the new orders are distributed.

In the staircase women line up in front of the stockroom, where the slave dealer takes and gives. My mother is inside. I wait in line with the other women. With their enormous, heavy tied-up bales, they have clustered into a single endless line of bodies. A line of human flesh. A sweaty, smelly, twisting, rearing, mutely shrieking line. Most of them don't know one another; they've never met before. A few sit on the steps. Others stand leaning against the wall. All of them are exhausted. Few of them converse, and only softly at that. Others puff away silently, gazing into space. Women of all ages and sizes. A fat one, whose bloated body certainly didn't get that way from overeating, gasps for air. Then there's one with enormous hips and drooping, milked-out udders; she must have birthed and nursed at least ten kids. She peels an orange with her teeth, spitting the pieces of rind out in all directions. Then, next to me, a young, lurking slut with heavy thighs, a bubble butt, and a small, sharp belly under the taut, too-short skirt, its ripped slit patched up grossly and clumsily. The sweat rings in her armpits have eaten their way to the charged, swinging boobs with long, hard nipples boring like nails into her shabby rayon blouse. To redden her parted lips, she uses a lipstick that smells sultry. A scrawny crone with snow-white hair clutches the banister to avoid toppling over. A very pregnant mom-to-be, likewise waiting with a gigantic packet, is carefully helped down to a step by two women. They unbutton her coat so that she can breathe more easily. But the oxygen has been totally drained from the air, and every breath you take hurts.

"If you don't like it, you can walk the streets!"

The slave dealer is bellowing behind closed doors.

The line of women winces. Their eyes take on a dangerous, leaden glow. The young slut next to me giggles soundlessly to herself. Her skirt is bursting at the seams. She is still applying lipstick.

"This humiliation is the worst part of it," the bloated woman gasps.

"Why?" the slut retorts. "You're richer by one experience."

"Or knocked up," says the one who's broad in the beam.

"You pig!" hisses one of the two women who are fanning the very pregnant one on the step.

My mother comes through the door. Bewildered she straightens out her dress, which is plastered to her body. She hastily yanks me down the stairs.

Long after we reach the street we're still dashing along. We don't talk. I just grab her strong hand tighter, kissing it as I hurry.

We scurry into Woolworth's and devour our red-hot Vienna sausages with lots of mustard.

Rat-a-tat-tat . . . Rat-a-tat-tat . . . Rat-a-tat-tat-tat-tat-tat. The sewing machine's rattling rattles everything to bits.

To keep me from getting on my mother's nerves all day, they send me to a part-time kindergarten at the grade school that my brothers and sisters attend. No one pays us any heed. There are neither toys nor picture books. When we play ring-around-the-rosy, we shuffle in a circle, apathetic, like old dwarves. The kindergarten teacher does her nails, keeps going to the toilet, and kids around with every guy. Our ears perk up only for the one daily meal. The rest of the time we timidly hang out in the stench, infecting one another with our whooping cough.

At last I'm allowed to go outdoors again by myself. So I start casing the neighborhood. There are lots of places to shoplift from.

I steal from markets and department stores. I grab food, clothes, linen, toys, books, lipsticks for my mother, and a doll for my sister. For my father I rip off garters, suspenders, a tie, and collar buttons, which keep falling off and which he can never find with his lousy monocle. I steal a soccer ball for my brothers, and if it's someone's birthday, I go to a park and take home lilacs or roses or asters, depending on the season.

Meanwhile I've started school. I believe that the female teachers get turned on when they make us bend over, so that our short pants stretch very tightly over our butts, before they cane us. Sometimes they grab our ass cheeks. When they do, they come very close, smelling of fish. I'd love to tear down the panties of some randy teacher slut and whip her bare ass until the cane shatters into smithereens!

I don't know which class bores the shit out of me the most. It's unbearable!

The religion teacher calls me up to his desk after entering an "A" for me in his book. He promises me the highest marks and gives me three suckers.

"In what religion were you baptized, my son?"

(Where does he get off calling me his son?)

"None."

"None?"

"None. I was never baptized."

"Why, that's horrible . . . ! Then how come you know the entire New Testament by heart?"

"I'm a fast learner."

"But how in God's name can you go to church if you've never been baptized?"

"I've never been inside a church."

"What about your parents?"

"How should I know?"

"Have your parents prohibited you from going to church?"

"No."

"What do your parents say about church?"

"My father goes nuts when he hears church bells."

"What about your mother?"

"My mother says that you people torture little Jesus."

It was a good thing I'd put the three suckers in my mouth right away, for I'm convinced the religion teacher would have fished them out again if I hadn't already sucked them into tiny remnants.

He erases my "A."

Since we still don't have a bathroom and we wash in the kitchen, my sister has started to feel self-conscious. She's got a big, bad ass now, and her cotton undershirt has long since gotten too snug for her impatiently growing tits. In her cotton panties her bursting chestnut stands out sharply under her juvenile belly.

I live almost entirely in the street. In winter, when we're frozen through and through, we lie on the grates of the subway shafts. Whenever a train thunders by under the asphalt, a smelly stream of warm air squeezes up through the bars, thawing our bodies for moments at a time. In summer the asphalt is hot and the street stifling. The municipal pools charge admission. Wannsee Lake, a mass swimming hole, where we can climb over the barbed-wire fence, is twelve miles away, and transportation costs money. The Havel lakes are likewise too far off. At Grünewald Lake it's wall-to-wall people. The so-called paddle ponds are blacker than a mud bath and as warm as piss; sometimes a turd comes floating straight toward you at mouth level. But oh, yes, there are possibilities. We can latch on to the door of the rear car in an urban train and ride all the way across Berlin and even farther. If another train comes along, you have to flatten yourself against the closed door, otherwise you'll be crushed between the two trains.

Sometimes we lie down in the gutter and enjoy getting a shower from the street-cleaning trucks. The water is cool and not stale, because it's tanked up fresh and used right away. Once the truck has lumbered past us, we jump up, catch up with it, and throw ourselves in the gutter, in the path of the shower. We keep repeating this until they turn the water off.

The drivers of the sanitation trucks hate us and they kick any kid they manage to grab. One kid actually bleeds to death in the gully. What happens is that he's lying in the gutter, and I'm just about to throw myself down next to him—when he suddenly straightens up. One end of the water pipe on the side of the truck slices through his carotid artery.

The Berliners' oxygen tanks are their summer shacks in the countryside. These are the mother animals that suckle them. And they suckle me too.

There are so many of these gardens in Berlin that I can't even count them all. There are thousands. I know nearly all of them and I've stolen fruit in nearly all of them.

It's stressful climbing into one of the gardens; the suspense is awful. The biggest problem is the dogs. Outside some gardens I can't even stop to catch my breath without some mutt baring its teeth at me. Others foam at the mouth, hoarsely yapping behind their fences, as if they had rabies. These are dogs that absolutely have to bite something. Preferably a human being, of course.

The most dangerous dog by far—it's always a German shepherd—is the kind that neither barks nor gives you any chance to defend yourself, because it doesn't attack you. It just gawks at you. Nonstop. With its cutting amber eyes. Wolf eyes. It watches you. Controls each and every one of your moves. God help you if you so much as stir. And heaven protect you if you so much as think of sneaking away quite inconspicuously. You can barely afford to breathe. Don't even think of running away. That would be a bad joke.

You have to talk to these wonderful mutts. Very softly, of course. First very faintly, yet loud enough to make them curious. Don't talk very clearly as yet; they needn't understand every word. Let them puzzle it out, keep them on tenterhooks. Then you have to get to the nitty-gritty very slowly. You have to arouse their curiosity, their emotions. . . .

I start crying to soften the dog. I bawl so convincingly that tears bounce down my cheeks. The dog is embarrassed; it turns away. And lo and behold! The delightful little doggy actually licks away my tears. I'd love to dognap it, but it wouldn't fit through the barbed wire. I can't toss it over the wire either—the mutt's too heavy.

Last time I came away unscathed. This time I don't. All night long I've been padding around a garden like a panther. No barking. No dog has shown up. It's three thirty A.M. The full moon illuminates everything clearly, including the drunken faces of gigantic sunflowers. I've had my eye on this garden for a long time because it's got a small tree with the biggest apples I've ever seen. They're the size of my head and weigh at least two pounds each.

These apples cast a magic spell on me. I can't sleep at night; I'm scared the owner might pick them. I'm gonna have to twist every single apple from its stem. I mustn't bruise them. They're as shiny as if the owner had waxed them.

Sniffing in all directions I move toward the tree like an Indian. What a slender tree, I think. It's like with women. There are very delicate women with gigantic boobs, they get knocked up after the very first fuck and bear very strong babies.

I stretch my hands toward the apples. . . . At that instant I think of one of the hounds in stories, for right before me, a giant of a hound is standing. It can't be! He's the size of a calf! I didn't see him coming; I was too fascinated by the giant apples. And he didn't really come. He was lying under the tree. All he had to do was stand up to block the way. He doesn't bark, he doesn't growl. Not a peep. He stares at me mutely. His blond amber eyes bore into mine.

My arm is still stretching through the air. I can't take it down. The calf won't let me. This giant simply won't allow me to take down my arm. He won't allow me any movement at all. He merely twists up his lips as if he were drawing a sword from its scabbard. He knows that's all it takes. His canines, which now appear, are over an inch long.

What should I do? I can't stand here forever. My situation is so hopeless that, paradoxical as it may sound, I can barely choke back my hysterical mirth. Just don't laugh now! I think. He might take it as an insult. The shiny giant apples derisively sway to and fro, as if shaking their heads at my inexperience. My raised arm starts to hurt. I'm getting a cramp. When my arm falls down on its own, the dog leaps at me.

I'm not exactly feeble for a twelve-year-old boy, but his weight alone knocks me over. I try to cling to him as tight as I can. But I can barely reach around him. He's got the fur of a bear. There's no question of my struggling. His teeth snap on my underarm like a fox trap. His bite isn't deep, but I'm caught. Even though I'd love to strangle him, I don't hate him. He's too beautiful. Nor do I believe that he hates me. He's merely doing his job.

Now my opponent's face is right in front of mine. Our lips are almost touching. Desperate, I bite him. First his lips. I feel the hot, slobbering flesh in my mouth. This is useless, so I bite him in the nose—so hard that he yowls, opening the fox trap of his teeth for an instant. My salvation is the thick shaft of a shovel that tumbles in my direction as we brawl. I grab the shovel and wedge it into his gaping maw, locking it. His long, sharp teeth dig in so deep that he can't remove them from the wood. Luckily I always have string in my pants pocket. Grabbing his head together with the shovel shaft in his maw, I knock it with one hand into the sweat box and tie the two halves of his mouth together with my free hand. "Sorry, boy," I think, "but now we're even." Then, bleeding like a stuck pig, I dash out of the garden after grabbing at least one super-apple from the tree.

I rob other gardens daily, hourly. The trick is never to step into the same garden twice.

All I can see is the tops of high plum trees. Just the tops. For I can't see into the garden itself. Try as I might to circle the garden and locate the splendid plums, I keep running up against gigantic thorny hedges of wild roses, real hills of roses that grow into mountains, totally blocking my view. Yes, they are so rankly entangled that I can't even guess which property these fat plums belong to. The only possible route is the thorny one.

The goddamn wall of thorns is very hard at one point, and that's where I enter.

My hands and legs start bleeding after my first few steps; the thorns tear off pieces of my skin and drill deep into my flesh like dull knives. Who cares? I have to have the plums, no matter what it takes. But the farther up I work my way toward the plum trees, the deeper I get into the chaos of entangled rose branches, which are as thick as arms. I have to keep shifting my weight to a single part of my body—a foot, a shoulder, a knee, a hand, a single finger. I don't know how I'll ever get out of this jungle, which instantly closes behind me like an enchanted fairy-tale forest.

I've almost made it—there's only a single thick branch in front of me. I have to grab hold beneath me and pull myself over an abyss. Then I'll be able to peer down into the garden as if I were looking through a tiny open window. I no longer feel the pain of the thorns, but I do feel them on all sides, nibbling my body like sharks. I try to resist as little as possible to weaken their piercing. It's not easy because my situation requires all my energy and muscle power, and I have to exert my body to the utmost.

Now I grab a branch and pull my chest across it. My feet, with no way out, are deep in the chaos that tangles below me and above me, so that my lower body hangs like a suspension bridge over the thorny abyss. Another inch—and there I am! What I see knocks me for a loop! Naked women! I'm too horny to count them, but I figure there must be ten or fifteen! They loll in beach chairs, sit on chairs, or lie on towels on the ground. Their bodies are oiled up. A few sport deep tans; others are still light, some white. One is as red as a lobster, and she sits in the shade. All of them are stark naked. They change positions. Stretch sensuously. Open their legs. Draw in their thighs. Spread. Lie on their sides, on their backs, on their bellies. Stick out their assess, their tits, their pussies. Who would have dreamed that such plums were waiting here for me! The whole thing is so overwhelming that I think I must be dreaming. They barely say a word, barely make a sound. Everything is harshly lit, overexposed, as if I were looking into the white sun.

I get a raging hard-on, which is a problem in my position and in my tight pants, which I've long since outgrown.

One of the women is right in front of me and under me. She has broad shoulders like a swimmer and short, flat breasts with huge, almost swarthy nipples. A sturdy, fleshy pelvis. Embedded in it is a small belly with an umbilical bulge. Huge, outstretched thighs, robust calves, and strong, wide feet and hands. Her crotch hair, growing thickly across her pelvis and belly, reminds me, oddly enough, of the thicket I'm hanging in—and her unusually arched mound of Venus rises above her fat vaginal lips, which open like a crater. I can see the rosy interior of her twat, where a sweet drop glitters.

Another woman, her skin all white, rolls over in her beach chair, revealing her small, gaping butt, so that I can see straight into her open asshole.

I must be right over the toilet, for a young, naked girl with immature tit buds and skimpy crotch hair comes toward my thicket prison and vanishes beneath me. I hear a door close. Then the bolt. And then the relieving piss.

As I strain to the utmost to move forward and get a better view of the other naked women, my torso smashes deep into the thorny jungle below me, and I hang there, bleeding, unable to stir, my head dangling, until I black out. . . . When the complete hush tells me that all the women have gone home, I struggle my way out of the wilderness of roses.

I stalk through another garden. Not a sound. Not a soul. . . . I'm just loading my shirt chock-full of velvety apricots, which I always raise to my lips as if they were very young little cunts. . . . All at once, from the corners of my eyes, I glance through an open window—and see her! She can't be older than I. She sits there legs akimbo, masturbating. Her eyes are shut tight. . . . She moans . . . whimpers . . . reaches orgasm. . . . I open my trousers . . . in a trance like a tomcat in heat . . . I'm as drenched as if I'd pissed in my shorts.

My outings to the garden colonies are always brief. I have to return to my asphalt jungle.

"Coal! Get your red-hot coat!"

I ring every buzzer. The people hate me. It's not working; I have to talk to the coal dealer. He pays my salary in coal. At worst, I can sell it. The more I carry in one day, the more briquettes I earn. I can lug up to a hundred briquettes on my back, and I drag them until all I can do is cough bits of coal.

I beat rugs until I almost choke on the stench of dust and filth. But with every stroke I knock a little more of my poverty dead.

I tote dirty clothes to the laundries. I soak them in troughs, scrub them on the washboards till my fingers bleed. I heat the irons. I put sheets and feather-bed cases through the wringers. I stretch curtains on the drying frames. I mix starch for collars and home-deliver the clean wash.

I shine shoes. Five pennies a pair. I help the sanitation men gather the scattered garbage in the cans. I pull the carts of the street sweepers when they take five to grab a smoke. I collect butts in the streets, make new cigarettes from the tobacco, and sell them to jobless people, re-tirees, and war invalids. I push crippled and injured people around in their wheelchairs when they want to go to the park for a game of cards. I assist the hurdy-gurdy men, picking up the five- and ten-penny coins tossed from the windows and carrying the sad, threadbare monkey on my shoulder when the man has to go take a leak. The monkey's always chained to the hurdy-gurdy.

The most lucrative work is helping the pallbearers. This is pos-sible only if the near and dear are paupers who can't afford to tip the pallbearers and who pay no attention to my presence. I'm paid by the pallbearers, whose breath always reeks of booze; they give me be-tween fifty pennies and a mark per cadaver, it all depends. My job is to wash the stiff body before it's put in the coffin. If the dead person has to wear something, then the pallbearers help me dress him because I can't turn the heavy corpse over by myself, and his arms and legs can't be bent.

I'm supposed to strip a dead seven-year-old girl, wash her, and slip her into a little frock. No mother is to be seen. No father. No siblings. Nobody but an old man sitting in the corner and talking to himself. The girl is holding a one-eared teddy bear. To undress, wash, and clothe her I'll have to extricate the clinging teddy bear.

"I can't," I tell the pallbearers.

One of the men gingerly tugs at the teddy bear, which the little girl refuses to release. Then he shakes it. No use. When he tries to wrench it away, the brisk pull makes the corpse sit up as if she means to say, "You can yank all you like, it won't help!"

I dash out of the place.

The most gruesome labor of all is trucking the hospital refuse to the garbage dump. I don't sit with the driver; I have to hold the cans fast during the trip. They contain not only pus-smeared gauze, blood-soaked muslin, and encrusted bandages, but also—incomprehensible as it sounds—amputated human legs, hands, feet, and bowels. If the wrapping paper spontaneously opens up, a bloodless human arm looms out.

Whenever I have no work, I break into cigarette machines and pay telephones. I don't like doing it—you never know whether you're being watched. I can't afford to wind up in juvenile jail.

I wash fish at the markets. I can't get the stench out of my clothes. I believe there is no stench that I haven't stunk of.

On account of the sewing machine we get an eviction notice. My mother ODs on sleeping pills. My brother describes how my father ran weeping alongside her when the orderlies carried her down the steps on a litter. Her head kept sliding off and bumping against the staircase walls.

"We've got an apartment!" my mother exclaims once they pump out her stomach and she's back on her feet. "It costs a fortune. But we'll have light and sunshine and flower boxes with flowers and a balcony!"

It's true. She's found a fourth-floor apartment facing the street; it has a three-foot-by-six-foot balcony with a southern exposure. So we'll have light and sunshine. But I mustn't think about the sewing machine. None of us wants to think about the sewing machine. And yet we feel it like a heel on our necks.

The apartment has four small rooms, a kitchen, the first private toilet we've ever had, and a bathroom with a stove that has to be fueled from the hall. The rent is exorbitant—my mother's right. It's sixty-eight marks a month. But we'll manage somehow.

Every morning, when Inge goes to the toilet, she passes my bed, wearing only a much-too-short cotton shirt and much-too-short panties. If she's certain that everyone else is asleep, it's even worse: after pissing, she wears only the shirt, which doesn't even reach over her stubbly cunt and her aggressive buns.

What in the world can I do? Should I follow her? And what if someone else has to shit or piss and sees me coming out of the john with her? So when? Where? I don't even know if she'd let herself be fucked. Besides, I share a room with Arne and Achim between my parents's bedroom and Inge's. Her bed is separated from Arne's by a wall. And it squeaks. Achim's bed is about three feet from Inge's door, which creaks like an old cart. Inge spends each morning in school. In the afternoon she helps my mother. Or she does homework. So do Arne and Achim. Evenings are impossible because no one ever misses supper. I have to find a way! I can't take it anymore!

My kidneys are infected and I have to sleep a lot. In the daytime too. That's no good. I can't get my mind off Inge or my hands off my hard cock, day or night.

This afternoon nobody's at home. Where can they all be? Someone's in the toilet; I hear it flushing. I quickly turn over and pretend to be asleep. Someone enters my room—I don't know who it is—bends over me . . . raises the covers . . . gets in bed with me. . . . I hold my breath. It's Inge! I'm dumbfounded! My eyes are still shut, but I know it's Inge. Her flesh grazes me. I smell her. She climbs over me, turns her butt toward me, and likewise pretends to fall asleep immediately. In any case she doesn't touch me. Nor do I touch myself. But her ass cheeks touch my prick, which is so hard that it hurts. She still doesn't move. She doesn't pull her ass cheeks back, either, or squeeze them together. Anything but. They feel like they're opening. There's no doubt about it: She must feel my cock all the way to her cunt.

We can't keep lying there forever like this. If she didn't want something from me, she wouldn't have climbed into my bed. That's obvious.

I act as if I'm tossing and turning; I murmur in my "sleep" and place my lower arm on her pelvis accidentally on purpose. I let my hand slide down her small belly to her twat. I work my forefinger through her scrubby crotch hair and let it wallow in the twitching clam, whose warm shell opens promptly and gladly because she raises her thigh very slightly—and pushes my hand away. Naturally, as if she were doing it in her sleep. I quickly withdraw my hand and greedily lick it off. It's as gooey as if I had thrust it into a bowl of oatmeal.

Now she reaches for my hand on her own and places it back on her horny clam as she yawns and rolls over on her back. I instantly stick my finger back in. The more she shoves my hand away, the wider her sturdy legs spread apart. Her head writhes as if she were having a nightmare, while her hands grab her thighs. Just as I roll on top of her, someone opens the front door!

Inge leaps out of the bed, races to her room, and locks herself in.

I talk to no one and eat nothing. At night I can't sleep a wink, I just stare at the ceiling. Every so often I go to the toilet and examine my hard-on. Then I lie down and stare at the ceiling again.

It must be about three A.M. Three thirty at the latest. I sit up and listen for a long time. Arne and Achim are asleep. I can hear their regular breathing. In the room with the balcony my father snores, and my mother, whose nose is stuffed up, emits a whistling sound. I tiptoe to my brothers' beds and lean over. Arne is on his belly like a sack. Achim's head rocks to and fro as it did when he was a baby, lulling him deeper and deeper.

When I turn the knob on Inge's door, I press against the door panel with all my strength to prevent even the slightest noise. Naturally the goddamn door creaks, as usual. I should have thought of that and oiled it.

Earlier we couldn't sleep because of the sewing machine. Now we've got air raids every night. Every night! Every night we're yanked out of sleep three, four, five times and we reel into the basement shelter. Soon we don't even get up anymore; we just roll over when the bombs come hailing down, shattering the buildings around us.

Just why are we so poor? Why can I never sleep at night? Because bombs keep dropping! Why does my mother have to torture herself like that? Why didn't anyone give my dad a break? Why is there a war? Why? Why? Why?

When I walk through the streets, I keep bumping my head, because I always whirl around or walk backward so the passing girls and women won't escape me. It happens quite automatically. I can't help it. As soon as one goes by, I turn and look after her until she slips around a corner or vanishes somewhere else and is replaced by another, who comes toward me, from in front, from behind, from the right, from the left. The worst is when they show up from all sides and I keep spinning like a top so as not to miss a single one. Usually my brow or the back of my head then bangs into a cast-iron lamppost.

I don't care how old they are, how young, how big, how little, how thin, how fat, what kind of hair they have, what kind of skin—they all cast a magic spell on me.

The first time I kissed a little twat, I was seven. We were alone in the staircase. I put her on a step, spread her legs, and sniffed around on her like a puppy.

Now I'm thirteen and try to plug every hole. In the school toilet, in bushes, in hallways, in basements. Sometimes even in their beds.

In the second back wing of our building there's a young redhead with huge blond freckles on her transparent white skin. Her husband is a garbageman. She constantly loiters outside the front door as if waiting for someone. She's bound to have a guy who comes and fucks her whenever her husband's at work. Her eyes gaze blankly from her big skull like empty sockets in a death's-head. I never see her shopping or working. Just hanging out and waiting for something. Her legs are really twisted, she's bowlegged, and she always looks so feeble, as if she had to lean on someone. I've heard she's got TB, but I think she's weak from fucking so much.

Her apartment's on the ground floor, and the bedroom window, which is always open, faces a vacant back lot. Sometimes I hang out there, poking in the rubble, and one morning I heard a guy moaning and a woman shrieking through the open window. The moans couldn't have come from her husband. He leaves the house at four A.M. and doesn't return until afternoon.

There she is again. I stare at her spellbound, until the death's-head turns toward me. She's one big pussy. Her face. Her eyes, which now have a dim, gray glow. She takes my hand in her damp, hot hand and pulls me along.

The bedroom is clammy, and barely any light filters in even though it's sunny outdoors. And even though the window's open, the place smells of fried potatoes.

She dashes out of her clothes like an addict whose fix is way overdue. She has an almost childlike torso with clearly visible ribs and practically no tits. To make up for that, she's got an unusually broad, bowl-shaped pelvis, with sharply converging bones that threaten to pierce the thin skin. She's got short legs, which makes her lower body look even wider. Everything else is pussy, pussy, pussy.

My balls are as hard as stones. She promptly shoves them in too.

A hailstorm of bombs. The tenants have crept into the air raid shelter. My mother and I are alone. We have nothing to eat. It's almost dark. We're tired and freezing. What else can we do but go to bed? My mother takes off her clothes in front of me. Her panties, too.

"Come to bed" is all she says.

For three days aerial mines shatter the buildings all around us.

At sixteen I get drafted. When I read the draft notice, I cry. Not because I'm a coward—I'm not afraid of anyone. But I don't want to kill or be killed.

Urban rail, Westkreuz Station. I have to change trains and go to the paratroop barracks. I detach myself from my mother's lips. She remains in the compartment, riding on to Schöneberg. She gazes at me through the dirty panes. Her eyes will leave the station with the train.

"Mom!"

In the paratroops I run into a kid I know.

"Hey, Buddy!" We hug for a long time.

They shove weapons into our hands and say, "Kill the enemy!"

The Limeys'll beat the shit out of us. My buddy and I never hit the ground when we hear the grenades yowling. We play a game: The guy who can hold his unpinned grenade longest is the winner.

Sometimes fighter planes hover in the sky like vultures. Then we hop around like crazy, flapping our arms, until they spot us, nose-dive, and shoot at us. When they miss us we grin and thumb our noses at them. We haven't the foggiest notion what it's all about. For us the *rat-a-tat* is like New Year's Eve, when we never had enough maroons and firecrackers.

Now my buddy's gone, and I've got no one to play with. I've gone astray. Like a lost kid. Not like earlier at the lake, when a kid lost his brother in the crowd. The kid's name was announced over loud-speakers, and you could hear him crying through the mike. Someone always showed up after a while and took the kid away.

Someone ought to shout over the loudspeaker:

"Boy, sixteen years old, gold-blond hair, huge, violet eyes with long, dark-brown lashes and a big red mouth, wants to get back to Buddy. Stop that stupid *rat-a-tat!*"

The thought makes me laugh. But here no one will take me back to Buddy.

"Volunteers for patrol, step forward!"

Kiss my ass.

In the abandoned houses, from which the inhabitants have fled, I find civilian duds. I toss my uniform into a garbage can and put on whatever I find. A child's shirt with green and white checks and over-size women's panties.

The people must have jumped up from a meal. The plates of food are half eaten, the glasses half full. Everything is moldy, like in "Sleeping Beauty."

I strike off in the direction of the grenades and live on mushy apples. Apples everywhere, lying in water under the trees. The whole area is flooded with water and apples. I've got the runs so bad that I eat only in a shitting position. In the daytime I can't even straighten up to piss. I do it lying down, my body freezing to the ground with my pissed-up pants.

This is my sixth night of feeding on mushy apples. All at once, on an inundated meadow, in the gaudy light of signal rockets, I see: a cow. There are carcasses of cows and horses and even pigs wherever you look. But a live cow! Grazing in a pasture. It's absurd! The cow shines gaudily in the light. More and more signal flares burst high up in the air and then slowly drift to the ground, melting into nothingness over the cow's head. Maybe they're doing it for Christmas, I wonder. It must be Christmas about now. . . . Maybe I'm hallucinating because of all the mush and the endless shitting.

I have to try to get at that cow. Then I'll pounce on her and slice a chunk of meat from her body. Maybe I won't even have to kill her. I'm bound to find matches or a gas burner in a deserted house. Then I'll build a fire and roast my chunk of beef. Maybe I'll find a pan. Or at least a pot.

I yank loose my pants, which are frozen fast to the ground. Now it dawns on me that I have no weapon. I have no rifle, no pistol, not even a knife, not even a penknife—nothing. Not even a cord to strangle her with. How am I supposed to kill her? How am I supposed to slaughter her? I can try to bite through her throat. Yeah, that's what I'll do. I'll hang on to her neck. After all, I've bitten off bottle stoppers with my teeth. Her throat can't be harder than a bottle stopper. I'll chomp out only a piece of her flesh and then let her go. At worst I'll eat the meat raw.

To get to the cow I have to climb over a barbed-wire fence, the kind that's usually found on a cow pasture. I'm no more than thirty feet away from her when she jerks around and gallops off.

"We'll see who can run faster," I yell as if she's broken our agreement to let me nip off a piece of her living flesh. But I'm wrong. I'm not in my asphalt jungle here and I don't have sneakers on, I'm wearing hard, waterlogged boots that are much too big for me. Nevertheless, near a stretch of barbed-wire fence, I get close enough to grab one of the cow's legs. I bury my teeth in the soft inner side of her thigh, right next to the ass cheek. At that instant her asshole opens, and a stream of green shit splashes onto my face. Still shitting, she jumps over the barbed wire. She doesn't quite make it and she tears her udder. But that doesn't faze her. She storms from one stretch of fence to another. She never quite manages to hurdle the barbed wire. And, as if she's lost her mind, the cow, with her raggedy udder, doubles back like a billy goat—while I, drenched, covered with shit, floundering calf-deep in the morass, with chattering teeth, curse her. Then I have to find a place to take a dump myself.

Since I don't have a compass, I run around in circles, right into the German lines. They catch me, and I'm sentenced to death for desertion. The firing squad is detailed. I'm to be shot tomorrow, at the crack of dawn.

The soldier who's assigned to guard me has the hots for me.

"What do you care?" he says. I say I don't care.

When he drops his pants and tries to fuck me up the ass, I punch him in the skull to daze him.

This time I escape in the right direction. At dawn I bump into the patrol that I didn't want to take part in. The corpses of the boys are frozen iron-hard and contorted like dolls with movable limbs.

Drumfire. The Limeys must be preparing an attack. I lie in a shallow hole on the only approach route where they can attack. Everything else around me is under water.

Rat-a-tat-tat-tat-tat . . . The machine-gun fire zigzags across the sand, which spurts up in tiny fountains.

Thick fog. You can barely see for thirty feet. I finally have to stretch my legs. *Rat-a-tat-tat-tat!* A tommy-gun volley. Five bullets hit me. The guy standing in front of me fired only because he panicked when I suddenly came out of the ground. Now I'm surrounded by a whole bunch.

"C'mon! C'mon!" they say in English, skewering me with their tommy guns. At least five are aiming at my head. Another at my heart. At my belly. All that's missing is one in my ass! When it finally dawns on them that I'm not armed, they send me back to their own lines.

More and more Limeys emerge from the dense fog as I stagger past them toward where they're coming from.

My lower right arm swells up as big as my thigh. My head is bleeding and so are both my arms and my chest. I throw away the jacket.

"Go on! Go on!" each soldier says when I show him my wounds and try to get him to help me.

"Go on! Go back! Back!"

They simply have no time for me. They've got enough to do for themselves. The air is polluted with whistling bullets and bursting shrapnel, and the low-flying German aircraft are swimming around in the air like sharks.

Nevertheless the Limeys walk upright. Their helmets are tilted back. They're probably tired of throwing themselves on the ground and even of crouching. Some have a cigarette dangling from the corner of a mouth.

My pants are sliding down. My suspenders are ripped, and my swollen, bleeding arms can't hold my pants. My belly is bare; my kid's shirt doesn't even reach down to my navel.

Behind the lines they shove me into a rowboat while they themselves wade hip-deep in the water. I'm so happy that I start singing, weeping, laughing. . . . Slowly my head sinks down to my chest.

In a surgery tent they remove my bullets. When I wake up from the ether, a military chaplain winks at me and places a small, thin chocolate bar on my chest.

"He's just a child," he says, as if to himself. Then he lights a cigarette and inserts it between my dry lips.

I'm loaded into a medical train. I don't know where it's heading. I just keep my eyes glued to the wonderful tits, asses, and bellies of the nurses in their tight uniform skirts as they keep panting along from one moaning patient to the next.

Snowflakes are falling outside. It's Christmas. Frost flowers are back on the windows. Like when I was little and dreamed about glittering Yuletides.

I'm handed pants, a jacket, a coat, and a pair of lace-up boots without laces. No shirt. No underwear. No socks. No gloves. No caps.

"Take your hands out of your pockets or I'll whip them out!" A red-haired Scot with a ludicrous sea-dog beard waves his riding crop in the air as he receives us at the entrance to a POW camp. I'm so riled that I yell back:

"I'm not playing with my balls, you red rat! I'm cold!"

Another POW tugs at my sleeve and whispers: "Don't let him get to you. Take your hands out."

I take my hands out although they're frozen stiff.

After hours of being counted off we enter our cages with frozen bones. The other POW tells me: "You'll see, they're not all like that. On the average they're okay."

The brick-drying sheds, which are about twenty-five yards long, are so low that we have to kneel down to crawl in. Once you're inside, you can't straighten up. You have to crawl around. We sleep in two rows on the cold, slimy earth. We lie so tight together that you have to lift up your body if you want to turn over on your other side. And so close together that our feet touch and we kick one another. Each man has a thin military blanket to cover himself with, and that's all.

Using our fingers we eat from old, rusty tin cans. Sauerkraut with water every day, and a can of tea. I never realized there was so much sauerkraut in the world.

Incredible the things that go on in the camp. Not only swapping, robbing, loan-sharking, prostitution, and killing, but grown men reciting poems, going from barrack to barrack, reading aloud from the Bible (the devil only knows where they got it from!), reading palms, telling fortunes, trying to "convert" one another to some kind of crap, and fighting over the last ladle of sauerkraut.

Tobacco is the most important thing. Even more important than fucking. The men pounce on one another insanely, beating each other bloody over thrown-out tea leaves which have been steeped so often that they're totally tasteless. The leaves are dried and made into cigarettes with newspapers, which we sometimes get for wiping our asses. An old POW literally eats up a "genuine" English cigarette. Using a rusty razor blade, he slices off a thinny-thin slice every day and luxuriously devours it in its paper.

After a while we're interrogated. They call this an interview. The guy who cross-examines me is a Berliner. He gabs about his school days, his high school, the street it was on, and so forth. Who cares?

He's stuffed to the gills, and he lights one cigarette after another without giving me even one. He's probably never suffered any lack and has always had enough to eat. Even now, in the midst of war, he's got everything. I've had nothing and I've got nothing now, not even warm clothes in winter. I wish this whole gang would go to hell with their loudspeakers, their yellow lines, and their eternal barbed wire.

After two months in the brickworks we're supposed to be shipped to England. On the way to the docks in Ostend, the people along the road spit at us. Oh well, who cares?

While crossing the Channel, we're torpedoed by German U-boats and nearly go down. By the time we reach England and crawl out of our cargo holds, the war is over. But they transport us to POW camps all the same.

The camp latrines in Colchester, Essex, are where we all get together. The latrines are long, very deep ditches spanned by raw beams, where you sit and shit. And during the shitting everything is discussed, planned, and concocted. Everything is prepared here: burglaries, escapes. Conspiracies develop here, and this is also the marketplace for the sex hustlers: A fuck costs a piece of soap, tobacco, or cigarettes, depending on whether it's the ass, the dick, the mouth, or the hand. The prisoners make a lubricant out of mutton fat.

A young boy is fished dead out of the shit. Even though the war is over, insane Nazis charged him with "high treason" and condemned him to death on the latrine, and that was where he was executed. They shoved him into the shit, where he suffocated.

Colchester is a transit camp for released prisoners from Canada and the United States. They bring our first samples of Lux soap, blue jeans, chewing gum, Camels, and Lucky Strikes.

Now it's our camp's turn, but transport home takes another year. First the sick. I'm not sick. All night long I stand naked against the icy barracks wall to get a kidney infection so there will be protein in my urine for the examination. I wolf down a pack of cigarettes and hot sardines in oil, and I drink my own piss so as to get a fever. There's no gimmick I don't try. But to no avail.

"He stays," says the asshole of a doctor. There's nothing wrong with me. I'm unkillable.

At last I manage to get into the final transport. I've spent one year and four months in this zoo! Truck after truck lumbers out of the barbed-wire dump.

"C'mon! C'mon!"

If I had said I live in Berlin, I would have had to stay in the German reception camp. For the time being, no one's allowed into Berlin. I tell them I'm from some provincial burg. Then I forge my release document. Profession: newscaster! I don't know how I ever hit on that perverse idea. I've never heard a newscast in my life.

I have an American haversack, blue jeans, a sleeveless shirt, a pair of shoelaces, two cakes of Lux soap, a tin of Goldflag tobacco, and seven marks to my name.

I sell a cake of soap on the black market and keep moving, always zigzagging. I sleep in bunkers or bushes.

In a railroad station a girl with curly hair flashes a smile at me. She's already in the compartment. I join her. During the ride we chew each other's tongues up. We go to the john and I put her on the commode. I don't even pull down her panties, I just yank them aside. Her hole is warm and wet, like the mouth of a cow.

We get out of Heidelberg.

She lives in a pretty garret near American HQ, where she carried on with everyone. The Yanks pay with food, coffee, chocolate, cigarettes, liquor, and cash. And, of course, with soap, nylons, and toilet paper.

Toward morning, when the girl, with her lipstick smeared, climbs into bed with me, the fucking really gets going. She's only sixteen, but she knows the most diverse positions, and she teaches me all of them. I've never lived this well.

We fuck for three or four hours. After breakfast I take a walk and let her sleep till noon. Then we have lunch, and she goes back to the Yanks.

After six weeks I'm fed up. While she's off with a client, I grab my haversack and split.

The trains are so mobbed that people are spilling out of doors and windows. I bore my way into the human tangle and for the entire trip I hang head-down in the compartment while my legs stick out through the window.

Stuttgart. Kassel. Karlsruhe. I don't have the foggiest notion where they are. In every town I reach, I borrow from the theater directors. Some give me more, some less. Some give me cigarettes.

In Tübingen I send a telegram to Berlin. I put down the Tübingen theater as my address. My mother's sure to respond immediately. Maybe she'll send me a little money or some candy—the way she sent them to me in a vacation home. At that time she sent me "spring leaves": These are green leaves, like on trees, but made of candy sugar. They don't cost much, and they always stick together in clumps inside the bag. But I love eating them, and my mother's love stuck to them too.

I stroll a lot, warbling to myself. I haven't got a care in the world and I'll soon be with my mom. I've got food and tobacco, and at night I sleep in the parks.

The secretary at the theater schedules an audition for me. During lunch break we go to the park and I show her where I sleep. The bed, made of leaves, is still there from last night. Dense bushes protect us from the eyes of passersby, but I have to clap my hand over her mouth, because she shrieks out at every thrust as if she were being skewered. Her underwear is soaked with blood. Her hymen was so tough that I had to smash in brutally.

Even though I've been out in the street for a long while, I keep rereading Arne's wire: "Mother not alive stop Know nothing about the others."

I don't cry. I see everything in gaudy, shattered splinters, like a kid peering through a kaleidoscope. You had to shake the tube so that the glass splinters froze into a different, exotic pattern. I don't see the people coming toward me; I run into them. I don't see the cars either. Only the multicolored splinters that keep changing their crystal patterns, which are never repeated. I dash about aimlessly. It's only toward morning that I go to the park and lie facedown on the earth. I wanted to buy her a winter coat and mittens and warm shoes for her frostbite, and genuine coffee from beans, and rolls with butter and real honey. And it was all meant to be a surprise.

This morning I audition for the part of Melchtal in Schiller's *William Tell*. When I come to the words "Into the eyes, you say? Into the eyes . . . ?" I think of my mother's eyes, and my tears prevent me from going on. Then I yell: "The day will brightly dawn within your night!" I dash off the stage and out of the theater.

The secretary catches up with me in the street and tells me I've been offered a contract. I go back with her, sign the thing, take an advance of fifty marks, and split forever.

I join a wandering troupe. They do operettas and I have to sing. I don't give a damn so long as it brings me closer to Berlin. I can't believe my brother's telegram. I can't believe my mother is dead.

The troupe director's wife is very young. She has rosy raspberry lips that have been crushed with kisses and she has deep rings under her black cherry eyes. I'm gonna screw her no matter what it takes.

We act in taverns and meeting halls. The stuff we put on is not to be described. To top off all the stupidity we're to mount *Charley's Aunt*.

We travel in open trucks and sit on cast-iron garden chairs. I curse this brood, but we're heading north. In one village they even let us perform in the lousy theater.

The Offenburg park is thronged. But I have to memorize my idiotic part in *Charley's Aunt* somewhere. I'll go bananas if I remain in the stall where I'm billeted.

In the bright sunshine a Moroccan soldier is sitting on a bench. He grins at me with his yellow tooth stumps and points to his fly while brandishing a pack of cigarettes in his other hand. Then he motions toward some bushes behind him. He repeats his pantomime quite unabashed: fly, cigarettes, bushes. The guy must have a screw loose. He expects me go join him in those scrawny bushes? In the middle of the flower beds with everyone trudging by? Besides, he's sure to have syphilis. And then those yellow Gauloises he's holding are totally unsmokable. They're made especially for the Foreign Legion. You can't get beyond the first drag, it explodes in your lungs like a hand grenade. Who the hell does he think he is?

On Sundays we do two of those vile performances. I've already got one behind me, and so I rip off big, fleshy cherries on the highway outside the village tavern where we're performing.

Next to me a Moroccan soldier is also pilfering cherries. When he sees me grab a fully laden branch, he tries to yank it from my hand. I kick him in the butt. He pounces on me and, holding out his rifle, he drives me into the barracks across the road.

A moment later I'm surrounded by a gang of Moroccans. I don't get what they're jabbering but they gesticulate like ogres and threaten me with their bayonets. A couple of them are feeling up my fly. They seem to lust especially for blond boys.

A ghastly trumpet blare summons the horde to roll call. That's my salvation. They shove and kick me through the barracks gates. The sentry draws his rifle bolt. I very clearly hear the bolt snap in. The cartridge is now in the barrel. He aims at me.

"Get the hell outa here and go fuck yourself!"

I've never run so fast in my life.

The director and his young wife spend the night at the inn where we've been doing our repulsive performances for two weeks now. During the day we rehearse *Charley's Aunt* in the meeting hall.

I've got at least two hours to kill until I'm on with my shit. So I go take a leak. The toilet is one flight up.

To get there I have to walk past the double room where the director and his young wife sleep. And where they fuck, even in the daytime, during lunch break, before and after the performances, nonstop.

It's ten A.M. Her door is open. The room's untidy. I listen to make sure no one's coming; then I enter the room. The bed's a mess. The sheet's covered with stains. Some are quite fresh, still damp and creamy. I get a hard-on. When I turn around, she's standing behind me.

"What do you want?"

"The same as you."

"What do I want?"

"To fuck."

"You creep!"

Her face turns crimson. Her raspberry lips turn dark red. Her eyes get a silvery glow. She breathes heavily.

I take a used handkerchief and put it over the keyhole. In the mirror above the wash basin I see her yanking up her skirt. She pulls off her panties and stands before me with open legs, protruding pelvis, and slightly bent knees. Her rough, swollen tongue fills my mouth. Her belly pushed against my dick as if she were knocked up. She moans. Her abdomen works like a machine. She shpritzes and shpritzes. Our knees buckle. I shove my dick into her from behind, right up to my nuts, and I writhe as if I were touching a high-voltage line—while she, impaled, and with her tongue hanging out, rattles like a slaughtered calf.

Her husband won't pay me an advance. We're out in the street, and I punch him in the nose. Once again there's a Moroccan soldier—he drives us apart with his bayonet.

I skip town before dark, after stuffing my tux into my haversack. I tell no one I'm splitting. When the evening performance gets going they'll notice I'm gone.

The only trains heading for Berlin are freight. I have to buy a ticket for the next one-horse town so I can get through the barrier. When it's dark I'll run across the tracks. The freight train for Berlin arrives at six A.M.

Everyone who passes the military barrier is frisked. A woman is carrying a bottle of milk for the infant she's holding in her arm. The French sentry smashes the bottle on the station platform. This thug won't smash anything of mine. I've got nothing but my haversack and my tux. I've also wedged a pack of cigarettes between my ass cheeks.

I hide out till morning in the brakeman's booth of a sidetracked train car. I chain-smoke to avoid falling asleep. My freight train will stop only briefly to hitch on a few cars. I don't dare oversleep.

I make it as far as Frankfurt. The train stays put. I was misinformed.

I sleep in an air-raid bunker. A short, plump girl is also lying on a cot. We go outdoors—too many snoopy eyes in the bunker.

I have to wait days on end for a freight train that's going to Berlin. At the freight station in Berlin I take the urban rail to Schöneberg. From there I hike the two and a half miles to our place.

A couple of firebombs have smoked out the back wing. But our apartment has survived. Except for the shattered window panes and the charred frames.

Arne tells me how our mother died. He heard it from a woman who was with her when it happened. Low-flying American airplanes shot my mother in the belly. As she bled to death in the gutter, she smoked a cigarette and worried about us kids. Then she was buried somewhere or other. The woman couldn't say where because parachute mines were coming down, and she had to get into the air-raid cellar.

No one knows anything about my father. He remains among the vanished. Achim hopes he's in a Russian POW camp. Inge has written from Schliersee.

I'm even hungrier than in my childhood. It's impossible to dig up any food if you don't have jewels or whatnot, or get involved in some racket. We trudge from farmer to farmer, twenty or thirty miles on foot, trying to get potatoes or turnips which they feed to their pigs. But the farmers want jewelry or genuine Persian rugs.

After running around I'm so wiped out that I fall asleep on the urban train. When I wake up, a plastered G.I. is babbling away at me. Some sort of bullshit about "you German . . . You were . . . Boom, boom . . . No good . . . No boom, boom." I ought to yell into that moron's drunken face that it was American pilots who killed my mother! They shot her in the belly! In the womb! The womb she carried me in and from which she gave birth to me! But I don't know any English. All I know how to say is, "Fuck you!"

Arne tells me he's gotten an ax. He wants to hide behind a tree in the park, wait for a passerby, and mug him, because he's totally at the end of his rope. He trembles like an aspen leaf.

A week later I realize I've caught my first dose of the clap. Who knows from whom? I'm gonna have to get used to this from now on.

I audition at Berlin's Schlossparktheater. I lie brazenly, claiming I've played Hamlet, whereas I've never even read or seen the play.

I don't know whether anyone believes me. Barlog hires me after my first audition.

I debut as the page in the prologue of *The Taming of the Shrew*. The page has nothing to do but wear drag and hold on to the drunken tinker so he can watch the show from a box. During those stupid two hours the page has to grab the liquor bottle from his hands the instant the tinker tries to drink. Naturally this is not real booze, not even rotgut, just some sort of warm stuff. A piss drink. Not even Coke.

After a whole month I'm fed up. I pour booze into the bottle. Whenever I grab it away from the tinker, I take a deep swallow. By Act III, I'm totally bombed. . . . I start grinning from ear to ear, slurping from the bottle and reeling around the stage—and I step into the stupid prompter's box. Curtain.

Backstage, Barlog confronts me, so I hurl the empty bottle at him.

At five A.M. I wake up on a bench near the Zoo subway station. I don't know how I got here. Someone is groping me. I shove him away. The old people say that this is the worst winter in decades. The mercury plummets to fifteen below, I still don't have a coat, and Barlog doesn't seem to give a damn. Like all the lousy actors he's always nicely wrapped up, and he's always got a huge thermos bottle and sandwiches. He gets the best ration book, No. 1. I get the worst, No. 3. I can't spend the night at home anymore. We cover ourselves with rags, newsprint, and cardboard, and wind strips of cloth around our hands, feet, and heads. We still have no windowpanes; the icy wind whistles into the room day and night, the snow falls into our beds and our faces.

Tonight, when I take the unheated trolley to the theater, I cry. It's not my poverty I'm crying about, and not the pain caused by the lump of ice that went through the hole in my shoe sole. It's my fury at that theater riffraff. The starvation wages that Barlog pays me. Not enough even to buy a little food.

After each performance I hide in the heated theater and sleep on two chairs in the wardrobe. The janitor doesn't fink on me. But when Barlog finds out about it from some shithead, I'm strictly ordered not to do it anymore.

I take along food from home. Barley porridge. I cook enough for several days in advance. After a couple of hours the porridge gets as stiff as bread. Every day before heading out to the theater I cut off a slice of ice-cold porridge, wrap it in newspaper, and stick it inside my shirt.

Since I have no rehearsals, I don't know where to spend my days. I'm not tolerated anywhere for long.

So-called "warmth halls" have been set up in every neighborhood, and here people can huddle around iron stoves. In their homes they die like flies.

These "warmth halls" are no bigger than normal rooms—at best, they're the size of a tavern. They're always mobbed. The overseer makes sure that nobody outstays his welcome. So I have to commute from one warmth hall to the next. The distances are huge, and I draw up a precise schedule. Once I get into a warmth hall, I remove the frozen rags that are wrapped around my head and hands as if I were a leper, and I place those rags on the stove until they almost burn up. Then I put on my "clothes" again and race, cringing, to the next warmth hall. I can't do it at one fell swoop. Every hundred yards I have to look out for a way station—a building entrance, a covered driveway, a basement entrance, a subway staircase—in order to shield myself against the relentless cold.

Hygiene is catastrophic. In our apartment I can't even wash, much less take a bath. Wood and coal are nowhere to be found. The pipes in the toilet and the kitchen are frozen. Even the razor is frozen fast. I wash wherever I can—at the theater, in public rest rooms.

The worst of the cold is past, and the sun is timidly peeping out. Only now, after I've been asking him all winter long, does Barlog have someone tailor an American army blanket into a coat for me.

The coat is never completed. The costume designer who's making this coat monster for me claims I grabbed her pussy in the costume room.

When Barlog refuses to cast me as the lead in *Ah, Wilderness!* I smash the windowpanes of the Schlossparktheater. My one-year contract is not renewed. But I would have lost my mind anyway and starved to death among these barnstormers.

From now on I just wander around. I eat and sleep wherever I can. The main thing is to avoid dying of cold or hunger and to put my head somewhere or other, preferably between a girl's legs. Once it turns warmer I'll sleep in bushes again.

Meanwhile I've learned that there's such a thing as acting schools. I use them to steal books, and normally I also steal a girl into the bargain. Besides, the acting schools are always heated, and the girls always have sandwiches or an apple or a hardboiled egg.

What they teach in these acting schools is incredible, hair-raising crap. The Actors Studio in America is supposed to be the worst. There the students learn how to be natural—that is, they flop around, pick their noses, scratch their balls. This bullshit is known as "method acting." How can you "teach" someone to be an actor? How can you teach someone how and what to feel and how to express it? How can someone teach me how to laugh or cry? How to be glad and how to be sad? What pain is, or despair or happiness? What poverty and hunger are? What hate and love are? What desire is, and fulfillment? No, I don't want to waste my time with these arrogant morons.

Books and girls, yes. These girls are very young. The youngest is thirteen. The oldest sixteen and a half. She's a slut, but she's hard at work studying acting, and she gets food and whole cartons of cigarettes from the Yanks. She's had syphilis, but says she's been cured. She's very sweet, but a boring beanpole. I fuck her just once, on a steep slope over the railroad tracks near Halensee Station.

As for the very young one, I devirginize her at her home. She lives with her mother in a small apartment near Treptower Park. I believe her parents are divorced, but I'm never sure. I meet only her mother. She leaves us alone in the parlor all afternoon because I tell her I want to rehearse the bed scene from *Romeo and Juliet* with her daughter. When the girl strips naked and pulls on only her transparent nightie, the mother plays safe and leaves the apartment.

Once she's gone, we rehearse the scene on the parents' double bed. But the mattress is too soft. We need something that doesn't yield, that offers resistance—otherwise I won't be able to penetrate her closed-up cunt. We lie down on the hard sofa. It's the right stuff, but I can't manage to penetrate her no matter how spread-out she lies. I pull her off the sofa, turn her on her belly, pull her up on her knees, and force down her head, so that her face is on the floor and she can hold tight to the legs of the sofa. Then I bore my fist into her back, hollowing it, so that her ass sticks up. But I can't drill her even from behind. She's incredibly tight. The stiff little wads of her vaginal lips keep springing together like two halves of a rubber ball.

And now she has to piss in the bargain! She can't even make it to the door—she stands there, pissing wide-legged on the floor. Her piss pelts downs like a cloudburst. I yank her back on her knees and shove it in. I explode deep inside her.

For a short time Ulrike K.'s acting school becomes my refuge. That is, the apartment she shares with Agnes, her adopted daughter. She doesn't expect me to endure the garbage of acting classes. She simply takes me in, shares everything with me. Food, drink, a little cash, and the mattresses. In any case, Agnes gets into my bed every night.

The first I see of Agnes is a nude in red chalk; it's on the wall of the waiting room in the school. I get a boner. Everything on this body shines like marble. The butt. The boobs. The small, round belly.

The convex pussy.

Usually I don't get back from my scouting expeditions until the night. I climb through the bedroom window, which she keeps open for me as if I were a cat. I crawl right into bed with her and warm up on her hard butt. But before I get warm, my dick stands up like a hammer, and we toss away the covers. Her body stiffens and writhes nonstop and quakes and twitches. We go through all positions, even up her ass, and everything oral. I feel her orgasms like electric pulsations, while I grow deeper and deeper into her like a root. When she's drained me dry, brimming over with me and so feeble that she can't even scream, I jump back out through the window and run through the starry night. My body, my hands, my face are more fragrant than the blossoms on the bushes where I lie down to sleep with my face toward the sky.

Prince Sasha Kropotkin is a gangster. In the daytime he deals in antique furniture and jewels, buying the very last spoons from old grannies. He takes anything—earrings, amulets, gold fittings of family albums, photo frames, even gold teeth. Anything, so long as it's gold.

He scratches it slightly and drips some acid on the scratch, and he can instantly tell the karat figure. His biggest profit comes from Russian icons.

He fritters his nights away with male hustlers, who rob him blind. Once, a boy even banged his mother on the head, trying to clean out the apartment.

Tonight, as usual, Sasha is hanging out in a bar with a boy, gaping at him with his glassy eyes as if the kid were a priceless icon. Meanwhile Sasha is getting plastered on vodka. He's very rich and always treats everyone. Until Gustl snaps and barks, cutting down the hustler with her snotty tongue and pushing Sasha into a cab. She takes me along, too.

Gustl is a beautiful woman in her late twenties. She got it into her head to marry a Russian prince, Sasha Kropotkin, and become Princess Kropotkin, because she's got a thing about nobility. But otherwise, lots of men have fucked her. She sponges off Sasha and other fat cats, getting her hands on whatever she can. She likewise deals in antique furniture, which she buys from a dead man's survivors in the very room he's just died in. The heirs want to take the cash straight to the black market and buy a lump of butter, eggs, milk, and meat. She deals in worm-eaten crosses, patens, tabernacles, and icons—even confessionals that she steals from bombed-out churches, headstones from torn-up cemeteries. She buys and sells jewelry for Sasha, on consignment, and she pockets a commission for the boys she gets him. She administers Sasha's fortune in her head, and at every hour of the day and night she reminds him that when he was crocked he promised to marry her. This, in Gustl's view, means he has to pay all her bills. Sometimes Sasha beats her up. Once he even broke one of her fingers, and it never healed properly. She talks about it to everybody, holding up her crooked digit. Most people laugh. But Gustl is cunning. She doesn't mind being laughed at if she can arouse pity.

She's always cheerful by nature; this, she says, is due to the fact that she was born in the Rhineland. She never holds a grudge, even after the heartbreaking tragedy that she plays at least once a day with Sasha.

She takes me along to fuck. I promptly shack up with her. She buys me a toothbrush and a razor and a minimal wardrobe—she even orders a custom-made suit for me; it's made of the finest English wool.

Then she drags me along to all sorts of parties and to other hookers in order to show me off. She feeds me nutritious first-class food, even cooks wonderful delicacies, and buys pounds and pounds of meat at exorbitant prices. And she squooshes my balls dry like an orange squeezer. If there are any tricks or positions I don't know, she teaches them to me. She also tells me a lot about other men. Hans A. had her suck him off—but she wasn't allowed to swallow his come, she had to give it back mouth-to-mouth. He wanted to swallow it himself. Gustl is a fabulous whore, and I'm in good hands here.

But eventually she gets on my nerves, and so I see her only occasionally, at Sasha's place.

The Kropotkins are one of those White Russian families that managed to get out in time with their stuff, and no matter what nook or cranny on this planet they may be in, they're eternally scared of the Bolsheviks. Sasha and his mother got stranded in Berlin, and he is always scared of being kidnapped by the KGB. His apartment, which is stuffed with priceless antiques and whose walls are jampacked with Russian icons, is equipped with steel doors and heavy window gates, like a penitentiary. This floor-through, which runs around an entire street corner, from Uhlandstrasse to the Kurfürstendamm, is a meeting place for black marketeers, aristocrats, high-fashion designers, thieves, whores, hustlers, artists, murderers, and top-ranking French, British, American, and even Soviet occupation officers.

Sasha truly loves me. He surely also loves my face, my body, and my Slavic soul. Above all, he loves me because I tell the truth and don't rob him. His confidence in me is unlimited: He leaves me alone in the apartment with diamonds and pearl necklaces. I can eat here and spend the night whenever I feel like it. His queer butler has orders to let me in at any hour of the day or night—but Sasha never gives me money. Nor does he ever pay me a commission. When I tell him I want to deal on the black market, he laughs at me.

Instead he tells me about Russia. About Dostoevsky and Tolstoy, about Tchaikovsky and Nijinsky. He plays Russian records for me, and he weeps the way Russians do when they listen to their music. And like the Russians in the novels of Tolstoy and Dostoevsky, he gets bombed out of his mind and confesses all the nasty, filthy things he does, and he then begs me for redemption. He should worry!

Sasha takes me along to the Paris-Bar. I dance with a Polish cunt. She works as a stripper at a nearby club and lives in a rooming house on the corner. I reach into Sasha's trouser pocket and fish out whatever I need for the Pole.

The Polish cunt must have a magic technique. My dick stays hard nonstop even after I've shot a couple of times. After every fuck she pushes out my boner, rolls over, and dozes off. There's no way I can sleep; I wait with my trigger-happy cock until her big ass squeezes toward me—that's the signal. She's gotta have it six or seven times a night. She barely talks, only when it's absolutely necessary. Besides, I don't understand her gobbledygook.

It might look as if all I do is loll around in beds and fuck. No way. Frequently I isolate myself from everybody for weeks on end, lock myself in my room, and don't even go outdoors. During such periods I do language exercises ten, twelve, fourteen, sixteen hours a day. Or all night long. If the neighbors complain—and they always do—I have to leave whatever room I'm in. I change rooms more often than girls. Sometimes I have to leave a room the very same day I get it.

I spend days strolling through the parks, nights walking the streets. Barely conscious of what's going on around me, I recite some text or other. If I get tired during my language exercises or I don't think I can reach my quota, I slap my face. I just have to make it! I'll show them!

Alfred Braun, the former star reporter of Berlin Radio, casts me in *Romeo and Juliet*. With my pay I rent the first studio of my own. It's really just a laundry room on the top floor of a building. But it has a large studio window with light flooding through it. I paint the place white and scrub the floor. I have a bed, a table, a chair, and my own toilet, where I wash myself with cold water under the faucet. That's all I need. What meager laundry I have I do myself. At night I don't sleep on my bed; instead I walk through the parks, and when I can't walk anymore I lie down on the bare ground and peer at the sky. When day finally breaks, like a long-awaited birth, I go back to my studio and lie down fully dressed on my bed. I don't need much sleep, just three or four hours.

Jean Cocteau's *La Machine à Écrire* ("The Typewriter"). In one scene I have to have an epileptic fit. The director has never witnessed one. Neither have I. That's why I go to the hospital and ask the head of the psychiatric division to describe an epileptic attack. He wants me to watch a patient getting shock therapy. The reactions, he says, are the same as in an epileptic fit: When the patient is electrified by the heavy current, her body writhes and convulses. Her teeth suddenly bang so hard that they would shatter if it weren't for the piece of garden hose between the two rows.

She foams at the mouth. Her eyes pop.

The patient is wheeled into the treatment room. She's very young and beautiful. But her face and body are as gray as a street. All she has on is a hospital gown. She sits up halfway, but doesn't seem interested in her surroundings, she just stammers softly and unintelligibly. The doctor says that the girl was ditched by her boyfriend, and the trauma was so great that she lost her mind. They're using shock therapy to trigger a countershock, which may help her if everything works out.

"What if it doesn't work out?" I ask.

"Then she's out of luck," says the doctor coldbloodedly.

The girl is strapped to the bed. The electrodes are applied. On her arms, her feet, her temples. Like in an electric chair. A piece of chewed-up garden hose is wedged between her teeth. The power is switched on. Jerking dreadfully, she opens her legs wide, simultaneously yanking them in, so that her gown rides up and I can see her open vagina. Her abdomen rears as raunchily as if she were shrieking after love and not after an electric shock. Then her legs lurch forward, as if she were kicking something. I turn and leave the room.

I succeed in performing the epileptic seizure on stage. But I keep seeing the girl. Her abdomen exposing her secret, which was not meant for me. Every woman's magic secret.

Edith E. plays opposite me in *La Machine à Écrire*. After performing we often hang together all night. Sometimes I visit her in her apartment in Westend during the day. Though she's fifty, she's never had a man in all her life. Initially I satisfy her with my tongue. Soon I get her to the point of letting me fuck her with my dick. The entrance to her vagina is as tiny as the slit in a piggy bank in which you can only insert pennies, and she gets agonizing pains. Nevertheless she squeezes my pecker greedily and she doesn't want me to stop plugging her.

All her life she's licked girls and women and all her life she's only let girls and women lick her—at school, in the girls' boarding school, and later as an adult. She tells me about passionate muff-diving feasts.

About her first touches. About the teacher who first seduced her. About a nurse who brutally raped her, who controlled her completely, whom she hated yet was in complete bondage to, and who eventually committed suicide because Edith managed to dump her. She tells me about romantic, dreamy women who were like herself, like little girls, crawling under the blanket because they're scared. She tells me about the uninhibited obsession of a Catholic nun who left the order for her sake. And about her own sister, who was her idol. And she tells me about her relationship with Marlene D. when they were both just starting out. Marlene tore down Edith's panties backstage in a Berlin theater and, using just her mouth, brought Edith to orgasm.

Jürgen Fehling, the only living genius among stage directors, calls me in. I audition for him. Seven hours straight! It's six P.M. The staff is already arriving at the Hebbel Theater to prepare for the evening show. Fehling has a young usherette to do the death scene in *Othello* with me.

"Just keep your trap shut," he tells the flabbergasted girl, "no matter what Kinski does to you, you just stay as motionless as a bump on a log, don't let out a peep. I want to hear nothing but his voice." What does he mean, "No matter what Kinski does to you?" What can I do to her here anyway?

I hate this guy. I'd rather fuck the usherette, whose panties smell so intoxicating that my nuts ache. Seven hours aren't enough for him! He must be wacko.

We have to break. He has me read to him from a phone book in a dressing room. I read and read and make him laugh and cry.

From then on Fehling never lets me out of his clutches. I accompany him for weeks on end, watching his rehearsals, eating with him, and spending whole nights in bars with him. He talks and talks, and sometimes I'm so tired that I slump over with my face in a plate of food.

Fehling is to become artistic director of the Hebbel Theater.

"When I take over, I'm gonna save on everything—sets, cos-tumes, and especially those foul-smelling officials, and all the other stuff." He grows angrier and angrier as we sit in a corner of a dive. "But I'm not gonna save on my actors' salaries. They'll get everything they need. Everything. Then I'll demand everything from them, and they'll have the strength to give me everything!"

Otto Graf wants to cast me as Oswald in Ibsen's *Ghosts.* I sign the contract, getting an advance of five hundred marks. When I tell Fehling, he replies:

"You're not ready to do Oswald. That's gonna be a high C for you. You have to break the contract. I, Fehling, will defend you in court. Never forget: The Good Lord has plans for you! And I'm gonna make something of you! If you're gonna do Oswald, then only under my direction. Never for anyone else. Above all, you should never work with Gründgens. That pissoir slut is an ignoramus. He claims there's no such thing as feelings. Because he has none himself. If you need money, tell me, I'll give you money."

"No thanks. I've still got some."

It hits me that I shouldn't have said that. Have I gone bananas, turning down money?

"Fine," he says. "Let me know if you need anything. I'll always be here for you. I'll protect you."

I'm so convinced by what he's said that I go to Otto and repeat it verbatim. I also tell him that I want to get out of my contract. Otto is very crestfallen. But he's scared of Fehling and doesn't dare contra-dict him.

"Then I won't do *Ghosts,*" he says.

The next morning Otto takes a final stab. He wants to go to Fehling with me and ask him to release me.

Fehling tells me to wait in the next room while he talks to Otto.

He's very charming to him. But he makes it clear that Otto should keep his hands off me. I eavesdrop at the door and hear every word.

"You'll only destroy him," says Fehling to Otto. "But I can turn him into the greatest actor of the twentieth century!"

Fehling tells me that I'm the first actor he'll hire as soon as he takes office at the Hebbel Theater.

The chief of the American Military Police in Berlin (I met him through Sasha) gets me a ticket for an American army plane to Munich. From there I take the train to Schliersee, where Inge lives. She's married a lumberjack. I feel as if Paul Bunyan were standing in front of me when, shouldering his ax, he crushes my hand in his viselike grip.

Since neither I nor they have money and we have to sleep in the same room, I'm forced to hear their fucking, which they indulge in as shamelessly as if I weren't even there. "How randy she is," I think, "she can't even control herself for one night." Or maybe she's doing it deliberately to remind me of what we did together. In any case, she keeps moaning and coming until dawn, and all I can do is jerk off under my blanket.

By the time I get back to Berlin, Fehling has become artistic director of the Hebbel Theater but has then been instantly tossed out on his ear after announcing that he first wants to do a movie in which he himself plays God. After his lecture at the university, students throw rocks at him, making his head bleed. He then vanishes.

I go to Otto and promise to do Oswald. I need money. Mrs. Alving is played by Maria Schanda. After the scene in which Oswald loses his marbles, she holds me in her arms for a long time because she's worried about me.

Before the premiere Otto gives me some cocaine because my throat is so hoarse that I can barely speak. After I inhale some of the white powder through my nostrils, my air passages and vocal chords are magically liberated. But the coke dries out my mucous membranes;

my tongue grows heavy and fails to obey me, while I have the delusion that I can speak trippingly and feel so powerful that I can tear out trees.

At the performance everything goes well. Spectators shriek during the mad scene. A few dash out of the theater. One woman faints.

Otto shouldn't have given me the coke. He also left me with a pouch containing one gram. After using up half of it, I ask around, trying to find a dealer. I've spent a week's salary on one gram and snorted it up when it strikes me that I've no appetite anymore. I haven't eaten for days. Instead I lick the last few crumbs from the paper the coke is wrapped in.

I order a meal in a restaurant. Upon handing me the bill, the waiter gapes at me, dumbfounded. The full plates lie there untouched. I've pushed away the soup, the entree, and the dessert, and done nothing but chain-smoke. I haven't even realized what I've been doing. When I see my face in the bathroom mirror, I know there'll be no escape if I don't stop cold turkey.

Ghosts day after day. Even in broiling heat. Even Saturday matinee. Even Sunday morning. A girl brings me the first sunflowers.

A newspaperwoman wants to interview me. She's deliberately left the top button of her blouse unbuttoned and she's not wearing a bra. Her pearlike tits bounce wildly with every step she takes in her high heels; they almost hop into my face. I keep looking at them. Her body is young and lithe, and yet so tense that I get the impression that if her tight skirt didn't cage her in, her thighs would spring apart like a switchblade, and her bodacious butt cheeks, which fit nicely into a male hand, would burst like chestnuts from their shells. Her beautiful, narrow mouth is almost too small for the strong, white teeth that keep the lips apart. She never even looks at me with her light-gray eyes. But I know that this interview will last for a long time.

Forty minutes later we're alone in her apartment on Reichskanzlerplatz. She stretches out on the bed, fully dressed. She lies very quiet, still not looking at me. She stands up again, lights one cigarette after another. She vanishes into the john for a long time. She fixes coffee and sandwiches. She lies back down on the bed. She smokes like a chimney. She doesn't say a word when I lie down next to her.

But whenever I so much as touch her, she flinches in terror. After two hours of this torture, I rip off her blouse at one swoop, and the pear tits lose control. They actually do a Saint Vitus's dance and shove their way into my mouth. We yank at our clothes, stumble, fall on the floor, gasp, yelp, shriek as if our lives depended on our getting rid of our clothes.

By the time we're naked, we're both crouching like two beasts about to pounce on each other. Then we do pounce, we dig our teeth into each other. We hit each other on the body. The face. The breasts. The genitals. Attack each other more and more violently. Sink our teeth in more and more painfully.

She pushes her abdomen up to my mouth as if performing a gymnastic bridge. She does a belly landing. Stretches her butt in the air. The cheeks gape apart, opening up her asshole and the gullet of her ravenous pussy—which snaps at my writhing eel like a feeding predator.

Sixteen hours later, when I leave her apartment at seven A.M., there's nothing we haven't done.

A short time afterward I read in the papers that she and her husband have committed suicide.

Seven months ago, Wolfgang Langhoff, the artistic director of Max Reinhardt's Deutsches Theater in East Berlin, refused to hire me. I even had to wait for weeks before he saw me. When I finally auditioned, shrieking at the top of my lungs, weeping my eyes out, and banging my hands and arms bloody, Langhoff didn't even listen. He wolfed down sandwiches and rubbed a splotch of sugary tea from his tie.

Why are these lowdown directors always scared they'll starve to death in the theater?

"Come back in a couple of years," he says to me with his mouth full. "Maybe something'll work out. And eat. Eat, eat! You're so skinny that people are worried you're gonna be shattered by your emotional eruptions. So eat heartily."

I should have smashed that jelly fish in his jelly belly. But I thought to myself: "You'll be crawling to me someday! And in a couple of years you're gonna kick the bucket anyway!"

He comes crawling earlier than I figured. After *Ghosts* his managing director sends me a polite letter, inviting me to come to the Deutsches Theater.

Langhoff signs me up for one year at a monthly salary of three thousand marks and says that when the season's over I can decide whether to renew my contract. Naturally, for a much higher salary.

The first play is Shakespeare's *Measure for Measure.* I'm Claudio. He's sentenced to death for deflowering a young girl without first marrying her. (Me, of all guys!) In the dungeon cell he has visions of his corpse being chewed up by worms.

It's hard for me to picture the worms eating me. I never think about death. I haven't even really started living yet.

Nights, I sneak around cemeteries and enter tombs. The rusty cast-iron portholes are heavy and I can barely open them. I squeeze through. I lean against the canvas-covered coffins. I listen, trying to catch something. I put my ear on graves and call the dead, who never respond. I have to find the answer. But how?

At a performance everything works out on its own. I've solved the mystery: You have to submit silently. Open up, let go. Let anything penetrate you, even the most painful things. Endure. Bear up. That's the magic key! The text comes by itself, and its meaning shakes the soul. Everything else is taken care of by the life one has to live without sparing oneself. You mustn't let scar tissue form on your wounds; you have to keep ripping them open in order to turn your insides into a marvelous instrument that is capable of anything. All this has its price. I become so sensitive that I can't live under normal conditions. That's why the hours between performances are the worst.

I'm fed up with doing *Measure for Measure*. I sniff around everywhere like a puppy, trying to find something better. Eventually Bertolt Brecht wants to meet me. I watch a rehearsal of *Mother Courage* with some cast changes. This is the third month he's been rehearsing this very same scene. He goes through an actor's every word, every motion, a thousand times. My mind gets numb from so much stupidity. They must be illiterate!

When he asks me if I want to join his Berliner Ensemble, I try to come up with a clever reply. But Brecht himself is clever enough and reads my silence in his own way: "I myself would have to advise you against it. I can do as I like here in East Germany, but I doubt if they have the sense of humor they'd need for you."

I wrack my brain, trying to figure out what I can do to avoid performing each and every evening. I plunk down, fully dressed, in a tub of ice-cold water and with dripping clothes I creep through the ruins of the bombed-out section of Wartburgstrasse, where I remain lying in the rubble until evening. I want to catch pneumonia. But I don't even get the sniffles. The Good Lord must really have something in mind for me.

As a member of the Deutsches Theater I receive coupons for one meal a day at the Theater Club. This club has been set up by the Russians and is open to anyone working in opera, ballet, or theater. The restaurant has everything, including Crimean champagne and malossol caviar. I don't eat caviar or drink champagne because I can't afford them, but one day I indulge in a second meal. Lunch, and then another meal after the evening performance because I'm starving. I promptly get a warning. The manager of the Deutsches Theater, who always eats two meals a day there, saw me and reported me.

One week later that same manager refuses to give me an advance on my salary.

You can get from the dressing rooms to the offices directly through internal stairs and corridors. I'm already in costume for the evening show, except for my long boots, when I grab the shithead's necktie and slap him until his bleating attracts other office employees. Now Langhoff appears, too, and orders me to take off my costume, firing me on the spot. But I have no intention of removing my costume. I storm into my dressing room to pull on my boots.

The boots are still at the cobbler's. I can't get in there because Langhoff, the manager, and the other office workers, who follow me like a string of geese, would block the way. So in stocking feet I go downstairs to the lobby, the string of geese behind me.

The first few spectators are gathering at the evening box office. I storm past them into the street. It's filled with people heading toward the theater. Here! The theater pub! The barkeep's a friend of mine. The joint is likewise crowded with people devouring a meatball or having a drink before the performance.

The string of geese, headed by Langhoff, has used a different stairway, which leads from the theater lobby directly into the bar. I run right into their arms. They chase me over tables, chairs, customers. I jump onto a table.

"If you want your costume back, here it is!"

I rip bits of the costume off my body. I chew it up into bits and pieces.

"This is for you! And for you! Here! Eat it up if you like! No one else'll ever wear it after me!"

That rat of a manager suffers with every shred of cloth. I mince the costume into such tiny scraps that it could never be patched to-gether again. There's no way they can stop me. I stand with my back to the wall, and if anyone tries to get at me I'll kick him in the head!

Then I'm naked! The barkeep throws a coat over me and tries to calm me down, for I'm shrieking with fury and disgust at this rabble. The string of geese goes away with their tatters.

After the business at the Deutsches Theater, I'm back on the street, and so I go to Sasha. "Don't give a fuck!" is all he says, and hands me a vodka. That's just like him. When another gangster ripped him off by replacing a pearl necklace worth three hundred thousand marks with a bunch of phony pearls, Sasha merely gulped down a vodka. When I tell him about the ruckus at the Deutsches Theater, he laughs.

"Don't let it get to you, and thank the Creator for your talent. Look at me. I'd give anything to switch places with you. I'm forty-two years old and all my life I've done nothing but suck out other people's blood, run after hustlers, let them rob me blind, and get looped under my icons. Do you believe I enjoy this life? You've got every reason to be happy! Someday people will cluster around you! They'll have fist-fights over you. You're gonna get everything you want. Don't worry about people who threaten you. Hide your fists from them. They can't hold a candle to you. Go find a new studio, it'll be on me. Or sleep here and get fed. Or live in my apartment on Königsallee."

I don't move in with Sasha or to Königsallee. Instead I find a nice studio on Brandenburgische Strasse.

Helga is the girl who brought me the first sunflowers in the theater. Her parents ordered her not to come to me; her father is a Protestant minister. But even though it takes forever for her to let me fuck her, she keeps returning every day. At last she allows me to place her on the altar and sacrifice her hymen.

When her parents ground her, she marries a student. Now her parents can't order her around anymore. Every morning she slips into my bed, remaining until the student comes home from campus, when she has to cook him dinner.

I need sunflowers! I walk many miles, trying to find some. If they're fresh, I kiss their honey faces. If they're dried, I put them on my windowsill, where they continue glowing.

I saw a gigantic sunflower in a garden in Tempelhof. I can't risk stealing it, so I ask the owner to sell it to me. He lets me have it for free.

I carry it by its light-green six-foot stem from Tempelhof to Brandenburgische Strasse. Its black, sticky face is framed by radiant yellow petals, while I wear jeans as blue as cornflowers and a T-shirt as red as poppy. I got both items from someone who has a friend in America. Since it's summer, I go barefoot.

It's Sunday, and the streets are full of strollers. I try to escape people by using side streets, for no matter where I go they all laugh at me and my sunflower.

To avoid running this gauntlet, I break off the head of the sunflower, press its face to my chest like a baby's, and jog on toward Wilmersdorf.

I try to climb into a bus, but the conductor can't help entertaining the passengers with stupid remarks about me and my sunflower. They roar with mirth. I leap off the moving bus.

The street becomes more and more unbearable. I'm so bewildered and offended by the brutality and narrowmindedness of these people who laugh at me and my sunflower that, surrounded by all these pedestrians, I see no other solution than to tear the yellow sunflower head into pieces and run away.

Achim is home from a Russian POW camp and already locked up again. He was part of a gang that ripped off fur coats. I visit him in the Moabit remand prison, bringing him chocolate and cigarettes. He's ecstatic at seeing me again, and we hug and kiss. He begs me to get him a lawyer.

On the way to the lawyer on Fasanenstrasse, I see a policewoman dragging and shoving a weeping woman with a knapsack on her back. Passersby gape but hold their tongues.

"What are you doing with her?" I ask the uniformed nanny goat.

"She sold stuff on the black market," she replies.

"So what!" I retort. "Aren't you ashamed, you female Cossack, arresting this poor woman for that? She must really be needy, otherwise she wouldn't have done it. Let her go!"

The uniformed nanny goat releases the terrified woman for one instant and grabs me by the wrist.

"Your ID card!" she shrieks hysterically.

I twist out of her sausage fingers and laugh in her face.

"I ain't got none!"

This is too much for her uniformed brain. She raises her whistle to her thin lips and blows it until the traffic cop lets the cars drive as they like, and without asking what's happened he jumps on me. Now the passersby feel confident enough to call me an "agitator" and a "dangerous element." The traffic cop twists my arms behind my back, and I and the woman with the knapsack have to go along to the precinct.

"You've insulted my colleague's uniform and resisted the authority of the state!" a cop says at the precinct.

I can't help it, I have to laugh.

"Stop laughing!" he yells, beside himself. "Or I'll lock you up!"

I laugh all the louder. "You want me to cry?"

"I want you to shut your trap and speak only when you're spoken to!"

I have to laugh so loud that I choke.

"You're making me laugh again, I can't help it."

I get a kick in the small of my back and land in a cell. There are serial cages as in a zoo, with a cop walking up and down like a zookeeper guarding predators, his ego boosted by my raging against the bars. He must have been depressed before I got locked in the cage, for the neighboring cages are empty. Now he grins scornfully, so he must feel just fine and dandy. He slides his keys through his fingers like a rosary.

I shout at the top of my lungs, explaining that I'm friends with the mayor of Berlin, who's bosom buddies with John F. Kennedy, president of the U.S. of A., and that I'm gonna get all the thugs of this precinct fired. So the officer on duty lets me out of the cage and apologizes for the incident.

"What's gonna happen to the woman?" I ask him when he pushes me toward the exit to get rid of me.

"Nothing bad'll happen to her," the officer lies brazenly. Once I'm out in the street again, I piss on the building.

After his release from prison, Achim tries to go straight. He watches dogs, baby-sits, and donates blood twice a week. For every pint he gets twenty marks and a big steak.

I figure I might as well hock my corpse. I've learned that while you're still alive you can sell your carcass to a medical school for a nice handsome sum. My plan is to sell my "remains" to as many medical schools as possible. But this idea goes awry because the onetime sale of your corpse is noted on your ID card.

I hop a bus for Munich. I've heard that the Mardi Gras is just crawling with half-naked chicks.

The Haus der Kunst is putting on a Van Gogh exhibition. This is the first time that I've seen originals by Van Gogh. I dash outdoors, weeping and wailing.

At the Art Academy carnival, I bump into Gislinde and Therese. They're both made up as Pierrot, wearing leotards that emphasize their thighs, their little bellies, their teensy asses, and their sweet thick snail shells. Both are drenched in sweat. I dance the night away with them. I swallow their tongues. I knock both of them up that very same night.

Therese's family forces her to get an abortion. But Gislinde carries the baby to term. Therese is very sad. She wanted the kid, even though she knows I can't marry both girls. Nor do I ever talk marriage to Gislinde. She just looks forward to having her baby.

I can't fuck all the time; I have to make money too.

Fehling is at the Bavarian State Theater, so I make an appointment to see him. He reads my dramatization of *Crime and Punishment* and says, "I'll produce it with you, but not here. I take the theater so seriously that I can only feel sorry for these pathetic hicks. Let's try and figure out where and when. Relax, you look very worn out. Go to the country—my treat."

Fehling is as charming as he was in Berlin, and he radiates the same tremendous warmth and energy. But I'm worried that he'll never direct again.

As I climb into a streetcar, a girl stops dead in her tracks and flashes her snow-white teeth at me. I jump off the now moving trolley. I don't know the girl. This is the first time I've ever seen her. She introduces herself as Elsa. Elsa has a brownish face, long, black, stringy hair, eyes that shine like metal, stiff lips, and greedy, sensuous hands.

Elsa's relatives all have high positions in the Catholic church. One uncle is the pope's "right-hand man." The instant this clan finds out that Elsa is whoring with the devil, they kick out the little lamb as if she had the pox, and they cut off all support. Previously she was having an affair with the Berlin head of the American secret service, and he's still after her. He came here specifically to track down Nazis hidden in the Bavarian mountains. They wear lederhosen and live somewhere or other, tending goats.

For a while he keeps giving her money. But then this source dries up, too, because she has absolutely no time for him since we're "fucking like bunnies," as she puts it. We live in a cranny at an old-ladies' boardinghouse in Schwabing and we get up only to find food. Mostly we gobble raw eggs to keep our strength for fucking. But when we can't keep up the rent for our cranny we continue fucking in the English Garden, at a graveyard in Bogenhausen, and in the circular corridor around the Angel of Peace.

Elsa shares a room with some church lady; I'm in a Catholic seminary dorm that was founded by her grandfather. They haven't get gotten wind of the anathema inflicted on Elsa because of me, nor do the small parishes know that Elsa is being screwed by Beelzebub. We go begging in the churches, for the business about the uncle in the Vatican and the grandfather who founded the dorms still has a certain clout. At the church door the priest fobs us off with one lousy mark from the cash register. You can imagine how many churches we have to trudge to.

We'll never get anywhere on these alms. But then two old madams, Elli S. and Ilse A., who run an acting agency like a call girl ring, take me on. This is how it works: I'm to live in a dressing room at the Bavaria Film Studios so that I don't wander off. Besides, the dressing room doesn't cost anything—it's a kind of storeroom that's included in the rent for their office space. It's a two-by-four cell in which you'd go stir-crazy if you had to stay there alone. Whenever some director or producer walks into the agency office, which is one flight below my loony bin, my hair is wet down with water and combed, and then I'm shown off like a well-behaved brat. For this act I get a per diem allowance of seven marks as an advance against any later salary. I share the money with Elsa. I sneak down the fire escape and fuck her in the forest, which starts right near Bavaria Film Studios.

The wife of an American photographer named Jones or Bones or Clones or whatever arrives in Munich to make the rounds of the German movie producers. At Bavaria she runs into me, of all people—and even though she's constantly chaperoned by her mother-in-law to keep her from noshing on any dicks, we manage to grab a moment of privacy in the Court Garden of the Feldherrnhalle.

She scratches up my face and chews me out because I won't fuck her standing against a tree after fingering her hot, drooling cunt. It just won't work. I can't fuck her standing here. The bushes are too low and so sparse that passersby would see everything.

We try the bombed-out synagogue. But it seems to have become a latrine. Men are standing everywhere, pissing. Or jerking off.

Furious, she agrees to come back with me to my dressing room at Bavaria Studios.

But stupidly, we're spotted climbing the fire escape. At that instant the two agency madams happen to have a client in the office, and they want to display me like a hooker. They rattle the dressing-room door, firmly convinced that we've locked ourselves in. I stop up the keyhole and we try not to make a sound. This is very difficult because the photographer's wife pulled off her panties in the hall, and I can't manage to get my trousers off because she's knelt down, opened my fly, and is simply gobbling up my prick, so that I can't yank it out. I spurt in her throat. Then she grabs my head and squeezes my face between her widespread legs; and she comes so often that I lose count.

Now she's really raging and things get going. We keep switching positions, as if we were doing floor exercises.

The two madams keep coming upstairs and fanatically rattling the door, shrieking that I'm spoiling a big opportunity and so on.

When the yelping at the door lasts too long, we cautiously continue. But the dyed-blond beast keeps wanting to scream. No scream, no orgasm.

Outside it's night. We can't anymore. Besides, she suddenly remembers, she's got a mother-in-law at the hotel. Before she can clamber down the fire escape in her crumpled, splattered dress, I jump her once more from behind—and as she returns my thrusts, even deeper and more brutally, we crawl on all fours toward the fire escape.

Since I can't get anywhere in Munich, I have to head back to Berlin. Elsa gives me the ballads of François Villon as a going-away present.

I read them in the bus. As we arrive at dawn, I know: I am Villon!

At the Café Melodie on the Ku'damm, I present my first recital of the ballads of François Villon. The students of the art academy use colored chalk to write "KINSKI READS VILLON" on the roadways of the Ku'damm. Admission is free. I'll pass the hat.

The Café Melodie is so mobbed that people step on each other's toes. The ones who can't get in smash the windows, trying to force their way inside. When a policeman interferes, they beat the shit out of him.

I climb onto the nearest table and speak, shriek, yell, whisper, puff, gasp, weep, laugh the ballads of François Villon out of my soul. I'm barefoot, in a tattered sweater, and I have a peaked cap in which I collect money after every ballad.

Sasha tosses a hundred-mark bill into the cap; others put in from one to twenty marks, poor students fifty pennies or just ten, one even throws in his last penny. In less than fifteen minutes the cap is full.

Gislinde is in her ninth month and wants to give birth in Berlin because I can't make it to Munich. I rent a run-down but huge studio near the Ku'damm. I paint the whole place white and buy a lot of stuff on the installment plan: an iron bed with a mattress, a raw-wood table and two chairs, a laundry basket as a crib for the kid, baby blankets, baby linen, and diapers. I don't have enough money for bed linen. But I do buy sunflowers, which I stick into pitchers that someone lends me. I always take along one of the little baby shirts.

If it's a girl, I'm gonna name her Pola. That's the little girl in *Crime and Punishment* who runs after Raskolnikov and hugs and kisses him. Even though he's a murderer.

My daughter is born at the clinic in the red-light district. I'm so happy I tell all the hookers who walk up and down across from the clinic. They all know me. They give me flowers for Gislinde.

When Pola first opens her eyes, she looks around angrily. A thunderstorm breaks outside.

I don't want these goddamn nuns to take my daughter from my arms. The nuns get snotty. I curse them out. The mother superior asks me to step into the corridor. There two policemen are waiting for me.

"You desecrators of Jesus!" I yell so loud that Gislinde must hear me, for she emerges from the room with her suitcase and the baby, and we hop a taxi to my studio.

I can't keep up the payments for the furnishings, so the court bailiff hauls them off. We sleep on the floor for one night. The next morning I send Gislinde and Pola to her mother in Munich.

Eisenstein's *Ivan the Terrible.* Since I have no money, I dub the Russian film as well as two British movies starring Sabu.

Sasha leases a theater on Kaiserallee for me. I'm to play the woman in Jean Cocteau's *La Voix humaine* (*The Human Voice*). The whole thing is a monologue—a woman on the phone with her lover, who's dumped her. In the end she strangles herself with the telephone wire.

When I read the text all I can think of is being this woman. Why not? In Shakespeare's time there were no actresses. All the girls and women, including Juliet, were played by men. Even the Mona Lisa was a man. Anyway, who cares? I'm that woman, and that's that!

The monologue fills twenty-four typewritten pages. I memorize it in twenty-four hours. Then I dash over to Sasha and recite the hour-long monologue to him. It takes all night: He keeps wanting to hear it over and over again. At six A.M. his mother, Princess Nina Kropotkin, comes stealing by in her nightgown and chews Sasha out in Russian because she's learned he's invested a lot of money in the theater. Tears of avarice run down her cheeks, even though she herself is a millionaire and Sasha earns his own living. Her greasy hair reminds me of the pawnbroker in *Crime and Punishment*, whose head Raskolnikov splits open with an ax. Sasha now grabs a burning gold candelabrum and hurls it at his mother.

"You shouldn't do that, Sasha," I tell him. "She's your mom." But Sasha is beside himself, and I can't get him to calm down. I leave him alone and walk over to his floor-through on Königsallee.

However, I can't breathe among this antique plunder and the chichi gewgaws he gathered together for his weekends with hustlers but never uses himself. I crawl into bushes in the villa garden and try to nap.

Opening night is in four weeks. The theater is sold out for two months. But then the production is prohibited by the military government!

Sasha sends Cocteau a telegram in Paris. Cocteau wires back the very same day:

I'm happy that Kinski is playing the part. I congratulate
him for his courage. I'll do my best to attend the premiere.

Jean Cocteau

But the shit-headed military administration refuses to rescind the ban.
Their asses are licked by the art-and-culture riffraff, who are scared of
a scandal.

Time passes. Sasha won't keep paying because he's under pressure from his mother, who knows about the prohibition.

Sasha is drunk again and begs me on his knees to rescue him from
his unworthy life. I hurl the vodka bottle at the silk-covered wall and
tell him that he makes me puke. He yanks open the door of his safe:
"Take it all!"

Then he heads for a bar and drowns his hatred of his mother and
his own shitty life, which he never knew how to use.

I stand at the open safe, which is stuffed not only with packets of
banknotes but also diamonds, pearls, rubies, emeralds, and mountains
of gold. I don't know why, but I give the safe door a kick and leave the
apartment without touching anything. I'll never forgive myself.

I don't want to go back to the villa. I walk to Wartburgstrasse.
The front door is locked. I smash the colored-glass pane and ring
Arne out of bed.

Arne now works in the editorial department of a newspaper for
housewives and has pulled his way up the ladder. He's repaired his
apartment, bought furniture, owns suits, and wants to buy a car on the
installment plan. He doesn't know what Achim's up to, though Achim
drops by every now and again. Arne gives me the money for a bus
ticket to Munich. The vehicle's shaking is agony, but I miss my
daughter.

Gislinde lives with her family on Mauerkircherstrasse near the
Isar bridge—that is, right across from the English Garden. Hexi is the

youngest sister, she's fourteen or fifteen. All she cares about is hammering away on the piano. She has a face like Beethoven, and her touch is so wonderful that I burst out crying when I hear her play. When they no longer let her play in the apartment, and she can't find another venue, she kills herself.

Even though the family's nice to me and I've married Gislinde, I don't live in their apartment. I spend my nights in the English Garden or under the Isar Bridge. I'm happy that I've finally got the sky overhead, otherwise I'd die.

Once a day I meet Gislinde, who brings me my daughter so I can play with her, and sometimes she also brings some food or a couple of marks. If no one's at home, I go back with her and wash and shave. At such times I also get a hot meal. Otherwise I wash in the icy mountain water of the Isar. If it rains, I make a bed of leaves and cover myself with branches. I leave my face exposed so that it rains on my mouth and eyes. The raindrops are like hands caressing me, and I fall asleep. Best of all I like thunderstorms. They make me truly happy.

When the nights grow colder, Gislinde brings me a blanket under the Isar Bridge.

A director who wants to cast me in a Russian play gives me an old baby carriage. I now wheel Pola through the English Garden. The carriage is made of wickerwork, and I slip daisies into the gaps until the entire carriage looks like a flower bed.

In the English Garden I encounter Wanda, who's married to a Bulgarian. She's also wheeling her baby. Two hours later we're lying in the bushes. She's a maternal animal through and through. Her mouth. Her boobs. Her hips. Her butt. Her thighs. Her crotch. With every thrust we wallow deeper into the ground. We've left the carriages within our line of sight. It's pitch-black out by the time we separate, smeared with soil. She can't find her panties. I hurled them away.

I visit her daily, first thing in the morning, when her husband heads off to Radio Free Europe. They live in a furnished room, and everything smells of urine and diapers, which are scattered over the floor. I poke her in her double bed and drink from her long, full teats, which, like the udder of a well-fed cow, are almost bursting and have to be milked all the time. We're so horny that we're still banging away when her husband comes home from work. I have to hide in the hallway broom closet.

In Berlin the fashion photographer Helmut von Gaza calls up the two madams at the Bavaria Studios. He's got a studio the size of a meeting hall in his twelve-room apartment on the Ku'damm, and he wants to offer this space for the staging of *La Voix humaine.* The production can't be outlawed because he plans to register it as part of a theater club.

That same evening I hop the train for Berlin. Elsa has pawned her watch for me. She's now married to the general manager of the Bayreuth Gas Company, and while he drapes her with all sorts of gewgaws, he's very tight-fisted with cash for her.

Once again performances of *La Voix hunaine* are sold out for months in advance. I have no place to live. Arne uses only the balcony room and the parlor of the apartment on Wartburgstrasse, and I settle into Inge's room, where I'm bothered least of all. My food consists of hard-boiled eggs, hot water, and lemons.

But the premiere has to be put off again because I come down with a bad case of jaundice. I'm as yellow as a canary, but because I've ignored the doctors' warnings I collapse in the middle of the street. I had been walking to Tempelhof to fuck two girls who wanted to take care of me. Upon reaching their building entrance, I have no strength left and I drop down in the gutter. The girls drag me to their bed and call a physician, Dr. Milena Bösenberg.

She bends her pale, delicate face over me to listen to my heartbeat—and she's got such fine blue veins on her frail temples, and the biggest eyes I've ever seen, and wonderful silky lips, which hang over me like ripe raspberries, their skin about to tear and spray me with their fruit blood. So I kiss her on the mouth.

Startled, she pulls out of my arms while her red blood shoots into her white face as fast as it does into Snow White's, in the glass coffin after she's brought back to life by the Prince's kiss. Yet Milena opens her mouth as if trying to puke out the poisoned apple.

She places me in the hospital near the zoo. The two girls pay an advance because I'm to have a private room.

Milena visits me every day, but she won't let me pull her into bed.

"Your hepatitis is so serious that you have to lie still," she says gently.

Twice a day I have to swallow a long tube, and gallons of my bile flow into a pail.

A nun takes my temperature every evening; her tits graze my face when she unhooks or hooks the fever chart over my head. I grab her belly, but she acts as if nothing's happened.

She comes back that night. And when she climbs on top of me and straddles me and her thick pussy touches my mouth so I don't have to move, I eat her out.

The eight weeks in the hospital grind away at my nerves. I'm irritable and foul-tempered, and when the nurses apply a hot compress to my gallbladder I hurl the compress at them. Nor do I have the patience to read. I'm a caged animal with no other thought in mind than to break out.

Eventually I ask for pen and paper and I write an essay called "The Perfect Crime." The idea came to me a few weeks ago when I reread *Crime and Punishment*. Raskolnikov writes a similar essay, which an investigating magistrate subsequently uses as incriminating evidence against him. The novel doesn't reproduce the essay. But I write the text in case my version is ever staged and I play Raskolnikov.

I remember Holbein's painting of Jesus in the grave: stiff, dead, with a greenish face, his beard sharply pointing up against the soil that has been shoveled over him. Carcass. Carrion. Decaying. Dostoevsky was deeply frightened by the picture. He was afraid that the devout might lose their faith in immortality if they saw this painting.

This night I escape from the hospital. I can't stand it anymore. The doctors don't allow me out of bed, and I can't pay the balance of the bill anyway.

I walk to Tempelhof and ring Milena's bell; her apartment doubles as her office. She's worried. She undresses me, bathes me, and puts me in her bed. Then she switches off the light and undresses in the dark.

Her vaginal lips are as silky as her mouth. I piss my come deep inside her until she orders me to stop fucking. She says she only wants me to fuck her when my balls are heavy, about to burst. So after shooting several loads, I go to sleep and collect new come.

Whenever I visit her and try to force my way between her thighs, she first weighs my nuts in her hand to see if they're the right weight. She wants to make absolutely sure that I haven't spurted my semen into other cunts before she inserts my rod, which is so hard that it hurts.

Milena is from Yugoslavia, she's been a widow for years, and her only contact is with her sister, an eye doctor with a daughter, Vera, still in high school.

Milena not only lets me fuck her regularly, she eventually develops enough trust in me to take me along to her sister's. She wouldn't have done it if she'd had any inkling that Vera and I would instantly start fucking with our eyes.

I say I'm going to buy cigarettes, and Vera comes along. It's dark out. We come to an open construction site, where I have her lie down on a pile of boards. I stick my tongue on her clit, making it dance an Irish jig. When she rears up insanely, grabbing at my fly, I realize that buying cigarettes couldn't possibly take any longer, and I pull her home.

Neither her mother nor Milena notices anything. Vera instantly goes to the bathroom. Nor do they find anything strange about the fact that whenever Milena takes a leak I always dash out of the room and listen to the sound of the piss hitting the bowl. Or that Milena hangs around near the bathroom whenever I have to piss.

From now on I commute between Milena's apartment and that of Vera and her mother. Now here, now there. I also spend my nights in either place. When Vera's mother has to go to her office, Vera has to go to school. I pick her up at school every day, but when we arrive home her mother is already there, and she'd get suspicious if we were late. Soon I go to Vera's school during recess, when Vera dashes out to me in the street and sucks my lips hard.

We can't stand it anymore, and so today I go to Vera's school at ten A.M. I knock on the classroom door and tell the teacher that Vera's mother has sent me to bring Vera home immediately. Her mother's suddenly taken ill. The trick's an oldie but a goldie—it works. Vera doesn't believe my silly story for an instant, and I have to violently prevent her from hugging me in the teacher's presence.

On the final step in front of the apartment, we start pulling off our clothes, so by the time we get to her room we're naked. With one hand on the back of her neck and head and the other in the hollows of her bent knees I heave her up so that her ass with its solid baby fat sticks out. Then I turn her ass-backward toward the mirror.

"Do it already!" she begs hoarsely when I carry her toward the bed. Before I penetrate her, she throws her head back and starts moaning as she draws in her firm thighs and pulls her vaginal lips far apart with the fingers of both hands. Soon the head of my dick is so deep inside her that she shrieks and breaks into a cold sweat. . . . I keep pushing in. . . . The opening is so tight that I feel as if my pecker is bound up and being drained of blood. . . . I stick my elbows on her shoulders, grab her head with both hands on her skull, and by twisting my abdomen forward and upward like a fucking billy goat, I push and press with all my muscle power. She shrieks and squeals—and then I'm totally inside her.

Why does Vera's mother have to come home at this very moment? When we hear the door being unlocked, I yank my cock violently out of Vera, who refuses to give it up. Beside herself with rage and hate, she dashes into the bathroom. I toss the bedcover over the bloodstained sheet, stick my head under the water faucet, and walk toward Vera's mother in the corridor. I rub my hair and help her tote the shopping bag into the kitchen.

"Today is Yugoslav Christmas," she says, "and I have to do some baking."

I don't know what she's talking about; I just keep rubbing my hair as if it won't dry. She takes the towel from my hands and massages my head. I forgot to close my fly, and now it opens. When she sees my boner, she must think it's her doing. She drops the towel, kneels down in front of me, and *slurp!*—she deep-throats my whole dick like a vacuum cleaner.

She's not surprised that Vera is home this time of day. She's got only one thing on her mind: fucking. Nor does Vera think of anything but fucking. And I think about Vera, her mother, and Milena.

Vera must have done a good job of jerking off in the bathroom—I've never seen her with such dark rings around the eyes. Her eyes sparkle nastily. Her mother doesn't even look at her.

Milena arrives in the afternoon; the three of them speak in Serbo-Croatian, and I've got my peace of mind until evening. I lie on my bed and daydream about all three women naked: Milena, Vera, and her mother. Frankly, all three of them juice me up.

When the Yugoslav Christmas party finally comes to an end, Vera instantly goes to bed, probably to jerk off. Milena also says good night, because her sister says over my head, "He's spending the night."

As soon as Milena leaves, Vera's mother switches off the light, grabs my cock in the darkness, and pulls me into her bedroom. She rides me till morning and dozes off while crouching on me.

So far everything has gone smoothly. But the bomb explodes when Vera's mother sees me fucking Vera and tries to kill herself.

Milena and Vera instantly catch on. Milena hates her sister and Vera. Vera hates her mother and her aunt. Vera's mother hates the two others. And all three hate me.

The situation gets even more complicated when the two girls who summoned Milena to my sickbed come to her office and claim I've knocked up both of them. When they refuse to let Milena examine them, she slaps them.

Despite the family quarrel, Milena lets me keep living with her, and she keeps giving me money. When the dust has settled, she opens my fly, pulls out my dick, and weighs my nuts in her hands to determine whether they're heavy enough. When she's satisfied with the weight, she spreads her legs and fucks like a whore.

I now feel strong enough to schedule the first few performances of *La Voix humaine*. The premiere takes place at night. Some spectators come chiefly out of curiosity—they've never seen a man play a woman. "I'm only here to laugh at him," some creep says. But after the performance he tearfully holds his hands in front of his face and disappears.

Months later, when Cocteau arrives for the opening of his film *Orphée* (*Orpheus*), he asks me to reprise the role of the woman in *La Voix humaine*. When I'm done he kisses me and says, "Your face is as young as a child's and yet your eyes are utterly mature. They switch from one instant to the next. I've never seen such a face."

Since I wasn't fully healed when I fled the hospital, I have constant gallbladder pains. I find some pills in Milena's office, and I swallow them, not realizing they're the wrong ones.

I wake up in an emergency room, where they think I deliberately tried to poison myself.

After they pump out my stomach and bring me back to life with shots, I make a break for it, jumping out a second-story window. Before I can scale the hospital wall, the orderlies catch up with me, yank me down from the wall like bark off a tree, and violently drag me back.

Milena isn't scheduled to come until noon, and so I'm at the mercy of this riffraff. After the cattle doctor has ordered security measures as if for a criminal, I hurl the bedpan at him, so they strap me to the bed. A short time later the quack returns with a cop, who is supposed to hand me over to the district physician.

That louse of a district doctor wants every last detail. He asks me if I'm having an affair with Frau Dr. Milena Bösenberg. I piss on him.

He'd be delighted to lock me up immediately at the Wittenau Insane Asylum, but Milena suddenly shows up. She promises to cover all expenses if the district physician will be kind enough to turn me over to a private hospital institution instead of Wittenau. Milena can't really prevent her colleague from doing what he wants. She herself is partly to blame, because out of fear—and probably also out of jealousy over the family fucking—she refuses to admit to this medical creep that she whores around with me. On the contrary: She claims she barely knows me, and says she feels sorry for me because I've got no one to take care of me. Nothing can prevent my being transported to the loony bin.

"Why, this is quite an honor," the meat inspector purrs in the locked ward, "to have such a great actor visiting us."

I kick him in the balls.

"Wittenau! Take him to Wittenau!" the hyena screeches. Covered by two orderlies, the coward recoils. The door, which has no knob, snaps shut.

I examine the barred window, which faces the courtyard. Even if I managed to remove the tight mesh, I couldn't jump from the fourth floor down to the stones without smashing every bone in my body.

The knobless door is pushed open. Four orderlies pounce on me and bind me up in a straitjacket. Then I'm taken downstairs and loaded into a VW van camouflaged as an ambulance. Its motor running, its doors open, it waits for me in the courtyard.

During the drive I don't recognize very much. The panes are frosted—only the narrow borders around the crosses are slightly transparent—and for a few seconds I spot the Radio Tower. How often have I passed it en route to see Vera, her mother, and Milena, who have so shabbily run out on me.

Wittenau. Berlin's infamous insane asylum. The VW van is stopped, checked out, and then it passes through the heavily guarded entrance. I try to make out details through the borders of the crosses. But the van is moving too fast. All I grasp is that this is a gigantic complex (how many alleged lunatics there are!): asphalt streets, blocks, many other variously large or small stone barracks—probably laundries, kitchens, garbage dumps, mortuary. Everything is enclosed by a high wall.

The VW van stops outside the reception building. I'm unloaded directly into the waiting room.

They unknot the straitjacket, I promptly move and massage my lifeless arms and wrists. One of the bullies shoves me down on a bench. I have to wait. For a long time.

The room is high, bare, the walls are painted green at head level like the gas chambers in America. The blind windowpanes are densely barred. Bars everywhere. Knobless doors everywhere. Constant rattling of keys. Locking, unlocking, locking—always two, three, four doors in a row.

Other prisoners are led past me. You can tell they've been here for a long time. They shuffle along with the bullies, like robots. They let themselves be directed, shoved. The staff busily hurries to and fro. They wear grimy jackets, the sleeves pushed up the red butcher arms. The condemned wear prison outfits: long gray cotton gowns and something like slippers on their bare feet.

Then there are newcomers like me. Some resist. They refuse to be pushed and pulled despite brutal slaps and punches. They have to be carried.

Some are accompanied by a family member, who quickly says good-bye and dashes out. Most are alone, with only bullies right and left. Some aren't all there. Some cry. A woman screams. Her scream drills into my heart. She throws herself on the floor, lashes out. Knobless doors open. The woman is lugged away, her feet dragging along as if she were being hauled to the guillotine. Everything runs as swiftly and smoothly as an execution.

If only I could get something for my headache! A meat inspector assigns me to Ward III. It's catercorner from the next block, so we walk there. This time there are only two bullies. I try to get my bearings and memorize details. But everything looks the same: stone blocks, asphalt streets, stone blocks. We arrive.

One flight up I'm handed over to another slaughterer, and it never even occurs to him that I might resist. Behind us at least ten knobless doors have slammed shut. He assesses me with an expert eye but without looking into my face, as if he were calculating my height and weight. He can't be doing it for the asylum uniform, because he tosses a gray package and a pair of slippers in front of me without checking if the stuff fits. I'm ordered to strip naked. He resolutely grabs my clothes and stuffs them into a sack like garbage as if to say: "You don't need this anymore!" I'm weighted like a side of beef. Then I'm measured. Then I'm hosed down with an ice-cold stream of water.

The bare, barred, tubelike room contains a row of ten iron bathtubs like open coffins. If an inmate has a "crisis" he's shoved into a tub of ice-cold water. And he has to endure the ice-cold water until his "crisis" is over. If it doesn't pass he gets electroshock. And if that doesn't help, then the victim is thrown into solitary confinement. They take away his gown and slippers so that he won't tear or bite them into strips and hang himself. There's no toilet in the isolation cell. And no food. It's not worth feeding the inmates. Most of them become hopelessly insane, if they don't kick the bucket first.

I pull on the gray gown and the slippers and I'm taken to the room where I'm received by the permanent watchdogs.

In this room, where I'm locked in with some eighty to a hundred fellow inmates, everything takes place: sleeping, eating, pissing, shitting, screaming, raging, wailing, crying, agonizing, and the final collapse of anyone who survives. The stench is indescribable. This is hell! True hell!

Someone shrieks tearfully. Two watchdogs stifle his shrieks. They bandage up his mouth and strap him to his bed.

Just don't look! Don't look, I keep telling myself. Don't listen! Don't inhale that saccharine smell that triggers nausea, like those lumps of fat in the children's hell. My God! How many years ago was that—and now this! Now the adult hell!

But I mustn't bitch! I mustn't lose heart, no matter what! I mustn't even get sad! Sadness would reduce my hatred—and I need hatred! Not scorn! Scorn is tiring! I need nasty, vindictive hatred!

I talk to myself. Not too loudly or too softly—just loudly enough so I can barely hear myself. I reel off my date of birth, phone numbers, house numbers, names. I mustn't weaken. The tragedy is starting to befuddle me like a drug. I have to stay physically fit. I do knee bends, upper-body circles. Keep moving! Don't halt, keep going, going. But where? We're not allowed to move away from our beds except to piss or shit.

Food is handed out. I don't touch the swill. When the others notice that I'm not eating they pounce on my tray. The watchdog jots it down in his notebook.

My headache gets so unbearable that I ask one of the thugs for an aspirin. He pays no attention, even after I repeat the question. Don't let him provoke you, I tell myself. Just turn around, go away, forget I asked this creep a question. Forget I've got such awful pains.

But the pains get worse and worse. With every shriek from a fellow sufferer. With every rage, curse, threat. With every punch from the fists of these slavedrivers. With every dull blow that hits a Jesus Christ. With every gagged and weeping mouth. With every footscrape as someone is dragged out of the room. With every moan, curse, fart, piss, shit into the toilet that stands in the middle of the room.

I pray to God. Yes! I pray to God to increase my pains, make them worse and worse! We'll see whether my head bursts. That was how Jesus must have prayed in Gethsemane: "My God, if you want me to endure all this, then give me the strength!"

He gives me the strength. I do not go crazy. I visualize *Idea,* a linocut by Frans Masereel: A man in prison is illuminated by the idea of freedom coming to his dungeon as a naked woman and squeezing her breasts through the bars so that he may drink and gain strength.

I already think I've weathered it, but it's not that simple. When I approach the barred window to see a patch of sky, one of the watchdogs orders me to go back. I turn around and weep. A one-legged inmate whispers to me: "Don't cry! If you cry, it means you're not healthy."

At the barred windows, which reveal only the gray wall of another block, the watchdogs sit at a table, jotting everything down in a notebook: When you cry. When you laugh. When you eat. When you don't eat. When you eat another inmate's food. When you talk. When you don't talk. When you approach the barred windows. When you get too much sleep. When you don't sleep. There is nothing they don't jot down in the notebooks.

"Are you a lathe operator?" asks the one-legged guy. "You've got strong upper arms."

I can't tell him I'm an actor. He'd think I was trying to pull a fast one.

"Yes, I operate a lathe," I say, to avoid disappointing him.

His sad story is so shattering that I forget my own troubles. He returned from a Russian POW camp. During his captivity his wife, whom he loved more than anything in the world, had learned from the Red Cross that he was still alive, but that a hand grenade had ripped off one leg. So she had him declared dead. The one-legged guy, using crutches, limped into his house and found his wife in bed, fucking with some guy. Naturally he began smashing his crutch into them. Then he lapsed into a crying jag.

The wife and her boyfriend had him declared mentally incapacitated and dangerous and quickly got him into Wittenau.

"I just wanna live long enough to get out of here and kill them both," he said, concluding his tale.

The cattle doctor shows up every three days. When he talks to me, I turn my back to avoid jumping at his throat. He doesn't talk to me during the next few weeks. Then I'm taken to his office. I realize why when I discover Milena hugging the barred window. She doesn't have the nerve to look at me, and I don't say hello to her. I remain standing after the slimy jellyfish of a psychiatrist offers me a chair.

He demands that I sign a paper stating that Dr. Milena Bösenberg is not responsible for my incarceration in the asylum and that I agree to leave her alone in the future—that is, neither to get revenge on her nor to attempt any sort of contact with her, much less approach her. If I refuse to sign, they won't release me.

I'm so flabbergasted that I forget about this vile extortion for a moment and wonder what could have driven this flabby eunuch to pimp for Milena. Has she given him good head? She must be scared shitless that people might find out we've been fucking.

Maybe these cockroaches think I've gone crazy, for the Moloch whispers his good-byes to Milena and hastily sees her to the door. Nothing can prevent me from doing what I feel like once I'm free.

The myopic jellyfish grabs the document as if it were a love note from Milena, folds it neatly, and fussily slips it into his wallet.

"Everything's settled," he says unctuously, "but I'd like to have a chat with you. You interest me."

"But I don't wish to chat with you. I want to get out of this garbage dump for human brains, and right away!"

I'm certain that only the watchdog standing at the door could prevent me from killing this eunuch with the paperweight—a grenade shell. I can already see the ripped steel of the half-exploded grenade shell chewing into his disgusting fat scalp like shark teeth so that it can never be sewn up again. I see myself striking again and again between the bulging toad eyes, and again and again on the back of his head and smashing his cranium so that all that remains is a randy, bloody, pulpy, stinking lump. All I have to do is reach out for the paperweight. But I don't. Not yet.

"Why get so excited? Everything will work out. I give you my word."

Word. What kind of word can he give me? What kind of word can such a stinking piece of dung have? I would shit into his hand if he held it out to me.

"Tell your torturers to bring me my belongings!"

"All in good time. It can't go as fast as you imagine. First, your brother has to come and talk to me. Dr. Bösenberg has already notified him; he'll come here tomorrow."

"My brother? . . . Why does my brother have to talk to you?"

"I'd like him to tell me about you. I've already explained: You interest me. After all, I'll be responsible for releasing you. But you won't tell me anything."

"What?"

"For instance, what you do with your hands when you talk. Have you always done that?"

I'm convinced that this sadist is crazy—and why shouldn't he be? My hands are my language, like my eyes, my mouth, my whole body. I express myself with them. I'm itching to say: "You'll know what I do with my hands when I strangle you." But I hold my tongue. I say nothing more. I leave his office wordlessly, and the watchdog takes me back to the torture chamber. If Arne really does know where I am, he'll get me out of here even if he dies trying.

After endless eternities in the adult hell, we embrace, and Arne drives me in his new Ford to Wartburgstrasse. He asks me no questions and is very tender. He realizes I can't talk now. After taking a bath and stuffing my belly, I thank him. I accept the money and cigarettes he offers me and I kiss him good-bye. He cries.

It's spring, and I can see the apples growing in girls' blouses and I can smell their pussy plums ripening.

I'm in a mobbed bus, wedged in by shoving passengers, who make me feel claustrophobic. Panicking, I fight my way out. Merely being elbowed brings tears to my eyes.

I walk all the way to Clayallee. The British ambassador's villa must be located in a side street. Some time ago a young student offered to let me live with him and his mother in a wooden cottage on the grounds of the British embassy, where she works as a cleaning woman.

I lie in the flower beds for days on end, my face toward the sky. For the first few nights I sleep outdoors. I have to start living again. I don't leave the property for two months and I see no one except the boy and his mother. In the daytime I'm alone. The student is on campus, and his mother spends all day in the ambassador's villa. She must be about thirty-five. I always get very close to her because her skirt smells so sharp. I believe she is a terribly open person. Whenever she uses the toilet, the strong smell lingers on. I rack my brain, scheming about how I can fuck her.

I'm totally convinced that I've got the adult hell out of my system, for my physical strength is also restored. But then a wasp on the windowpane drives me crazy with its buzzing while I sit at the table by the window, staring at the sky. I open the window to let the wasp out, but it doesn't fly away. For a while everything is silent. Then the wasp starts buzzing again and drumming its head against the pane. Bang! You'd think the wasp was drunk. Or doing this to get my attention. It wants me to deal with it. Perhaps it enjoys teasing. I should try as hard as I can to catch it even though I'm certain I won't succeed. I should touch it, even graze it—without hurting it, of course. Brush its ass, and so on.

Its buzzing is so supersonic that I have to put my hands on my ears. This goes on for several hours. Whenever I remove my fists from my ears, the wasp starts in again, as if it were watching me and just waiting to fly headfirst against the pane. I try to hit it, but I miss. It hides. I know it's watching me. As soon as I sit back down at the table, hoping that I've killed it or it's flown away, the torture resumes. I press my fists against my ears until I'm certain that the wasp is finally fed up with tormenting me. But when I remove my fists, it starts all over again. This time it sounds as if the wasp were banging its skull against the pane more violently than ever.

I remain sitting for a while without covering my ears. While watching the wasp from the corners of my eyes, I pretend I'm not looking. In a surprise attack I rip the tablecloth—with the ink, the honey jar, and everything else—from the table and knock the wasp to the floor. The wasp is merely stunned. I tear a thread from the tablecloth and strangle the wasp. Then I incinerate it over the gas flame. As its charring body crackles and slowly fades out, I realize that the wasp is not to blame for what they did to me in Wittenau.

"How could anyone dare to keep him from me for years?" says Fritz Kortner after our first meeting. "He is the only actor the mere sight of whom shakes me up. In all the world there's no other Don Carlos for me!"

Four years ago those sickening actors at the Schlossparktheater laughed at me when I said that someday I'd be Don Carlos.

After a few weeks of rehearsing with Kortner I'm fed up with his unfair, dictatorial ways. I yell at him to go fuck himself.

Paul is an architect and he says he's been after me for a while. I find out why when I have dinner with him and his wife, Erni. After dinner he heads for the bathroom while Erni clears the table. Even though it would be a lot more convenient to get the dishes from the other side, she leans so far across the table that I get her gigantic ass right in front of my face. Her skirt hikes up so high that I can see the edge of her soaked panties. She has no choice but to leave the table as is, and we dash to the bed. When I shoot, Erni hits the ceiling.

"You've gotta hold back longer! What am I gonna do now? I'm so horny I don't know what to do!"

"Paul can continue fucking you," I snottily retort.

"That's just it! Paul shoots too fast, too! The two of you have to control yourselves for a lot longer! I need both of you, both of you for a long time!"

At four the next afternoon we finally have breakfast.

They live on the top floor of a huge villa that belongs to Paul's father, a famous architect. I don't move in; I just go over to fuck—which, however, sometimes takes several days and nights. Erni could keep fucking to the point of cardiac arrest. *My* cardiac arrest.

When Paul and Erni have to go to Frankfurt, where Paul has a project, I'm deliriously happy. Not because I have to fuck so much, but I'm sick of playing the stud for a little food.

Why am I a whore? I need love! Love! Nonstop! And I want to give love because I have so much of it. No one understands that the sole purpose of my whoring is to spend myself totally!

After turning down more than a dozen movie offers, because either the scripts were feebleminded or the producers thought I was asking for too much money, I've finally signed a movie contract today. The director is a man named Verhöven. I go to the location in Wiesbaden. Verhöven asks me to cue a young beginner in her screen test. Two days later they cancel my contract and pay me off, commenting: "Herr Verhöven feels that your face is too strong for the German screen."

This is the worst shit anyone's ever pulled on me. But fuck it, as long as I've got the bread!

I order a suit, buy a shirt and a handkerchief and finally socks so that I don't always have to wear my shoes barefoot. For my daughter, Pola, I buy patent-leather shoes, and I order a burgundy velvet suit for her with cuffs and collar of Brussels lace, plus tiny white kid gloves. At Braun & Co. I have them model the most expensive suit for Gislinde and I take the tall model to the Clara, a small hotel.

The model introduces me to the Maccabee girl. She runs an Austrian movie distribution firm, drives a big car, and takes me on a round trip to Salzburg.

She smells of sweat and cheap perfume and is hairy all over—on her arms, her legs, even her boobs. Hair sprouts from her ass crack, out of her panties, high up on her belly, and down to her inner thighs. I discover this on the very first day, because if we don't find a rest stop along the thruway we'll cause an accident. When we head back to the autobahn I have to drive because she keeps coming.

"Faster! Faster!" she wails. She wants to get back to her apartment at the Max II monument.

Soon I prefer fucking her in the elevator going up to her pad. She bends over while standing, and I shove it in from behind. A couple of times, from the ground floor to the top, up and down, up and down, and that's it. Then I let her get out on the top story, just as she is, with a hiked-up skirt and yanked-down panties, a messy butt and torn stockings. I press the main-floor button. While descending, I use spit to rub the stains from my fly. This way, I don't even have to go to her pad.

For once I'm there, I have to keep my dick inside her nonstop. Even in the morning, at the breakfast table, she sits on me with her naked ass, as if I were a throne. When she takes a bath, she sticks her naked ass out of the water. When she cooks, she wears nothing but an apron, which exposes her naked ass. Even when her upper body's all spiffed up and she's wearing garters, stockings, and high heels, and even some horrible hat, she sticks out her naked ass toward me. Everywhere and always her hairy naked ass, which glares at me like an order, like a command that I can't resist. Sleep is out of the question, even though I deliberately crash in the next room. Whenever I stagger toward beddy-bye, thinking she's finally satisfied after hours of fucking, she shows up yet again to give me a final good-night kiss—and then remains lying on me, legs spread wide.

The hell with her distribution firm: this Maccabee needs the entire Israeli army.

Letters from the court, judicial payment orders, subpoenas, reminders, threats: In short, I never open any letter with an official return address. I toss them in the garbage or into the Isar, where they briefly drift downstream before going under. So I don't have a clue that I've been charged with insulting a police officer and resisting arrest after a slugfest with some guy who turned out to be a police detective. Nor do I realize that I've been sentenced to four months in prison plus probation. I'm also supposed to pay a fine. If I don't pay the fine, I'll have to report to Stadelheim Prison with underwear, a razor, and toothpaste.

A young lawyer named Zieger lives at the Clara. But he can't take my case because he wants to make it in the movie business. He wants to gain a name for himself as a divorce attorney. He wants to file divorces; he wants to divorce actors and actresses from one another—divorce, divorce, nothing but divorce. He's totally obsessed. People in the business say, "He's making it!" and they all run to him.

So he can't occupy himself with prisons. Instead, he recommends Rudolf Amesmaier—luckily for me. Not only does Rudolf instantly becomes my friend and never run out on me, but he's also the best defense attorney. He does it all between sausages and beer. I don't have to go to prison or pay a fine.

I can no longer take the model from Braun & Co. back to the Clara: We need too much space, and I'm living in a two-by-four across from the toilet. Anyone who's sitting on the bowl, and there's always someone on the bowl, can hear her shriek. In itself, that wouldn't be a reason to stop fucking her here. But the queer journalist from the *Frankfurter Allgemeine*, the photographer from *Stern*, and all the others who live here go ballistic when they can't sleep at night, and Madam Clara can't gossip in peace inside her parlor, which is next to my two-by-four. That's the reason. And even if there were no reason, my cot would be too close to the walls of my pad for my model's long legs.

I would've gone to her place from the very start, but it's always so hard for us to separate, and I oversleep and miss everything I have to take care of. I can't oversleep at Madam Clara's because we all have to show up punctually for breakfast, otherwise we get nothing. So everyone wakes up everyone else.

My model lives over the car dealership on Leopoldstrasse. All these buildings contain stores, and at night her shrieks are heard only by the watchman making his rounds.

Alexander the Great is a completely idiotic play, which no one understands. Nevertheless, I play Alexander because I need money and I receive an advance.

There are three women playing opposite me: a tall, athletic eighteen-year-old; a fifteen-year-old with baby fat; and a short, skinny twenty-four-year-old divorcée with two kids.

I visit the athlete twice on Türkenstrasse. She babbles on and on about her movie-star dentist in Grünwald, who pretends to be patching up something or other on her healthy teeth. I believe he fucks her, for she has no money. I try not to listen to her, and I pull myself along her strong sprinter legs up to her teeth, which she intends to swap for jacket crowns, and without interrupting her flow of speech I do gymnastics on top of her. Then she forgets all about the dentist and comes quickly to the final spurt.

I don't finish up my affair with the skinny twenty-four-year-old all that fast. We wordlessly drag her mattress to the floor because the bed in her rented room is too fragile. Quickly and simultaneously we undress. Sex itself is as smooth as a baby's ass and without complications. Her legs come apart in a split, opening totally, while she digs her long, sharp fingernails into my body; her body encloses me like a diving suit, absorbing my itching and distortedly swollen dick over and over again without our mouths ever touching. I never even kiss her. None of this is unusual. But this divorced mother is like a hard drug that you shoot into your veins, like morphine or smack. The harder I try to get away—because I know she's gonna ruin me and because I don't even long for her—the more often I catch myself heading yet again toward her room, where she waits for me in her bathrobe day and night, as if she knows that I have to return to her.

She doesn't even look at me, she's so sure of me. Things go so far that I start absolutely hating her; I don't say a word to her, and yet I dash back to her two, three, four times a day. Eventually I curse her out, slap her face, and punch her body. She doesn't bat an eye; instead she gives me a triumphant and half-crazy look. Sometimes we cook in her place, but we eat less and less. She's all skin and bones anyway. We look like a couple of addicts; our feverishly glittering eyes lie deep in their sockets. The wide, dark rings notched underneath pull all the way to our cheekbones. Our throats are parched by a burning thirst. Our pulses are abnormally rapid, and all our veins swell. Our ears buzz. The weaker we get, the more immense our desire. I can feel my own painful orgasms all the way into my brain.

You can fuck yourself to death like this, even if you don't have a heart attack. I'm saved by the director, who hasn't been able to rehearse for several days because we haven't shown up. He threatens to stop all further payments if this goes on. I don't tell him I'm addicted to the skinny bitch. I tell him I can't stand her. He rehearses her separately so that we don't meet, while she herself has to keep rehearsing nonstop.

But I'm wrong: The director can't save my life.

Four A.M. We're raiding his fridge when his wife, wearing a corset, comes into the kitchen and joins our pig-out.

My eyes bulge. I'm so surprised that I don't notice right off that she's got nothing on but a corset. I just gawk, hypnotized by her thigh flesh. In the first place, the black corset, which reaches down to her bladder, melts into the luxuriant brownish-black seaweed of her mound and into the venomously sweet weeds in her armpits. In the second place, I would never have dreamt that such a huge pussy could possibly exist.

After our meals, she lets us tie her to their double bed. She's stark naked; her body shines with cold, sticky sweat. We take turns till she can't go on anymore.

We finally untie her in the afternoon. She remains in her spread-eagled position, and the three of us crash till the next day.

I perform in another bar: "KINSKI RECITES VILLON." Again I stand barefoot on a table. This time I charge five marks' admission. I empty the take directly into my trouser pocket.

Gislinde has gone to the country with a girlfriend. Pola is with her grandma. When she refuses to give her to me, I yank her out of the old lady's arms. I take along some clothes in a paper bag. The bag falls apart in the street. I wedge Pola's clothes under my arm and look for a room to rent in the rooming house on Giselastrasse.

In the daytime I take Pola to the English Garden and ride a buggy and a merry-go-round with her at the Chinese Tower. In the evening, I take her back to the hotel, wash her in the sink, and put her to bed. Then I walk over to the bar and recite Villon.

Tatjana Gsovsky, the Russian ballet mistress of the Berlin State Opera, summons me to Berlin for the International Theater Festival. She's staging and choreographing Dostoevsky's *The Idiot,* and I'm supposed to play the title role, Prince Myshkin. The whole thing is a mixed-media fusion of pantomime, classical ballet, and theater. The prima ballerinas, the dancers, and the corps de ballet are dancing in classic style; I'm supposed to adjust my gait, posture, and movements in pantomime and recite a long monologue.

The rehearsals won't start for another three months. Tatjana mails me the contract, asking me to let my hair and beard grow so that I won't have to wear a wig or paste up my face.

My long-hair period becomes a martyrdom. People in the street aren't used to seeing a man with long hair unless he's a Russian Orthodox priest. I'm cursed and yelled at everywhere, and so I go outdoors only when it's dark. Not because I'm scared, but it gets simply unbearable. At Munich's railroad terminal the people spit at me. Some throw stones.

Gislinde and I get divorced. We're both sad about it, but she knows quite well that I can never lead an orderly life and that's its better for us to give one another our freedom. The suggestion comes from Gislinde herself even though she loves me so much that she's willing to give up anything and everything.

Since I can't wait the required period for a divorce date, Rudolf Amesmaier makes it possible for me to testify in court ahead of time.

"When did you last have sexual intercourse with your spouse?" that louse of a divorce judge asks me.

"Even if I could remember with all my whoring around, I wouldn't tell you."

I don't contest the divorce, and the red tape is taken care of.

In Berlin, I live with Tatjana. She makes my bed, cleans my room, cooks for me, and takes care of everything else. She also trains sixteen hours a day.

The prima ballerina, Nastassja, is half Dutch, half Indonesian. Her smooth, silvery black hair reaches all the way down to the crack of her teensy ass. She's got the body of a teenage Balinese dancer, but she's a bit taller. I don't know where we draw the strength to train sixteen hours a day after fucking all night. But we're so horny and obsessed that all we need to stay fit is food and vitamins.

Jasmin, former prima ballerina of the Oslo Opera, has nothing to do with Tatjana's ballet. She's twenty-two and fresh from Paris; she's had to give up dancing because of a spinal injury. She introduces herself to me as a "journalist." The alleged interview she asks for never gets written. Since we can't fuck in Tatjana's apartment because of Nastassja, Jasmin rents a hotel room.

She clings to my body like a girl on the backseat of a motorcycle. I can't take a step without her. She even brushes my teeth, bathes me, and holds my pecker when I take a leak. If I'm on the telephone, she wraps her thighs around me or sucks my dick. The waiters simply place food outside our door. The maids never have anything to do because Jasmin has to sleep while I train.

Ramon, the Indian dancer who's friendly with Jasmin from God knows where, performs in the International Theater Festival.

He pays for Jasmin's and my hotel room. When the rehearsals begin, Jasmin is everywhere: in my dressing room, backstage, in the auditorium. And we fuck everywhere: on beds, on floors, in corridors, in the street, in the subway, in the movies, on the plane. And above all in the forests along the Havel River.

The Idiot is a smash hit, and we're invited to the Venice Festival.

I hate to leave Jasmin behind. During my absence she wants to go to Paris and try to earn some money. Then we plan to take an apartment together.

In Venice our troupe stays on the Lido, in a small *pensione* belonging to Duse's nephew. He gives us everything for free. The Italians are so warm, so hospitable, so overflowing with spontaneous love that I feel like an émigré who's returned to his native land. They are also uncontrollably nosy. Wherever the Dutch-Indonesian half-breed turns up with me—at the Piazza San Marco, on the Grand Canal, even in a gondola squeezing through the most remote canals—people instantly cluster around us. They talk, gesticulate, shout, laugh, throng, touch us as if we were rare, exotic plants, and do anything to make it clear that they love us.

I embrace you, Italy, you wonderland.

Meanwhile our troupe's been invited to perform in both North and South America, and Tatjana also plans to tour Japan and Australia.

But after everyone screws everyone else, an ominous atmosphere of hatred, jealousy, and revenge makes it impossible for us all to live together. In Venice we even quarrel about our wages after someone runs off with half the take. So now mayhem and murder dominate our troupe.

Jasmin is waiting for me in Paris, but I don't head there straightaway. Instead I fly to New York, where the half-breed is scheduled to dance at the New York City Ballet. Six weeks later I fly to Paris.

Meanwhile Jasmin has been hard at work. She refused a striptease offer because the money wasn't good enough. But she seems to be making a lot of money anyway. The dress she's wearing on her naked skin must have cost at least a thousand francs.

"Tell me."

"What?"

"About the men."

She laughs, embarrassed, and even turns red.

"How many did you have?"

"I didn't count them."

"How many a day? Or didn't you work as a prostitute??"

"I was a call girl. Those are girls who get hooked up by phone to businessmen, diplomats, politicos, movie stars, and so on. But also vice squad cops. They don't pay."

"I know what a call girl is. Keep talking."

"Our madam is an ex-hooker—Madame Claude. Her office is on Rue Lincoln in the Eighth Arrondissement. Everything goes through her office, the calls, the appointments, the payments, everything. We have nothing to do with any of it. She keeps thirty percent of the fee, and we get the rest. I've saved a lot of money. You can live with me now, wherever you like. If you want, I'll keep hooking as long as you say so. Are you furious at me?"

"No. But I don't want you to continue. So how many guys did you have a day?"

"It all depended. Three, four, five. Sometimes just one. Except when I was having my period. I only do that with you. Once I had eight johns in one evening, and once even fifteen—a whole party of guys. Each one came two or three times. I think it added up to forty-five or fifty. The next day I couldn't get out of bed, much less walk. But those were exceptions. On the average it was thirty to thirty-five a week. I have a small memo book where I enter my appointments. I get the date and time one week in advance."

"Did you enjoy it?"

" 'Enjoy it'? That's such a funny word. The more guys I had, the more I needed it. After all, you weren't around."

"How much did you earn per guy?"

"The girls get between a hundred and a hundred and fifty francs. Sometimes you get a tip. That doesn't go through Madame Claude, of course."

"When did you have to meet the men?"

"Usually from three P.M. till midnight, according to how we got booked. The evening appointments almost always include dinner. But sometimes you get a john early in the morning because he has to get to the airport."

"How long does a session last?"

"One to one and a half hours. It depends on how much the customer wants to spend or how much time he has. The time is precisely scheduled before the meeting. There are also all-nighters and weekenders. They cost a lot of money, partly because the john has the right to hand the girl over to other men—business colleagues, friends—and because the men take turns or fuck the girl simultaneously. One guy, for instance, always orders all of Madame Claude's girls at once. Or a girl has to fuck with two, three, or more guys at the same time. That costs a lot more, too."

"How were you dressed? Like a whore?"

"Not like a streetwalker, if that's what you mean. We have to be dressed decently."

"How?"

She opens her closet door.

"Look for yourself. Very normal, very middle-class. The skirt not too short, not too tight. And we're not allowed to use perfume; otherwise the men's clothes smell of it when they get home to their wives. Our underwear is white and also quite normal. Not slutty. We have to bare ourselves down there right away, in back and in front. It has to be uncomplicated and not take any time. Unless the men like that. Normally we strip naked. The men, too."

"Tell me about the men. What are they like?"

"They vary. Most of them are nice."

"Do they also fuck with rubbers?"

"Almost never; I don't like it. And most of the johns don't want to. They want to have the feeling they're shooting into the uterus, they imagine they're knocking me up. Some of the men do want a condom—maybe they're scared of catching something. Now and then I've put a condom on a guy's dick; I always have a few handy. But that was when I was doing the streets. Some wanna fuck right in a car. Sometimes standing against a tree. Often it was dark and I could only feel their cocks. With one guy I had to peel off the condom—he couldn't fuck in rubber and he got soft again."

"Have you ever had V.D.?"

"No, not so often. Once—no, twice. You know, you recover quickly. The clap, of course. We have to be examined twice a week. Hopefully, no one's had the syph."

"Weren't you worried about getting knocked up?"

"I've got an IUD. Otherwise I'd've gotten knocked up by you."

"Did you always take the dick in your mouth?"

"You mean suck it?"

"Yeah."

"Most guys want it."

"Have you also worked in brothels?"

"Yeah. There were various houses they sent some of us to. But only for two or three days at a time. Those were quickies. Sometimes I still wasn't done with one john, and the next guy was already in the waiting room."

"Did you recognize the men?"

"Not usually. But the girls say that some of the johns are high-ranking politicians and police officials. Madame Claude pays us for the cops so that we don't have to do freebies. The cops reciprocate by protecting Madame Claude's organization. Aside from movie stars, whom we recognize of course, all I know is that the shah of Iran gets girls from Madame Claude whenever he's in Paris. He was here just two weeks ago. But I wasn't included. You have to have worked with Madame Claude for at least five years and have the necessary experience before you service the shah."

"How old are the girls, on the average?"

"Very young. Most of them start at sixteen or seventeen. The oldest is twenty-six, I think."

"How'd you feel after servicing several men in one day?"

"I wasn't satisfied even after five or more guys a day—I mean, really satisfied. I was just a total wreck, I felt drugged, and I needed more and more drugs. It's different than it is with you; there's no comparison. You wipe me out totally, I'm completely feeble, but I feel redeemed, happy. Often, at the end of the night or at the crack of dawn, even before my first client, I dashed out into the street and looked for men. I let each man screw me as long as he could. I didn't want any interval between men. Sometimes I lay awake at night and couldn't sleep because I was thinking that somewhere out there some horny, raging hard-on is hunting a pussy like mine. And I drew a rag over my naked body, looking for him so that he could fill my itching, burning hole with his boiling lava. Whenever a car stopped, I first stuck my head inside to see if his pants were bursting. If they were, I got in. If not, I kept looking. Naturally I always demanded money. One guy took me to a miserable, run-down hotel. I had to pay for the room. He stank like a billy goat. He fucked me brutally five times in all positions and then he didn't pay, that sleazy bastard. I could have killed him.

"Sometimes I imagine being fucked by hundreds of men, thousands. For instance, by men in the Foreign Legion, who haven't seen a woman for months. They'd have to set up a makeshift brothel, a huge tent or a barracks, and the men would have to line up. Or on an aircraft carrier, as the only prostitute for thousands of guys . . ."

Those last few words are almost breathed, as if she were dreaming. In fact, she is as good as asleep while she twists and turns on top of me like a young dog looking for the right position for going to sleep. Then she curls up and cradles her face in my fly.

"Why are you doing all that?" I murmur very softly, afraid of waking her in case she's already asleep.

"You ask stupid questions," she mumbles. She crawls up my body and licks me in my ear. "Every woman has her favorite dick. You're mine. Do you love me?"

"Yes."

I fly to Munich to see Pola. Meanwhile Jasmin flies to Berlin to look for an apartment. But by the time I arrive in Berlin, she's dead. She was struck by a hit-and-run driver on Clayallee; they were bringing her to the hospital with a badly fractured skull and she died en route. I could see her—she's at the morgue—but I don't go. I couldn't take it.

I return to Paris and stay in the same room where Jasmin told me about Madame Claude.

When I run out of money to pay the hotel bill, I sleep under the bridges of the Seine. At first the clochards leave me alone, and I figure they accept me. But then they change their minds about letting me sleep near them. They drive me away, hurling rotten tomatoes at me.

It's icy out. When I was with the clochards, I could warm up because they have small stoves under the bridge. Now I wander around for a couple of days until I get so tired that I duck in somewhere and fall into a deep sleep. . . .

When I wake up, I'm snowed in, and a *métro* is thundering past, very close to my head. I don't know how I got here. Even my brain is frozen. It's early in the morning and still dark. In the street a man picks me up and takes me home. I tell him I only want to sleep, and he doesn't touch me even though we both sleep in his bed. Before going out in the afternoon, he serves me café au lait with a baguette. Then I wash and shave and dry out my clothes.

As I leave he asks me if he can help me out in some way. I tell him I need the train fare to Marseilles. I want to sign up as a sailor on a ship that's going far away. Preferably to Japan or Australia or the Fiji Islands. He gives me enough for a third-class railroad ticket and says I can pay him back someday. I hop the night train for Marseilles.

There I head straight for the Arab market to hock my suit. I want to use the money to buy sailor's gear and get a hot meal for the rest. The Arabs virtually yank the suit off my body and offer me the equivalent of twenty marks. They're crazy! My suit is almost new and cost me six hundred marks! I try a pawnshop to ask what I could get for it. But the shop hasn't opened yet, and there's an endless line outside. By the time I get in, they're closing up again. However, the creep at the window offers me the same amount as the Arabs. So I go back to the Arabs, make the deal, pick out work pants and a jacket at a secondhand store, and have the Arab pay for them. Then I go to a pissoir, where I change and get the wretched balance of the money.

I dash along the fences of the wharves, which are guarded by cops ready to fire their machine guns. Eventually I'm five miles outside Marseilles. I stop at a tavern which has rooms to sleep in. I eat French fries and drink a glass of wine. Then I collapse on the bed.

From now on all I think about is finding a ship as soon as possible. It isn't easy. You can't enter the heavily guarded harbor without special authorization, and the shipping agencies, which hire crews, are overrun by unemployed sailors, who get into free-for-alls over jobs. No one even glances at me, much less talks to me. I try British and American companies, but they hire only Brits or Americans. I try to be a dockworker, lugging sacks with black Africans. I spend the money on the hookers of Marseilles. These girls can't be picky; they fuck with men of all races from the four corners of the world and they probably catch every conceivable kind of V.D. But I not only screw them without a rubber, I also eat out their pussies. I know it's crazy. But I want to love them, I want them to feel that I love them and that I need love. That I'm dying for love.

"You've got a mouth like a whore," one of them says to me before kissing me good-bye.

"I know."

A trolley runs to my inn every forty minutes. But I prefer using the money for fucking and walking the ten miles. I don't care. Especially when I go to my whores.

There's no dock work for the moment, so I do odd jobs. I even work for the sanitation department for a week.

I can't keep body and soul together on the pittance I earn, most of which I spend on women anyway. When I stop paying rent, the landlord gives me notice. My room isn't really a room, it's a windowless concrete hole, smaller than a prison cell, with an iron bed on the concrete floor. But it costs money. I earn my food in his kitchen: Working under supervision, I prepare and serve French fries, meat, salad, and caramel custard for the workers and I scrub out the kitchen, plus the whole goddamn stable with its shit-covered toilets, I chop mountains of wood, and I lug wine vats. For all that, I receive salad and French fries once a day. The rent is not included. I have to earn it somehow, or else he'll throw me out.

The men are all sulfur miners. Spaniards, Portuguese, Poles, and Algerians, working in the sulfur mine near the inn. They fritter their earnings away on food and booze. On their day off they down ten Pernods by lunchtime. And each man washes down every meal with a liter of wine. The drudgery in the mine will kill them all. They know it; that's why they don't save any money. It's not worth it. They wear gas masks in the mine, but those aren't much help—the men all croak within a couple of years. One of my friends—the men who share their Gauloises and their last few francs with me—is thirty-five but looks sixty. He gives me a colorful Arab scarf, which I wear every day.

If there's any leftover food, I don't bring it to the kitchen, where I normally eat. Instead, I devour it while cleaning up, or if it's a piece of meat I hide it under my sweater. If it's French fries, I wrap them in a newspaper and stick them in my pocket.

I write to Cocteau, asking for money. In Paris it didn't occur to me to look him up. He writes back:

> *My dear friend,*
> *I would share everything with you. . . . Unfortunately I own nothing. I live off the generosity of others. I am ill and already have one foot in the grave. I am sending you this drawing; perhaps you can sell it.*
>
> > *Your friend,*
> > *Jean Cocteau*

The envelope contains one of his typical drawings, my portrait from memory. He's given me the mouth of a black man and eyes like stars. The miners will hardly buy the drawing from me.

The wind force is Beaufort 10. No one's outdoors. I sit on a rock by the sea, where I always watch the departing ships. The surf rages over fifty feet high, and the tempest whips the briny spray into my face.

The thunder brings down the heavens, and the lightning illuminates me. I've never been so happy in all my life.

The landlord wants to force me to work in the sulfur mine. I refuse. He kicks me out of the hole I spend my nights in, and now I sleep in a shot-up bunker on the rocky coast.

I can't look for a job. A boil in my throat, caused by inflammation, prevents me from working. The boil keeps growing; my throat closes up completely; I can't swallow, and I can barely breathe.

The miners bring me hot stones, which I place on my throat. At night one worker always keeps watch. In the daytime I'm alone.

One of them takes me to a family—I believe they're from Portugal. They give me a pile of lemons. Thirty. I squeeze the juice right into my throat, thirty lemons in a row. It doesn't help; the acid only gives me stomach cramps. Besides, I want to get away from these people. They keep birds in cages. Once a year they open the cages and then shoot down the birds as they fly to freedom. They kill them for sheer pleasure.

Going to a doctor makes no sense because doctors always ask for their fee up front, and none of the workers has any money until the next payday. And I'd rather not go to a hospital, because I don't know if that fucking landlord has brought charges against me. I couldn't even give them a place of residence if they asked me, and I don't want the immigration police to deport me for vagabondage.

After passing the hat, the miners take me to a nearby physician, who gives me a penicillin shot, which has to be paid for up front, cash on the barrelhead.

But there's no improvement. So I walk to Marseilles and look for a specialist. I want to ask him to treat me gratis because I'm afraid I'll choke.

I scan the names on front doors, house by house, nameplate by nameplate. Nobody can tell me where to find an ear-nose-and-throat specialist.

I roam the streets till the afternoon. It always takes me several minutes to swallow. The torment gets worse and worse.

At seven in the evening I find a specialist, but he's closing up. He's already got his hat and coat on, but he's very friendly. He checks my throat and says he can operate for free. I'm to come back in the morning. In the morning!

I hurry back to my bunker and spend the night with hot stones, which burn my neck and my chin, but don't help.

At night I sneak over to the inn. The dog, who knows me, doesn't bark. But he whimpers joyously, so loud that I have to hold my hands over his mouth. I reach through a tiny broken pane in the rear kitchen door and push back the bolt. In the kitchen I find a long, sharp knife. If everything else goes amiss, I'll operate on myself. I'll try to slice into the boil when I can't breathe anymore.

At eight A.M. I walk back to Marseilles, with the long kitchen knife under my jacket—just in case.

Today it takes me a lot longer to swallow. In Marseilles I go to the German embassy. Unable to speak, I write on a slip of paper: "I have a boil in my throat and urgently need an operation. Please give me the necessary money, I have none." I show them my passport, and they give me three hundred marks.

One hour later I'm en route to the doctor. Again I absolutely have to swallow. But I can't. It's beyond me. No matter how hard I try, I simply can't swallow. I hold on to a street light and think that this is the end. I pull out the kitchen knife and stick it down my throat like a sword swallower. And then it happens. The boil breaks! And I puke half a liter of pus into the gutter. Now I'm rid of everything and my pains are gone.

The three hundred marks in my pocket could tide me over for a while in Marseilles. I could move into fairly decent quarters, eat a hot meal every day, and bide my time until I find a ship that'll take me on.

But I've changed my plans. There's no way I'll sign up on a tanker and get kicked around. I want to earn enough money to build my own sailboat someday. Then I'll sail away and never come back. So for now I have to make movies.

I don't go to the surgeon. I don't go to anyone, not even my whores.

I buy a ticket for Munich. The train is to leave at six P.M. At noon I sit down in a good restaurant, take my sweet time making my selection, drink a whole bottle of red wine, leave a generous tip, and have a nap. I've told the waiter to get me up only if I sleep past five P.M.

In Munich O. W. Fischer has mobilized everything to track me down for the film *Hanussen*.

"I need your eyes," he tells me.

Now that's really no reason to hire an actor, as far as I'm concerned. But I accept the part, which is better paid this time. After all, I'm not making a movie in order to turn myself on.

I rent a modern apartment with a garbage disposal. The first thing I throw into the garbage disposal is the *Hanussen* script. And then I buy my first car—that is, I make a down payment and get behind the wheel. It's a used Cadillac Cabriolet.

At the Bavaria Studios building, one of the sweet young secretaries gets into my pearl-gray "sleigh," and she can't wait until we finally zoom off. Unfortunately it's raining cats and dogs, and we have to ride with the top up.

At a red light I step on the gas, as I always do at a red light. A truck swerves in from the right; we crash into one another. The

Caddy's heavy bumper bursts into three parts, which soar through the air. Nothing's happened to the trucker or his truck. He's only bumped his knee. The sweet steno and I reel out of the Caddy as if we'd been driving an amusement-park car. The Caddy has to be towed, so we take a cab to my pad.

"Last name. First name. Date of birth. Place of birth. Address . . ."

"It's all in the file. All you have to do is read it."

"I'm asking *you.*"

That sadism again. I want to jump up. Rudolf Amesmaier pushes me back on my courtroom chair.

"Fine. I'm Mr. So-and-So. Born on so-and-so. In So-and-So. I reside at so-and-so . . ."

"Marital status?"

"What's this all about?"

"Are you married? Single? Divorced?"

"Divorced."

"When did you marry?"

"I can't recall."

"You should be ashamed of yourself."

"What's that got to do with my Caddy?"

"*I'm* asking the questions here! Any police record?"

I turn to Amesmaier. "Do I have a record?"

"Yes."

"Yes."

"Why?"

I turn to Amesmaier. "Why?"

"For insulting a government official and resisting arrest," says Amesmaier.

"For insulting a government official and resisting arrest."

"Aha!"

"What do you mean, 'Aha!'?"

"If you talk out of turn again, you'll receive the maximum penalty!"

"What crime have I committed? Nothing happened to the trucker. My insurance'll pay for the damage to his truck. My Caddy's totaled. I'm the only one who's suffered!"

"You're an asocial element! You think that because you make movies and earn a lot of money you can act brutal and arrogant in traffic!"

"If you knew why I make movies, and if you knew why I was in such a hurry on the day of the accident—"

"If you get impudent, I'll lock you up!"

I turn to Amesmaier. "Can he lock me up!"

"Oh, bullshit," says Amesmaier. "Stay seated and let him talk."

"You know what? Give me the maximum penalty and lemme outa here," I say, disgusted.

Amermaier is crimson with agitation. I tell him that this asshole of a judge makes me puke and that I'll land in prison if I don't get the maximum penalty and get out of here.

"Counselor, did you hear what your client just said?"

"What?"

"He requested the maximum penalty. Right?"

"Yes, that's right, but—"

"I'm finished," the so-called judge breaks in, and packs up his stuff.

I get the maximum penalty. A ten-thousand-mark fine! All because I have no Caddy anymore. If I don't pay the fine, I'll have to go to prison for three hundred days!

While I'm filming *Hanussen,* Laslo Benedek hires me for his movie *Kinder, Mütter und ein General* ("Children, Mothers, and a General").

In Hamburg, everyone in the movie business stays at the Hotel

Bellevue, but not me. I go to a small rooming house around the corner. At six A.M. I'm arrested in my bed. The cops would never have figured out that I'm on their wanted list if I'd filled out the registration form correctly. Instead I wrote that I was born before the Christian era, that I have neither a permanent residence nor money nor a passport nor a job, and that I'm a whore. The landlady was unhappy with my data and brought me a new registration blank when I was already asleep. I put Chinese fantasy characters on the back. So she called the prowl car, and they found my name on their wanted list.

The reason why I'm on the list is not the ten-thousand-mark fine for the Caddy, but the old business about resisting arrest, which I've long since forgotten.

I'm led off in handcuffs, thrown into a Black Maria with other prisoners, and driven to the holding jail. There I get kicked into a cell.

In the morning they tell me, "Shut your trap," then "Bend over, pull your ass cheeks apart. Pull back your foreskin." They take all ten fingerprints. Photograph me with a number. Take my measurements. Make me hand over my belt and shoelaces.

"Do you have fleas?" a skunk asks me, tossing a dirty, raggedy blanket at my head. I'm supposed to cover myself with it.

"Not so far, you cockroach. But I'll probably catch all the vermin in the world if you don't get the hell away from me."

The blanket, which stinks of farts and sweat, drops to the floor, and I kick it away.

Two days later Rudolf Amesmaier gets me out of jail.

I move to the Hotel Prem, where one of the actresses, Ursula H., lives. I call her Uglymug. Uglymug is so ugly that I can only fuck her in the dark—to avoid putting a towel over her face. But her body is so young and firm and hot and horny that I think the Good Lord deliberately forced that face on her to punish all the guys who fall only for a pretty face.

Today I'm incapable of fucking her. After catching bronchitis in that medieval jail, I bought some codeine drops and swallowed the whole bottle. When Uglymug comes into my room, I'm sitting in a chair and I don't even have the strength to move. I feel as if Uglymug were floating into the room, running upside-down across the ceiling. But she undresses all the same.

Two weeks later, when Uglymug leaves town, I go to Hamburg's red-light district, where the girls flaunt their wares in the dim reddish light of the store windows. They straddle chairs or loll across sofas in order to entice the men.

I window-shop, fascinated. The faces and bodies of the young hookers turn into the faces and bodies of all the women I have loved in my life. It's like that whenever I embrace a woman: Her face and body take on the shapes and expressions of the other women I have loved or am yearning for, including women I don't know but am sure to encounter.

The girls in the store windows beckon to me. But I'm put off by the sleazy remarks of the men thronging the windows. I can't stand anyone deriding the woman who's about to become my beloved, and so I keep walking.

The street itself is unlit, so I can stand, unrecognized, in a house entrance or walk up and down if I avoid the clusters of men.

I sit down on the curbstone and fall asleep. When I wake up, the day is dawning. The reddish lights in the store windows are switched off. From a window one flight up an elderly prostitute calls to me, and I climb the stairs to her place.

She talks a blue streak. I merely smile without answering. Not because she's so old and used-up and I'm not the least bit excited, but because my thoughts are elsewhere.

"You're a papa's boy with a rich dad and you came here on a yacht, right?"

I nod. I don't want to blast her dream of the wealthy young man whose luxury steamer is moored in the Hamburg harbor.

"A guy like you ain't gonna be a cheapskate."

I shake my head. I'm uneasy about talking. If she keeps quizzing me, I'll have to lie. I'm always nervous about telling people I'm an actor. I'm sad to be here. But I don't want to leave; I don't want to hurt her feelings.

She strips and waits for me to strip. I don't because I'm not getting stiff, so she opens my fly and takes out my dick. Then she slips a condom over my dick, which still isn't hard, and massages it with her mouth. Then she soaps it up. Probably, I think, to lube it or disinfect it in case the rubber slips off.

I lie down on my back, uninterested, and she straddles me. When she starts riding me, she gasps randily and moans deceitfully, as hookers often do to make a john think they're reaching climax. The hookers know it excites a guy, so he'll come faster.

I'm extremely excited. Not because of her exaggerated and desultory moaning and whimpering, or the way she says, "C'mon, baby, give it to Mama. . . . Get it out. . . . I want all your juice." But because in reality she doesn't dare hope for any guy's horniness and because she lost all interest in fucking long ago. Her moans are one long self-derision. Her flesh is cold. She's trembling. Her body is devastated. Her boobs and her belly dangle like dead, alien creatures. The cellulite on her thighs is piled up into shapeless mountains. Her withered butt is pinched in as anxiously as a kicked puppy's. Her long pussy lips, which have been ground down by thousands of men, no longer close in front of the gaping hole, which I could easily fist-fuck.

I'm overcome with pain and rage: Rage because this clown of love has been tossed away. And pain because she has to keep turning her tricks because she has no choice.

And suddenly I see her the way she probably used to be, like the young whores in the display windows of the neighboring houses. When she could still be proud of herself because she knew that men lusted for her and their dicks stood up at the mere sight of her. And when her moans were still honest, because she felt the men inside her and really reached orgasm. In an orgasm every woman believes in love.

I throw her on her back, tear off the rubber, and shove my big, hard dick so violently into her hole that she breaks into a sweat. Her body quickly heats up, starts glowing. Her eyes under the half-shut lids take on an absent, silvery radiance. Her abdomen thrusts toward me as if her ovaries were fertile and she wanted to receive my semen. When she yells in her orgasm, I come.

I give her more money than she would earn from ten men. I'd like her to take the day off.

"I'll go shopping and then we'll have breakfast, okay?" she says, hurriedly covering herself so as not to destroy the illusion.

I thank her but point to my watch.

"I understand—your ship's leaving, you have to get to the harbor."

I nod and kiss her good-bye on her old mouth.

Yorka never leaves my side. Ever since I recited Villon at Berlin's Kongresshalle, she's been keeping her feverish Mongolian eyes glued to me.

She lives on Olympische Strasse with her mother. I sleep there on a lopsided couch, whose cushions are made up of something like small rag sacks, and I baby-sit for Yorka's children when she goes to work. It's on that sloping couch, which I roll down the instant I close my eyes, that I hatch the plans for my later tours. And on that sloping couch I first read Rimbaud, Oscar Wilde's fairy tales and "The Ballad of Reading Gaol," Tucholsky, Hauptmann's *Heretic of Soana*, Nietzsche, Brecht's ballads, and Mayakovsky.

First I perform in Berlin movie houses. Then in the university auditorium. Yorka sells the tickets in the campus restaurant, storing the receipts in a cigar box, which she hands over to me before my performance. Next I rent several theaters: the Komödie, the Volksbühne, the large Kongresshalle, the Titania Palace, and the New Philharmonic.

Fritz Kortner comes farting along and signs me up for his movie *Sarajevo* in Vienna. I'm to play the leader of the assassins, the guy who throws the bomb. E.R. plays opposite me. We fuck nonstop and so vehemently that I sleep even when I'm standing in front of the camera and Kortner talks softly near me, because he thinks I'm mulling over my lines. All in all he treats me a lot more cautiously this time.

Anuschka, the wife of a millionaire and a member of the Russian imperial family, has written me a letter offering to help me. I don't know what she means, but I can always use help. We make a date to meet in Salzburg, where her husband owns a house. She picks me up at the train station.

She bores her sharp fists into my armpit glands, my ribs, my groin; she chews up my entire body, sticks her tongue into all the openings that a human body has, and wants me to do likewise. Her animal shrieks don't stop until we move from Salzburg to Vienna.

Anuschka pays for everything. I have no money.

She gets no money from her husband unless she fucks him, so when her reserves are used up we have absolutely no idea where we're gonna get dough in the future. For the time being we move from one furnished apartment to the next, each more depressing than the last.

Eventually she lodges me in a ramshackle old-age home, where I settle in a room behind a secret door in the library while Anuschka steals food from the pantry of her husband's villa when he's not home. (Her little daughter and her mother-in-law also live there.)

When the Vienna Funeral Home celebrates its fiftieth birthday, it treats its employees to a matinee. The agency asks me if I'd like to participate in this variety program.

The agent wants me to recite a soliloquy from Franz Grillparzer's *King Ottokar*, in which the commander in chief or whoever is on a battlefield, reeling off claptrap about Honor and Fatherland.

I buy a thin paperback of the play and read through the garbage about the speech on the battlefield. At first I haven't the foggiest clue as to what it's all about. I try to revamp the text in a coffeehouse, but no matter how I twist and turn the nonsense, it remains battlefield drivel about Honor and Fatherland.

"I can't recite this sort of crap," I tell the agent, "not even for the funeral home."

"Fine," he says understandingly, "then suggest something else."

I suggest Hamlet's soliloquy with the skull in the graveyard; but that's too macabre for a funeral home.

"What about the *Faust* monologue?" I ask.

It's too long, says the agent. I reply, "Just let me try it."

At the matinee it's all over in exactly fifty-seven seconds. Running off the stage I sob the final verse—"The earth has me again"—and rake in a pile of money.

The pallbearers and gravediggers in the auditorium of the Mozart Hall still haven't caught on that they've just heard the shortest *Faust* monologue of all time.

The money tides me over briefly, but I can't wait until the funeral home's seventy-fifth birthday. So I recite Villon. I use the Mozart Hall, which I got to know through the funeral home. Then the Beethoven Hall, and finally the huge Concert House Hall.

After Villon I recite Rimbaud. Then Villon again.

And then both on one program.

At the Meat Market Theater I play the title role in *The King Is Dying* and at the Josefstadt Theater I play the cripple in *The First Legion.*

Next I recite Gerhart Hauptmann's *The Heretic of Soana.* This play is about a young Catholic priest who is excommunicated because he gives in to his love for a minor girl. As a result he is stoned. I want to proclaim the story of this Italian cleric from the pulpit of St. Stephen's Cathedral. But they won't let me.

Then it's back to Villon, Rimbaud, and again Villon.

Anuschka's husband keeps offering her money to return to him. But Anuschka goes back to the villa solely to pilfer some food.

We move before the first month's rent is due. Schönbrunn, Goethe Monument, Kärntner Ring, Naschmarkt. I can't stand it anywhere. When Anuschka is with her daughter I wander through Vienna. It's true what they say about the "sweet Viennese girls": They're all sweet, from the teenagers to the married wives and mothers and the hookers around Kärntner Ring.

Anuschka has become very suspicious because the hookers on Kärntner Ring wave at me. Understandably, she's now even less anxious than before to leave me on my own. She's made some kind of arrangement with her husband, and she's setting up an apartment on Judengasse. He's paying for it, but she wants to shack up with me there.

For the time being I remain in the creepy pad at Naschmarkt, but during the day I lie with the hookers in bushes and on green meadows and I go out to Ottakring with them.

O. W. Fischer, who has meanwhile learned that I'm knocking about in Vienna, writes to Rott, the director of the Vienna Burgtheater. Anuschka tells me that Rott is waiting to see me. He offers me a five-year contract at the highest salary. He talks a blue streak, allows me to choose my own plays, and says that he'll gear the whole season's program to my wishes. This is scary.

The first play is Goethe's *Tasso*. It's been scheduled for some time now, and Rott gives me a free hand to interpret Tasso as I like. All he asks is that I get in touch with the director, Raoul Aslan, and explain my ideas to him.

Aslan, who invited me to his home, talks such hair-raising bullshit that at first I don't even notice his heavy hand on my thigh. When I leave, his final words are: "So remember, Tasso is like a skier schussing downhill at sixty miles an hour!"

What've I gotten into!

Rott lets me have the rehearsal hall in the theater attic, where I won't be bothered by anyone for four weeks. The other actors never turn up for rehearsals, so I soon prefer the chairs, which replace them and keep their traps shut.

Rott has gotten into his head to present me to the public as Josef Kainz's successor. That's why he wants me to don the original costume in which Kainz played Tasso; it's now hanging on a wire dummy at the theater museum. But the costume doesn't fit me at all, even though Kainz must have had more or less my build. Besides, it's been devoured by moths.

A new costume, a replica of the original, is tailored out of pure silk, and a gilded dagger is made for me. Rott can throw around the millions he gets every year from the Austrian government. He wastes the money anyhow on his miserable productions, but in his treatment of me money is no object.

His effort to present me as the new Kainz is so obsessive that he sets up photo sessions between rehearsals, with me in costume. The photographers drag me to the Kainz monument, to the Kainz bust in the Burgtheater, to the Kainz portrait in the gallery, and to his tombstone! It's like advertising for Coca-Cola, I muse, except that I'm not getting paid for it! I'm disgusted by this grave-robbing. The creeps at the Burgtheater didn't start licking Kainz's ass until he had cancer and didn't have much time left.

At the dress rehearsal the other actors, who I have to perform with for better or worse, come toddling in. Most of them are very condescending, and as Burgtheater veterans they don't go out of their way with the new kid on the block. I myself am extremely surprised to be dealing with flesh-and-blood people, I'm so used to my chairs.

After the dress rehearsal Aslan wrings his hands. His dream of a ski champion has faded forever.

The performance is a triumph for me. The spectators refuse to leave and want me to stay in Vienna forever.

Kortner sends me a wire: "Please do Prince Heinz at the Munich State Theater."

Anuschka and I fly to Munich and rent a villa in Nymphenburg. Every morning I ride the trolley to rehearsals. At night we fuck and have fistfights.

Anuschka slices her wrists with a razor in the middle of the street. I bandage her hands with the handkerchief and take her home, where we fuck and fight again.

On the day of the premiere a warrant is issued for my arrest. The squad car is already en route. Once again it's about some sort of debt that I forgot to pay. Since I have no money left, and it's a matter of several thousand marks, Kortner rings up the minister of justice to cancel my arrest and then the minister of finance about the sum itself. Rudolf Amesmaier puts in his two cents' worth. He's got a brilliant idea: Every government, every German state, every city has a secret slush fund for unprecedented emergencies. My case is one of those emergencies, for no lead actor at a state theater has ever been arrested on the day of a premiere. If the performances had to be canceled, the financial damage to the state of Bavaria would be a lot greater than if my debt were paid out of the slush fund. Amesmaier gets his way. The slush fund covers my debt. In this way, the government pays the government with government money.

Anuschka and I return to Vienna. The apartment on Judengasse is ready, and in the romantic garret we rest up from all the stress and strain, which were worse for Anuschka than for me.

I have to go to Berlin for a movie. I realized long ago that I can't always pick and choose my movies, especially since I always need money. It's no use being selective. They're all alike, and the lot of them aren't worth the effort. What choice do I have but to make the best of this garbage?

Anuschka joins me for the next few films, but then my screwing around gets the upper hand again—from the extras, whom I fuck in the toilets and the dressing rooms, to the actresses, whom I screw next door while Anuschka waits for me in our hotel room, to the hotel maids, whom I poke in the bed I share with Anuschka. She returns to Vienna.

In Berlin I rent an unfurnished six-room apartment on Uhlandstrasse. Yorka helps me whitewash the walls. The furniture is quickly bought: a couple of beds, mattresses, a table, a chair, and some kitchen implements.

As soon as the word gets out that I've got an apartment again, the court bailiffs appear, like a plague of locusts. I hurl my only chair after one of them on the stairs.

Yorka was right when she told me to buy the chair. It's stable, and I can use it again.

So long as Yorka doesn't live with me, my pad becomes a real bordello. Every guy I've ever met anywhere buzzes at night so he can fuck here. Every one always brings a girl along. I don't switch on the light, so I don't see their faces. In the darkness we swap girls and no one knows who's fucking who.

There's an usherette at the Gloria Palace who kneels down next to my seat during a screening and brings me best regards from her friend, whom I've never even met. I have to take her to my brothel.

Unfortunately Yorka comes back from shopping with overflowing bags—and catches the usherette and me with my pants down in the middle of the room. We're wedged into one another. Till now I've always at least spared Yorka the sight of me carrying on behind her back. She drops her bags. Apples, oranges, carrots, and potatoes roll up to our feet. The slippery whites of the shattered raw eggs splash derisively across the floorboards, smearing Yorka's shoes. After dropping her bags, she dashes from the apartment.

For an instant the usherette and I stand there, petrified. Then her abdomen again starts moving rhythmically, and I can't help it: I take in her thrusts and respond with harder and harder thrusts.

I want to fuck her, fuck her! But I don't want to shoot inside her. I want to save my come, go to Yorka, beg her for forgiveness, and shoot inside her.

When I ring Yorka's bell, her mother opens the door. Yorka has taken a sleeping pill and is fast asleep. I take off my pants and shoot into her—shoot everything that I so violently held back with the usherette.

Yorka is carrying my baby. She knows I can't stay with her, and she's scared of being alone with two kids. I can't prevent her from having an abortion.

On the Ku'damm in Berlin I stand outside the glove store next to Rollenhagen, a gourmet deli. I'm not planning to buy gloves. Upon emerging from the deli, I ate up my salami outside the glove store. Through the window I spotted a blond kitten. She was slipping a glove over the proffered hand of a male shopper. I wipe my hands, which smell of salami, on my jeans and enter the glove store.

While the kitten serves a customer, I have time to take a closer look at her. She must be about seventeen. Her movements are timid and graceful, but this little kitty-cat can't hide the fact that she turns into a tiger in bed. Her snug, worn skirt, which is too short, and her tight, hand-knitted baby sweater, which she's long since outgrown, speak volumes. About the little tit balls, which quiver with every move she makes as if they knew that they had to behave here . . . About the shape of her small schoolgirl belly, which forms an S curve with her bodacious butt. Her eyes are greenish-gray, like those of many cats. Her flushed, bright-red lips are swollen and very slightly parted, like those of a thirsty baby. That's what her little twat must look like.

When she sees me, her face turns as bright red as her mouth. Her eyes shoot into my balls.

After finishing with her customer, she turns to me.

"What kind of gloves are you looking for, sir?"

"Very tight ones. I don't care about the color."

I should have worded this differently, but it's too late. For an instant she stands there, indecisive, and I regret confusing her. As if realizing that gloves are the farthest thing from my mind, she smiles and lowers her eyes.

She slips a tight glove over my proffered hand while I prop my elbows on the counter and splay my fingers. First she pulls the entire glove over my hand. Then she smooths out the leather on my fingers, from the tips up, as if massaging them. Finger by finger.

I can feel her hot fingers through the thin leather as if there were no glove. It's as if her skin were on mine. And all the while, I keep staring at her. She doesn't return my gaze, but she seems to feel what I feel, and this is probably the first time she's massaged a shopper's fingers. Who knows what she's thinking? As for me, I'm thinking that my five fingers are five dicks that she's massaging one after the other. I can't stand here forever with five stiff dicks.

"Would you like to come to my place? Live with me. Stay with me? Give up these glove fittings?"

She still won't look at me and she won't stop massaging my fingers.

"When?" she asks, barely audible.

"Immediately."

From behind the curtain of the back room her boss emerges; she looks like a toad.

"Are you satisfied, sir?" she asks, lurking like a madam.

"I'm satisfied with your salesgirl. I'll take her along. Please prepare her salary."

The toad is dumbstruck. Before she can pull herself together, Biggi and I are out of the store.

The toad won't pay the salary because Biggi didn't give proper notice. But Biggi doesn't need that pittance. I've signed up for several tours, and Biggi will have anything she wants.

Biggi's mother would worry if her daughter stayed out all night. So we send her a wire:

AM WITH MY FUTURE HUSBAND STOP DON'T WORRY.

BIGGI

As soon as I let Biggi out of my arms, she takes care of the apartment. So far we have no extra money, but Biggi grew up in modest circumstances and is thankful for every flower she buys at the market. Everything she touches becomes beautiful, and soon, with just a few more objects and furnishings, she's transformed my bare white six-room apartment into a romantic love nest.

Then I buy the barest necessary clothes for Biggi. Every rag she picks out and tries on looks tailor-made for her. She never wants the most expensive items, and she always asks how much everything costs.

Now I start running amok with my tours. Amok, with no end in sight. First Berlin, again the Sports Palace. Then Munich. Frankfurt. Hamburg. Then all the other cities. A hundred times. A thousand times.

Biggi is always with me. She never tires of taking care of every bothersome bit of crap. I can't because the performances drain every last ounce of my strength. She's in the audience every night. During intermissions she comes into my dressing room and mops the sweat off my face and body. She puts up with all my excesses, and her undying love helps me to endure the ruthless torture.

We travel by car; I've bought a Jaguar. By train. By air. We barely sleep—we usually have to hit the road again the very same night. During my first tour I give one hundred and twenty performances in a row. One weekend I perform five times. More and more sold-out houses. And I want more and more money so that I can fritter away more and more.

First I get five hundred marks for a performance. Then seven hundred, a thousand, ten thousand, twenty thousand. We stay in the most expensive hotels, the most luxurious suites, and we live like royalty.

Biggi can have anything she likes—I'll pay for it. But it doesn't go to her head. She remains as undemanding and down-to-earth as ever and delights more in a single rose that I give her than in a pricey ring.

"How many days are there in a year?" I ask my agent.

"Three hundred and sixty-five. Why?"

"Then get me three hundred and sixty-five performances a year."

He refuses to take part in my suicide, as he puts it.

Biggi is now in her ninth month and is still accompanying me. Even though the lashing sleet is turning the autobahn into dangerous slush, the speedometer needle in my Jaguar seldom shows less than 120 miles per hour. I can't take my foot off the gas if we're gonna make the evening show. We zoom through all the warning and stop signs and halt only to tank up.

Shortly before we reach Kiel a VW cuts straight in front of us from the left lane without flashing its turn indicator. I try to slow down. We skid, and the left side of the Jaguar is ripped by the steel fence of the highway divider.

Keep going! Keep going!

By the time we arrive in Kiel, the spectators are in their seats, waiting for the curtain to rise. As is, I dash onstage. After the performance we hit the road again.

En route to Hamburg, where I'm supposed to cut some disks for Deutsche Grammophon, we have another accident. When I try to pass a truck the Jaguar skids sideways across a patch of ice. I manage to regain control, but we're so close to the truck's trailer that I have to swerve left, and we skid across to the wrong side. About a hundred and fifty yards ahead of us a car is shooting our way. I'd have time enough to get back in the right lane—but a third car, which I haven't spotted, is racing in from a feeder road, closer and closer. I carefully try to steer the Jaguar to my lane. But it doesn't work. The third car is zooming straight toward us. I have no choice—I tear the wheel to the right. I've managed to balance the swing when the Jaguar skids out, rear first. It whirls around twice on its own axis. I lose control; we screech down a slope and turn over. The Jaguar is standing on its head.

The backs of our seats are shattered, but we're still belted in. When I come to, I hear Biggi whimpering. The doors are jammed. I manage to smash a window. I creep out and drag Biggi from the wreck before the car explodes.

She can't walk on one of her legs. She's also in shock and stammering confusedly. I try to calm her and take her in my bleeding arms. The trunk door has sprung open and some of our valises have catapulted out. But our coats are beyond help. I squeeze Biggi very tight to shield her from the cutting cold.

Meanwhile other cars have stopped, and the passengers are hurrying over to help us. Somewhat later, policemen and firefighters show up.

My arms are injured, and on my forehead is a lump the size of a fist. Biggi has pulled herself together and can walk now. She's unhurt.

The baby is kicking impatiently in her belly.

After the formalities are taken care of, a squad car drops us off in the next village, where we hop a cab to Hamburg.

Once there, I complete five records while Biggi finally sleeps her fill. Then I buy baby linen and a couple of baby shoes of light-blue kid with white tips; I roll a gigantic wheeled bear in front of Biggi's bed. Our baby will ride the bear. That same evening we fly to Berlin. Biggi's contractions have begun. I take her to the hospital. She gives birth that same night. It's a girl. I name her Nastassja. That's the young woman in Dostoevsky's *The Idiot*—the one who's crazy about Prince Myshkin.

The first night, I stay over in the hospital and sleep in Biggi's room. Then, after buying mountains of flowers, I go to Uhlandstrasse and turn our love nest into a sea of blossoms. For now, Nastassja will sleep in her perambulator. I got it from England. It's got huge wheels and it looks like a real carriage, pearl gray with a white cabriolet, like our Jaguar, in which Nasstja has raced over ten thousand miles of autobahn while inside Biggi's belly.

Much as it pains me to leave Nasstja and Biggi alone, I have to hit the trail again. I've got contracts to honor.

After another four and a half months I cancel the rest of my tour. It's a killer. Above all, I can't spend so much time away from Biggi and Nasstja.

We rent a villa on the edge of Grünewald. Seven rooms, three baths, a guest toilet, a garage, and a huge garden with a sandbox for Nasstja. The villa is a rococo pavilion with cupids on the roof and an outdoor stairway that curves down into the garden with its blossoming lilac and forsythia, roses and rhododendrons.

I clean out half a toy shop for Nasstja. I buy dresses and furs for Biggi as well as jewelry and the most expensive perfumes. I order custom-made suits, silk shirts, gloves, shoes, and even silk underpants. I order cambric bed linen with ruffles and lace, plus quilts and pillows filled with the finest down.

Biggi and I play tennis, and I buy a horse for us.

The dining-room table, groaning under the weight of our food, looks as if it came from a fairy-tale palace in the Arabian Nights. It takes hours just to set and clear the flowers, the mounds of fruit, the most diverse wines, the liqueurs in gaudy carafes of polished crystal, the whole roasts, the goose in any season, the venison, the marzipan, the candy.

We dine off the finest Meissen porcelain with gold knives and forks, and we drink from colorful beakers of polished crystal.

The urchin's dream has become reality. But I don't want any of it anymore. I've long since stopped yearning for it. Besides, I know that this idyllic happiness won't last. I can't go against my grain. Even though I'm sick with groundless jealousy, I have a relapse of screwing around—when up till now I haven't cheated on Biggi even once.

It starts with a trainee from the store where I've bought baby clothes for Nasstja. The girl delivers the huge package after the midday closing time. Biggi is breast-feeding in the nursery. I open the front door. The trainee is all dolled up in a very short, fashionable dress, with intense, gluey, aggressive lipstick on her mouth. She can't be older than sixteen. I take the package and ask her to wait a moment in the entrance hall while I dig up some cash for her tip.

When I return to the entrance hall, where a door leads directly into the guest toilet, the girl eyeballs me as though expecting something other than the money, which she doesn't even register as I hold it out.

As if in a trance, I grab the girl's pussy, shove her into the toilet, and lock the door behind us.

It lasts at most fifteen minutes. Then I bring Biggi the package, and we have Nasstja try on the little frocks all afternoon.

If Biggi snooped or had even the slightest suspicion that I cheat on her, I wouldn't feel such remorse. But Biggi trusts me so thoroughly that she never even asks where I'm going or why I often don't come home until close to dawn. I say, "I have to go out." That suffices for her. I myself can't explain why I'm now stepping out on her more and more often. I'm as horny for her as I was the first day. And she likewise gets randier and randier the more frequently and shamelessly I fuck her.

I receive a letter with a huge coat-of-arms. A British countess is inquiring whether I'd be willing to recite the Hamlet soliloquies for her, alone in her castle. Fee per soliloquy: ten thousand marks. She'd like to come to Berlin to get my answer personally.

One week later she calls me up. We are to meet in the Tiergarten. You never know. We take a long walk, and she rattles on about Hamlet. She's not pretty, nor does she turn me on particularly. If worse came to worst, I could fuck her right in the Tiergarten. Then I wouldn't have to go to England, where the beer is as warm as piss and has no head. Her Hamlet obsession is starting to get on my nerves.

It's drizzling. I suggest that we take cover in the bushes to escape the rain, and so we charge into a thicket. We find a place where we can't be seen from anywhere. I strip her naked and lay her out on the damp soil; she's embarrassed because she's having her period. . . .

Long past nightfall I say I have to leave. She remains lying in the bushes.

I get my bearings by the Victory Column; then I walk through the rain to get rid of the smell that clings to me. I see a clock: It's already midnight. I hail a cab.

Everyone's asleep in our villa. When I'm about to disrobe in the dressing room, I notice that my fly is smeared with blood. I sneak into the kitchen and wash out the stains under a cold stream of water. Then I hang up my pants with the wet part over the radiator. I crawl into bed with Biggi and shoot a heavy load while she hugs me in her sleep and spreads her legs.

Two weeks later Scotland Yard phones to ask if I know where the countess is; they say that she hasn't returned to England and that she left my address behind. I tell them I don't know her. That she did plan to visit me but never called.

So the countess has vanished. What's next?

Biggi believes she's pregnant again. But she loses the embryo in the toilet. She held her hand underneath, catching the embryo in a tissue and then showing it to me. It looks like a teensy white frog. Its arms, legs, hands, and feet are almost developed. The head is recognizable only by its shape, and the face has no contours. Two dark dots the size of pinheads are visible where the eyes might be expected.

For a couple of days Biggi is very listless and dejected. Then she recovers, and I try to take her mind off her terrible experience.

I'm supposed to do *Ghosts* with Anna Magnani. But we both have so many movies scheduled that we can't agree on a date.

Movies, movies, one after another. I don't even read the scripts anymore.

Der Rote Rausch ("The Red Intoxication") is being shot in Vienna— or rather, on the Hungarian border, some forty miles from the city. But we live in Vienna. Anuschka lets us stay in her apartment on Judengasse. She loves Biggi and Nastassja—I've written to her about them and sent her photos.

Nasstja is now almost a year old and she can stand in her crib. We go to the park; she walks for the first time, holding my hand.

I spend most of my time on location, sometimes sleeping over in the small border village if the roads are snowed in or I'm too tired to drive back to Vienna.

But there's a far more important reason why it's getting harder and harder for me to leave this one-horse town, which is famous for the storks' nests on its chimneys and for the wine, which gets everyone drunk. My reason: Claudia. We have to swallow drops for our circulation because between takes we slump in our chairs like two cripples, unable even to eat. This is because, aside from acting, we do nothing but fuck.

During the shooting that riffraff nearly burned me alive. I'm supposed to head into the reeds; there, according to the script, I'm to die in the flames. After pouring twenty gallons of gasoline into the reeds, they ignite them. The wind shifts, and the flames sweep together in front of me and behind me. I stamp through the ice crust on the shallow, muddy water and leap in so as to soak my hair and clothes; then, lowering my head, I charge through the fiery wall like a bull. I fall several times, cutting the veins of my lower arms on the reed stubble, which is as sharp as knives. The blood shoots from my injuries.

"Marvelous," some cattle driver in the crew bleats. This wretched gang of killers doesn't even have a Band-Aid, so I have to bandage my veins with strips torn from my shirt.

That's what a normal day is like in the biggest reed swamp in Europe. We can penetrate it only on vehicles with Caterpillar chains, otherwise we'd sink right in.

But neither this penal servitude nor my bandaged arms prevent me from spurting all my remaining energy into Claudia's hole.

Claudia has to see the dentist in Vienna to have a molar pulled. So that we won't have to be apart for even one day, I pick up a hammer and knock out one of my incisors. Now I have to visit the dentist too, since I can't be filmed with a gap in my teeth. So Claudia and I drive back to Vienna.

It takes us a whole day to cover the forty miles because we turn off into every side road for a fuck. In Vienna, I don't go to Judengasse. Instead, Claudia and I stay at a hotel.

After visiting the dentist, we call up the production people and tell them my tooth won't be ready for three days, which is actually true, while Claudia has to be treated for three days because the extraction of her molar left a huge hole.

En route back to the hick border town, we interrupt our drive more and more often. We move on only when we can't fuck anymore. With the onset of darkness we don't waste our time searching, we simply park on some frozen land. We lock the car doors from the inside and strip naked. . . . Covered with sweat, we're tangled into one another and Claudia is kicking her legs in her orgasms—when she accidentally hits the car horn. A flashlight glares into the windows, which are all steamed up from the heat of our bodies. Stark naked I get behind the wheel and burn rubber so fast that the country cop has to jump aside.

Claudia and I have a week off. But I can't fuck her during that week because her husband is visiting, and she has to let him fuck her.

Together with Nasstja, Anuschka, and Anuschka's daughter, Biggi has taken off for the mountains by Mondsee. She rang me up, asking me to join them. The superintendent has the keys to the apartment on Judengasse. Since there's no chance of Claudia's getting away from her husband, I make a date with Bärbel. She'll be coming by tomorrow morning at ten. Bärbel is another cunt in our movie, but I haven't managed to fuck her because of Claudia. In any case, I have to go by way of Vienna.

While waiting for Bärbel, I pack a few things for my holidays in the mountains. My train is leaving at 3:10 P.M. At ten A.M. on the dot Bärbel is standing at the apartment door. Before I can even shut the door she has already dropped her coat and her bag in the corridor and has started undressing. While peeling down her panties, she hops like a hare into the bedroom. She knows we've got only four hours to milk ourselves dry.

Bärbel is one of those cock-gobbling broads you get a boner with even if they're all wrapped up and you can't so much as sense their shapes. She's well nourished and as strong as a man. Plus, during the past few weeks she's been so horny she's nearly burst.

Two twenty-five P.M. I'm all set to leave. We don't even have time to wash up. The wind blasting into the train and the cold snowy air at Mondsee will blow Bärbel's powerful smell out of my skin and hair.

They're staying in a farmhouse, and when Nasstja sees me she comes storming toward me. I lift her high above my head and whirl her around until she's laughing so hard she can barely breathe. The earth is spinning underfoot, and we tumble to the ground. Next comes Biggi with Anuschka and her daughter. Her daughter hugs me so tight that I have to yank myself away so Biggi won't get suspicious. The girl keeps kissing me on the mouth with her wet lips and blabbering like a wound-up doll. She's extremely excited: "I love you. . . . I love you. . . . I love you. . . ."

It's fine with me, but not with Biggi. Anuschka smiles cunningly.

In Berlin I continue with Claudia. We shoot several movies in a row. While filming at the C.C.C. Studios in Spandau, we drive over to the Havel River during our lunch break. If there's not much time, I peel her panties down to just below her cheeks. She bends forward slightly and clutches a tree so as to have a solid hold and respond to my thrusts with her butt. If they don't need us right after lunch, we go deeper into the woods and undress.

When we film in Tempelhof, we drive back through the Grünewald in the evening. Usually we fuck in the car.

My next flick with Claudia is shot in Hamburg. We drive there in her car, and she calls for me at our villa.

Biggi and I have had a fistfight. It's the first time we've ever gotten into such a ferocious brawl.

Ever since I met Claudia there's been tension between me and Biggi, and it's gotten worse day by day. Now the tension explodes in insults and even physical violence. I don't think Biggi knows about me and Claudia; in any case, she has no hard proof. But Biggi is often sad and absent, which is not like her at all.

Claudia doesn't come into the house; she's been waiting in the car for half an hour. Biggi's eyes are swollen from crying, and she keeps bursting into tears. I'm desperate and at a loss, while the woman I cheat on her with and can't detach myself from waits in the car outside our front door. I can't put off leaving, because we have to reach Hamburg by nightfall.

Once there, I refuse to stay at the Hotel Bellevue with Claudia; I prefer the Prem. She takes offense and slams the car door so hard that the window shatters.

We have weekends off, so we drive to Travemünde, a seaside resort. When Claudia picks me on Friday evening, she's dead drunk. I tell her I'm going to drive. But she won't hear of it.

On the highway to Travemünde, she does over a hundred miles an hour. Her Mercedes won't go any faster. She doesn't even look at the road; she keeps glassily gaping at me with raunchy eyes.

"Keep your eyes on the road. You're drunk as it is."

"Does it bother you that I'm drunk?"

"No, it bothers me that you're drunk and doing a hundred and ten."

"Are you scared?"

"I'm not scared of anything. But I'd rather fuck you in Travemünde than lie separated from you in a metal coffin."

Her skirt has ridden up to her belly. When she catches me staring at her thighs, she spreads her legs without removing her foot from the gas pedal.

In Travemünde we try to get to the beach at least for a couple of hours just to clear our lungs. But when Claudia, who's not wearing panties, spreads her legs in front of me in the beach chair, we head back to our rooming house and don't get out of bed until Monday morning.

En route back to Hamburg, where we'll be heading straight for the studio, Claudia suddenly has to take a leak. She stops the car, thrusts her bare ass out the open door, and pisses. In the morning fog the cars, switching on their brights, roll past her butt.

Der Rote Rausch has its premiere in Hamburg. The distributor has invited Claudia and me as guests of honor, and we're supposed to take bows onstage after the screening. Next, an hour is scheduled for autographs. To endure this shit we get roaring drunk. We're sitting in our box during the screening, and Claudia, wearing no undies, puts my hand on her bare pussy. She grunts and squeals like a pig. I shoot even though I'm tanked, and I still have a boner when we're invited onstage. We haven't even watched the movie. We look as if we're still fucking and we're so weak we have to lean on each other. My face is smeared with lipstick, and my legs are buckling.

For the rest of the movie we're doing in Hamburg I have to be on a giant ocean liner in the harbor at night. I spend my breaks in the ship's toilet with a former Las Vegas chorine. Her pubic bone is as highly arched as half a coconut, and the inside is completely hollowed out.

At nine A.M. I arrive at the hotel, where Claudia has been waiting since eight to drive back to Berlin with me.

"Pussy pig" is all she says. Then we head back to Berlin.

Claudia is pregnant. Her husband can calculate that the baby can't be his.

Today I get together with Claudia for the last time. We want to try not to see each other anymore.

The International Theater Festival in Munich. I'm not interested in playing the stupid dauphin in *Saint Joan,* but I sign the contract anyway. First, because I can see Pola again; second, because I'll be well paid; and third, because I'm scheduled to make a TV flick in Munich at the same time.

While shooting, I make do with the script girl, who demonstrates her bathing suits for me in her pad.

The rehearsals for *Saint Joan* are so mind-deadening that I avoid them whenever I can. If I'm not rehearsing, the assistant director calls in sick, and we fuck in Grünwald, wallowing in the damp humus like wild boars.

During each performance of *Saint Joan,* I do whatever occurs to me. This is the only way I can survive George Bernard Shaw's lethal boredom.

Biggi has come to Munich with Nasstja. I've rented a furnished apartment on Ohmstrasse, right near the English Garden. We can get there on foot. Pola can spend the night with me. This way I can see my dear children at least when they're asleep.

After the festival I have to cut some disks in Vienna. Biggi and Nasstja remain in Munich.

During the recording sessions, which are slated to run till six A.M., I get fed up with talking alone into a mike surrounded by bare walls. I have to have live people in front of me if I'm going to prostitute my feelings. Besides, I've got a boner. At three-thirty A.M., I break off.

"Turn the three big records into three small ones," I say through the mike. "You can count my advance against my next recordings."

I have to go on tour again; my agents insist that I honor my contracts. I tell them that I want to recite my modernized version of the New Testament and the tour can start in one month. But the agents get cold feet. They suggest a tour with my famous classical soliloquies. I agree. I won't read from a script and drone out the words like John Gielgud on his American tour; instead I'll act them out, and in costume to boot, and I'll play each character myself. Then I put the program together: Hamlet, Romeo, Othello, Franz and Karl Moor, Tasso, Faust, Danton, Richard III, Melchtal, the Prince of Homburg. I choose twenty soliloquies. For the intermezzos during the breaks when I change costume, I decide on Tchaikovsky's Sixth Symphony, the Pathétique. Length of my performance: about four hours.

The costumes are tried on in our villa. I memorize my lines in a chair in the villa's library. I stand up only to eat or piss; otherwise I spend four weeks murmuring soundlessly to myself. All these soliloquies are full of outbursts, shrieks of despair, cries of joy. But I jealously hold back my energy and passion for the moment when I fritter myself away for the spectators. During those four weeks I never pronounce a single word audibly or hint at any movement. I know my voice and also my expressive capabilities, which have infinite range. The rest will come from instinct, from the situation, from the shock of the living moment.

During those four weeks of intense mental work and silence,

which I create around myself and which can be disrupted by the slightest and most distant noise, I am so irritable that Biggi and Nasstja suffer from it. But they're deliriously happy to finally have me back home, and even Nasstja, who's only three and a half, is so understanding and considerate that I'm ashamed and wish that so-called art would go fuck itself. More than ever before, Biggi devotes her entire life to supporting me with her boundless love in any way she can and keeping any possible disturbance at bay.

Finally the big day comes. For now, a hundred performances are scheduled in the largest theaters, arenas, and stadiums of eighty cities.

Next there'll be a second and third tour through Europe, America, Australia, Asia, and Africa.

My team is made up of a sound and lighting technician, a dresser who doubles as my secretary, a chauffeur, and two bodyguards. The premiere will take place at Berlin's Sports Palace.

My debut runs for six hours. The tumult of the jubilant and shrieking audience rages for over an hour, and after the performance they keep begging for encores and absolutely refuse to go home. This tour is the hardest I've ever done, but it's also my greatest triumph.

Frankfurt. On the front page of a daily gazette I find a half-page full-figure photo of me as Hamlet—and next to me the full-figure photo of a breathtaking, naked exotic dancer. She works at a nightclub, stripping to my Villon record, *I'm Just So Crazy for Your Strawberry Lips*. Finally the kind of honor I deserve!

After the performance I stroll through Frankfurt's red-light district near the main railroad station. The hookers want me to autograph their tits and also their panties—right over their cunts. But I have to save my strength, and not only for performing. A girl has written me care of the Hotel Frankfurter Hof, asking to meet me. She goes to high school, studies classical ballet, and has announced that she'll come by at midnight tomorrow because she'll be seeing her mother off at the station at eleven-thirty.

Without even knowing what she looks like, I'm obsessed with the thought of drilling this impatient swan. I go to bed and don't get up till the afternoon.

After the performance, I get into my car, sweaty as I am, and race over to my hotel. A quick shower; then I order raw egg yolks with honey and chain-smoke with my eyes glued to the clock. I listen to every sound that comes from the door.

Midnight. The doorbell rings. I almost fall on my face before yanking open the door. She's got chestnut hair flooding down to her hips. Her girlish face is pale. In it two black eyes glow, fringed by long, black, silky lashes; her mouth is like a burst wound. She walks on high-heeled shoes, wide-legged, like all ballerinas—which makes her even more aggressive.

I unbutton her blouse. Her pointed, girlish tits are like boils, and so hot. I pull her to the bed and start worshipping her. . . . But now the phone rings. The hotel manager orders me to send away my visitor!

I buzz my assistant, who's two doors away, and tell him I'll be in touch. Then the swan and I pack the barest necessities.

When we enter the hallway, two house dicks are posted at each end of the long corridor.

It's not easy finding a hotel, because my swan doesn't have any I.D. on her. Then I think of the hotel at the railroad station, where I've already stayed; the personnel, like staffs everywhere, will remember me because of my tips. And sure enough, at the reception desk they don't even ask to see my "wife's" papers. The night clerk, whom

I give a hundred marks, asks, "Do you have any special wishes, madam?" I signal this moron to hold his tongue.

I admire everything about her. For a long time. As if I'd never seen a naked girl before. And I really feel that way; I rediscover everything. Undressing the swan takes an hour. I want to relish it all. Before peeling down her panties I wait and wait. . . .

I touch the shapes of the vaginal lips, which are protruding through the thin cotton. She has high, solid tits. Sweat oozes out of her pores and runs down from her armpits and her ass crack. I walk around her, lie down on the carpet, view her from below, tell her to walk to and fro over me. Heat slams toward me, as if from a kiln. A tremor passes through the swan's body.

I'm spellbound. She lies down on the bed without throwing back the covers. She's feverish. . . .

Hamburg. Because of me the spectators get into a bloody free-for-all. Five squad cars surround the Theater am Besenbinderhof. Collin, the producer, weeps backstage.

"Be happy that people are fighting over me," I say, laughing. "Not even Jesus was loved by everyone."

After the performance the shitheads come into my dressing room and ask me whether I want to leave the theater through the back exit. Not on your life! As we drive out of the courtyard, some girls break through the barricade and cover the closed windows of my car with kisses.

And so it goes for another ninety-nine performances. Excited, agitated, jubilant, fistfighting, hysterically shrieking, weeping people everywhere, most of them loving me. Yes! They love me. Because, like nobody else in the world, I unabashedly expose my feelings to them, thereby releasing their feelings. The few who

don't love me hate me because of their liberated feelings, which
blind them.

The final performance takes place in Vienna's Grosse Stadthalle.
Eight thousand spectators. Afterward a court bailiff frisks my pockets
in my dressing room. Who knows who wants money from me now. I
don't even ask him. I eighty-six him.

Pakistan and India. And also my first Italian movie. Biggi wants to remain in Berlin with Nasstja. Magde is now staying with us temporarily; she keeps house and takes care of Nasstja, whom she idolizes.

I get vaccinated at the tropical medicine institute and fly alone to
Rome, where the Italian crew is waiting for me. That same day we hop
a Pakistani plane to our first stop, Karachi.

Flavio, the movie's costume designer, has billeted himself at my
right side on the endless flight. Scarcely have the "No Smoking" and
"Fasten Your Seat Belts" signs faded when he grabs my thigh. I don't
want to put him off; he's very nice. But I feel hot and queasy, and I
can't let his thick, steamy, two-pound paw remain on my thigh all the
way to Karachi. Besides, it wouldn't be enough for him.

I stand up as often as I can, and soon I'm eyeballing a slender but
big-assed Pakistani stewardess. Whenever I squeeze past the canteen
on the way to the toilet, my eyes insistently feel her up from head to
toe. From my seat I watch her every movement. I summon her with
the overhead light signal, racking my brain for an excuse, and I talk
softly so that she has to lean over to hear me. My arm dangles into the
narrow aisle, "accidentally" grazing her calves whenever she walks by.
If I spot her at the end of the aisle, I get up to run into her in a place
where she can't step in front of a seat to avoid me. Instead, she has to
squeeze past me. In a word, she doesn't have another calm moment.
She certainly gets the picture. She must know what I want before the

plane lands in Karachi. I can't tell whether that's why she smiles, or whether smiling is part of her charm. In any case, her smiles grow more and more alluring the more shameless I act.

Night. Everyone's asleep. They're wearing black blindfolds and slippers. The illumination is reduced to the minimum of a few emergency lights. Flavio has given up trying to fondle me and is snoring in his uncomfortable seat. And all the stewardesses but one are fast asleep. All but one. Except that I can't find her. I walk up and down the aisle, leaning over the sleeping girls to make sure I don't wake the wrong one. My stewardess is not among the sleepers. The aisle is empty. So she can only be in the cockpit or in the toilet. First the toilets. The two facing johns in the stern are empty.

I remove my shoes to avoid making any noise as I reel down the long aisle toward the cockpit, where the two first-class toilets are located. The right-hand one is vacant. On the door of the left-hand one the sign shifts from "Occupied" to "Vacant." But the door doesn't open. I don't know what shoots through my head during these seconds, or perhaps they're only tenths or only hundredths of seconds. I open the door and squeeze inside. And before the stewardess can turn toward me, the door snaps shut, and I bolt it. Now the sign says "Occupied."

She doesn't seem particularly surprised. She merely trembles slightly and peers deep into my eyes, which, with Indian eyes, practically amounts to fornication. In a patch of turbulence, the plane lurches leftward; our bodies press together, and I'm nearly lying on top of her.

I'm almost dazed by the animal stench of piss in the tiny john, which even a single person can barely endure. It's not easy stripping her. The PIA stewardesses wear shoe-length trousers, and over the trousers a sort of frock that reaches past their thighs. She can do a better job of unfastening it than I can. She opens her trousers and climbs out of them. Then she leans way down to the toilet seat and reaches over her shoulder to unzip the dress. I do it for her. She straightens up; I pull up her dress until she can reach it with her crossed arms, and she draws it over her head with a single supple but impatient yank. Now she helps me strip; by now I'm virtually intoxicated by her dark, heavy breasts with their huge, almost black areolae, her dark abdomen, and the smell of her even darker crotch.

I trample on my pants, rip my buttoned shirt off my body so hard that the buttons fly against the steel sink and into the toilet bowl, sounding just like dried peas. Another patch of turbulence tips the plane rightward and throws her body against mine, which is pressed against the door.

My dick is so hard that the collision hurts me. She reacts faster than I can moan. Instead of naturally clinging to my chest or shoulders, she cups her hands around my dick and my nuts to shield them against further collisions. The plane balances out again, and a Pakistani paradise opens up. . . .

When she hands me and Flavio our breakfast trays, she writes down her Karachi address in neat capitals. But I can't use it. We've got only two hours here. We switch to a twin-engine machine and fly a torturous eight hours through the foothills of the Himalayas until we reach our first location, Lahore. For two hours the plane can't land because a cyclone is raging directly over the airport. The pilot keeps trying over and over again to nose-dive out of the suction. By the time we start to land, the cabin is full of puke. There's no air-conditioning, and you have to have a totally empty stomach, as I do, to keep from throwing up.

As usual, I hurry to get rid of the others. After I dump my baggage in my hotel room, a greasy cabdriver in front of the hotel talks to me. I know what he's after, and all I say is "Show me the way!"

The Italian physician who takes care of our production crew has pressed a tiny bottle into my hand, ordering me to take a tablet every day for cholera. Just before our arrival an epidemic raged, taking five thousand lives. I pop a pill in my mouth and wash it down with some saliva. The most recent smallpox epidemic claimed fifteen thousand victims. But even though the vaccine doesn't necessarily ward off infection, I've got other things to worry about now.

The cab makes its way through unpaved, muddy streets and roads, through craterlike holes, ditches, and gutters. The ancient American Buick, so stiff with filth that your hand practically sticks to the plastic-covered seat if you touch it, knocks me from side to side. When no more houses and no more cars are to be seen anywhere, and only a camel caravan is visible with hungry eagles circling above it, and the electric sun is frozen in the green glaciers of the Himalayas, I ask the cabby why we have to drive so far to find a hooker.

"Special," he says in English, grinning into the rearview mirror and exposing an enormous gold tooth. He steers toward a lone, half-completed brick house. "I waiting," says Gold Tooth after stopping his jalopy, and I hope my suffering is over for the next few hours. I draw the pungently cool evening air deep into my lungs.

A door opens in the brick dump, and a young female giant bends forward in the door frame. She has to bend because she's truly gigantic—almost seven feet tall, and as broad as a heavyweight boxer.

Her stiff, horizontal tits are as huge as udders. Her arms are as strong as my thighs. Her hands could easily strangle me. Her strangely dark-blond hair, which reaches as far as her butt crack, is woven into a single braid as thick as a python. She's got the hips and ass cheeks of a young mare. I can circle her thighs only with both arms. She must wear size fourteen shoes. Her pussy is as big as my head.

Everything is perfectly proportioned and utterly harmonious. As in a breathtaking mammoth statue by Maillol. She's simply a giantess.

Her skin is tanned but not dark, and as taut and healthy as a peasant girl's. Her face is likewise rustic, but not crude—it's beautiful. Neither her face nor her body indicates that she's a prostitute. She has a naive, dreamy expression. She smiles timidly. Gold Tooth is right: She's special.

There is nothing calculating about her caresses. She's in no hurry. As if time has stood still. As if time didn't exist—only love.

Now I know. I didn't come to this country to make some stupid movie and get rid of my semen in every spare moment. I came here to give myself to this love giantess and have her drain me of my very last drop of energy. Her Indian eyes are feverish with sensuality. But she waits gently and patiently until she knows my desires. We communicate by smiling, by nodding or shaking our heads, by the slight pressure of my limbs, by my hands, which indicate the positions I want. She moves lightly, intent on distributing her weight so as not to crush me.

First we lie facing each other. I gobble her tits. Her tongue. I squash her lips with kisses, open them, push them up and down, and lick her huge, sharp, snowy teeth, which bruise my face, my throat, my body. I lick her paws, I lick every single finger. Her feet, her toes.

She turns on her side and lifts one thigh, and I fall furiously upon her. Her hole is nowhere as gigantic as I've assumed from her overall size. Her pussy muscles close tight around my dick. Never before has a cunt milked me so rigorously and yet so tenderly. While she prays in her native language with a grateful and loving smile, I dip my face into her streaming fruit, which she holds out to me like an overflowing bowl, and slake my thirst.

After she's nourished me, restoring my strength, I get out of bed and signal her to join me in front of the mirror. By grazing her inner thighs, I make it clear that she should spread her legs. I tap her on the shoulder, and she understands that she has to bend forward. She sticks out her ass without being told and props her arms on her upper thighs as if playing leapfrog. Except that she pulls in the small of her back.

Even though she's bent over, the giantess's back is as high as that of a fully grown horse. Now I benefit from the Cossacks' lessons: They taught me how to jump on a horse without stirrups or saddle just by grabbing its mane. I clutch her braid, and I'm on top of her in one fell swoop. She hasn't budged. I mustn't slip no matter what, for my spread legs, which barely envelop her hips, are high above the floor. If I slide down, I'll have to repeat my leap every time.

I hold on to her strong braid with both hands and ride her like a jockey. She trembles. Her flanks quake like those of a thoroughbred. Not because I'm riding her, but because she's having such powerful orgasms. I lie flat on her back—this is the end spurt—but my abdomen is working furiously. Goal! I bite into her braid and twitch on her trembling ass cheeks.

I've fallen asleep on her back. When I open my eyes, she's still in the same position, bent over at the mirror. Once again we gallop down the course. Then I glide down to the floor.

I pay the cabby. Under the rising white sun, the old Buick, in which you get stuck to the filth-caked, plastic-covered seats, moves away from the stacked diamonds of the Himalayan glaciers, which shimmer wanly in the white sky. Hungry eagles circle overhead, and a camel caravan heads our way. And from the brick block a gigantic hand waves good-bye.

The shooting is indescribable. I'm supposed to play a fanatical Indian ringleader who stirs up the masses against the British. For that reason, a makeup man—if you can call him that—paints me with a chocolate-colored solution and glues a Santa beard to my face. This morning procedure takes hours. Next Flavio puts a kind of white angel shirt over my naked body, and the cloth tortures me like flesh-eating ants. Which induces Flavio to touch all parts of me between the skin and the fabric. Then he ties a gold sash around my waist. He also wraps the turban, which makes the Indians shake their heads in pity.

Since I haven't read the script—no one's given me one—and can't understand the eternally screaming director's Italian, all I do is try to shield myself from the clouds of dust that swaddle us from morning to evening. The infernal heat burns out your innards. There's nothing to drink but boiled water. Boiled because of the threat of disease. A meal comes out of a package wrapped in greasy, filthy paper. I never unwrap it. If someone does open a package it instantly turns black with flies. All you can do is hurl the package as far away as possible. It's best not even to take it.

I can't find any peace in the hotel. First, because the heat prevents me from breathing and sleeping (even the ceiling fan produces only an earsplitting noise but no breeze), and second and foremost, because my mind is haunted by the giantess.

I can't locate the cabby who drove me to her. I can't even recall his face. The gold tooth isn't much of a lead, since every cabby has one. I ask them about the giantess, but no one knows a woman as big as I describe her.

My blood seethes, I have no choice. I let the taxis take me wherever they like. Empty, filthy, spit-ridden, pissed-up, shit-smeared hovels, where pockmarked girls are brought to me from brothels;

labyrinthine courtyards behind high walls, where I'm locked in so I won't try to split without paying, and where I grope my way in the darkness through low clay huts and stumble over female bodies lying on the ground. I fuck away furiously without ever seeing them. But even this dangerous whoring, which doesn't even bring me a dose of the clap, much less cholera or smallpox, can't console me for the loss of the giantess.

During the final shooting, which we do in some sort of catacombs in Rome, I still haven't forgotten the giantess. I have to complete the scene in which I rouse the Indian populace against the British. At the Indian temple I shrieked out a text without knowing what I was shrieking. This time the camera is far away, and the moronic director is content if I gesticulate wildly and yell whatever I like. I scream:

"Grab a hammer and smash the mouths of all the riffraff. Just let me get back to my giantess!"

It's only my second day back in Berlin when I get a call from the distributor with whom I have a contract: "You have to fly to Mexico this weekend to do a drag-racing movie."

"I'll go right out and buy a Spanish dictionary!" I shout back— and I can already hear the predatory roaring of Ferrari engines.

That was yesterday. Today these bunglers buzz me back: "The Mexican flick's been put off. You have to get to Madrid in two days to shoot a Western."

I know I'm a prostitute. So I fly to Madrid.

On the first day of shooting I refuse to put on a lice-ridden cowboy hat with a rotting sweatband. Let them send their rags to the dry cleaner, if you please. The Spanish director—the people who call themselves directors nowadays!—flips out and orders me to put the hat on.

"You can drink water from my toilet bowl," I say, and skedaddle.

But things don't go that smoothly. A contract with a distributor is sort of like a contract with a pimp. You can't just up and vanish. And pouting doesn't help. So to punish me they send me out to make a flick in Prague, the "Golden City."

I don't see any gold, but I do see girls who are famous for their fucking! So first I have to get a car. I order a new Jaguar from Munich. That takes care of that!

When the secretary at the hotel desk takes her lunch break, we go to the nearby park. The bushes are in full blossom, and we don't even have to be careful. The Czech girls all live up to their reputation. Unfortunately, the secretary's late getting back, and the hotel manager demands that I clear out on the spot. I move into another dump across the street.

Next comes Tonya, an actress in the film. She's seventeen, with gold curls, and she's sort of the Czech Shirley Temple. The Commies have confiscated her passport because she did secret nude photos for *Playboy*. I have to smuggle her into the hotel. Not that the Commie snoops have anything against fucking. They're only opposed to having people who don't live in the hotel fuck in the hotel.

There's really nothing wrong with Tonya, except that she never lets out a peep when she climaxes. We might've stayed together for the entire production if my other costar hadn't shown up: Beatrice Benito, part French and part Italian. A vampire who sucks out a man's marrow, if not his blood. She calls me up and asks why I don't live in the same hotel as she. I sarcastically reply, "For political reasons." She tells me to come to her. Tonya, sitting next to me on the bed, doesn't understand because I'm speaking French with Beatrice. I tell Tonya that I have to meet some friends who are gonna be in

Prague only for the day, and I promise her I'll be at the hotel punctually in the morning in order to take her along to the studio.

I'm supposed to meet Beatrice in her hotel lobby because there's a police agent posted at the elevator and another at the stairs; everyone has to show a room key. Beatrice sort of prostitutes herself in front of the stairway sentry: Cunningly dressed, she struts up and down the carpet runner from the reception desk to the dining room, as if she were streetwalking, and she sticks out her bodacious ass. Next she drops her Italian mini-purse. The stairway sentry dutifully bends over, turning crimson. At that instant, I race up the steps. . . .

Beatrice is still lying on her belly. I've fucked her all night in that position, and she shrieked so loud, at the top of her lungs, by the open window that the police patrol in the street sent the night clerk up to her room. Through the locked door he asked her what was wrong. Was she hurt? "I bumped into something," she replied, keeping her wits about her.

Beatrice has to go to the studio, as I do, and naturally she wants me to drive her. I ask her what we should do with Tonya, since my Jaguar can only seat two. But Beatrice doesn't give two hoots about Tonya. I tell Beatrice we have to hurry. Tonya may turn up late, and we could then get away before she arrives. But Beatrice deliberately stalls. She knows quite well that I would never swap her for Tonya.

When Beatrice and I arrive on time for my date with Tonya, and Beatrice gets into the car, Tonya scoots out from behind the kiosk on the other side of the street and tries to drag her out of the Jaguar by her hair. But Beatrice won't give up her seat; she likewise yanks Tonya's hair, scratches, spits, kicks, and inundates her with a flood of special French and Italian expressions, the hottest possible.

Tonya slaps me and dashes away in tears.

That same day, Beatrice transfers to my hotel. Anything I don't know she teaches me, anything she doesn't know I teach her. She no longer wears undies, because I won't let her. Never again. Not in the street. Not at the studio. Not in the restaurant. Nowhere. When we're not shooting we stay in bed or in the bathroom.

I have to go to Yugoslavia to shoot some lousy Western. The flick in Prague still has a long way to go, but since both movies are being done by the same distributors, they came up with the idea. Beatrice is furious because she can't come along. She still has some scenes to shoot without me in Prague.

In Yugoslavia I try to telephone Beatrice. But that's impossible in this hick country. I spend fourteen, sixteen, twenty hours waiting for a connection, and when it finally goes through we can't understand each other, or the line goes dead before we even start. The next hookup takes another fourteen, sixteen, twenty hours.

One week later I return to Prague. Beatrice picks me up at the airport and we race into bed.

One more week and I have to return to Yugoslavia. Again I try to call her up. Again we have to wait fourteen, sixteen, twenty hours for a connection, and again we can't manage to talk.

After yet another week I'm back in Prague. Again Beatrice picks me up at the airport. Once again we race directly into bed, and we don't get up until the next day of shooting and we never order any food.

I haven't called Biggi even once from Prague, though it's not that difficult to get through. When she telephones and reproaches me, I lie, telling her that I've been shooting day and night. I'm powerless against Beatrice, who binds me closer and closer every day. She's likewise nuts about me and begs me to fly to Rome with her and stay with her. I promise I will.

Fellini wants me for his next movie and summons me to Rome. I tell Beatrice to fly on ahead while I drive the Jaguar back to Berlin. I spend one day in Munich to hug Pola, and I visit Erika.

In Berlin, Biggi and Nasstja spend twenty-four hours with me, delirious about my return, until I leave for Rome. I'm haunted by Beatrice.

Biggi makes me promise to take her and Nasstja along to Yugoslavia, where I still have five weeks of shooting left. I can't refuse her. But I don't know what's going to happen.

In Rome Beatrice drives me to see Fellini, who's her good friend. Fellini circles me for hours on end, speaking French because I don't know Italian. He starts getting on my nerves. How important it all is! I never take my eyes off Beatrice for even a second and I whisper to her that we should go.

Beatrice has a huge, sunny apartment in Cassia Antica, with all of Rome at the foot of the gigantic terraces. Her maid is used to her long-drawn-out shrieks. She walks in without knocking, taps us on the shoulders even when we're in the midst of climaxing, and says, "Soup's on."

Beatrice loves to dress me. She buys me all sorts of Italian jerseys, swim trunks, pants, shirts, shoes, necklaces. She earns a nice living. She's also friends with Agnelli and owns a whole lot of jewelry.

Forty-eight hours later I have to leave for Yugoslavia, this time for Split. Getting there is an endless torture. You have to keep switching planes and then take a car in Trieste and drive for two hours. I don't want Biggi and Nasstja to travel alone and so we agree to meet at the Munich airport. Both are ecstatic and impatient to be spending five whole weeks with me. Furthermore, Split lies on the sea, and so Biggi has packed bathing suits, tubes, balls, and shovels.

I'm irritable and absentminded because I'm trying to figure out some way of telling Biggi the truth. I do have to tell her—I have no choice. I must. First of all, it's only right, because who knows how long my thing with Beatrice will last, and besides during these five weeks I'm going to fly to Rome as often as possible because I can't stand being without her. So how can I explain why I want to endure these tedious trips just to spend a day or even a few hours in Rome? The company won't let me get away for any longer, since we're behind schedule in Prague and they're waiting only for me.

Fellini can no longer serve as an excuse. The contract is ready and is to be dispatched to Yugoslavia for my signature. The more honest I am with Biggi, the better for her and for me. But I can't tell her here. Not here at the airport. I have to wait as long as possible.

During our first evening in Split, when Biggi, Nasstja, and I are having supper, the telephone rings. It's Beatrice. She asks me when I'm coming to Rome and why I'm acting so strange on the phone. I can't speak freely; Biggi and Nasstja are eyeing me. Besides, I have to shout so loud because of the poor connection that the entire hotel can hear me.

Biggi doesn't know French, but then I lose control and yell, "Je t'aime! Je t'aime!" into the receiver, while Biggi holds Nasstja tight so that she won't make a sound and bother me. I can no longer hide the truth.

"Does that mean you want to be alone, without us?" asks Biggi after I've stammered that perhaps we should live apart even though I love both of them.

"It means we have to separate—at least for a while."

"You mean you need peace and privacy for a time? I understand. But for how long?"

"I don't know. Maybe for a long time."

"But you'll come back to us?"

"No. . . . Yes. . . . No. . . . Yes. . . ! Of course I'll come back. I mean, I won't abandon you. And it's not that I have to be alone. I have to be with another woman."

Biggi suddenly eats all the grapes—probably without noticing, because before the phone call she was no longer hungry. She chokes down the grapes as if gagging on the word "woman," which she can't comprehend.

"Woman? What woman?"

"A woman. I have to be with another woman."

"Then you don't love us anymore?"

"My God, of course I do! I love you and Nasstja as much as I've always loved you. But I have to be with this woman, do you understand?" I scream, being even more unfair than I've already been.

"No," says Biggi in a hoarse voice.

"Forgive me. I'm a total moron. I don't know what I'm saying."

"Oh, but you do. You know what you're saying. I'm starting to catch your drift."

"What?"

"You love us, but this woman means more to you than we do. They why did you have us come to Yugoslavia? Nastassja and I were so happy to be with you."

I'm at a loss for words. My head is one big garbage disposal, in which everything is in total chaos.

Once again the telephone rings! Once again it's Beatrice! Once again I shout into the receiver that I love her. And so it goes all night long. She calls up three more times, demanding to know when I'm coming to Rome, which I can't tell her now, much as I'd like to. Biggi and I stay up all night. But we can't find the right words to communicate. Something is busted. She doesn't cry, but she seems timid, defenseless, as if fate were giving me a foretaste of what's going to happen once I leave her.

Mainly she just can't grasp what I've told her or what she can read between the lines. Biggi is by nature an independent person, capable of standing on her own two feet. But during all these years she's given me everything, given herself up to me without holding back in any way. I've taken everything, and now suddenly she's standing there empty-handed. It won't sink in that I, who had the most dramatic fits because of my exaggerated and groundless jealousy, am now leaving her for another woman. And she thinks I'm lying when I say I still love her.

During those five weeks I drive or fly to Beatrice in Rome nine times. Once I drive two hundred miles round-trip and change planes four times just to fuck Beatrice for half an hour.

At every stopover en route to Rome I dash to a phone booth and call up Beatrice, telling her I'm on the way. En route back to Yugoslavia, I shout, "I'll be back!"

The shooting moves from Split to a different location. Biggi's nerves are shot and she does nothing but cry. She wants to leave—right now. Climbing into the studio car, I accompany her and Nastassja to Venice, 270 miles away. Once there, they can't get a flight until the next morning, so they go to a hotel on the Lido. As soon as their silhouettes vanish in the wake of the ferry across the Grand Canal, I jump into a speedboat and race across the lagoon to the airport. I'm the last passenger boarding the plane to Rome.

Biggi arrives in Berlin with a raging fever. She writes me that only Nastassja prevented her from killing herself in Venice.

The manager of the hotel where I'm staying in Yugoslavia is a woman. If she's the one who gave me a dose of the clap, then I can't go to Beatrice for the time being.

The filming is done. I stop off in Munich, get a penicillin shot from Gislinde's father, and hop the plane to Berlin the next morning.

Biggi hugs me as I come through the door. But she's changed and she'll never be the same. That night we fuck. Biggi fucks as shamelessly as possible to show me that she can be as big a slut as Beatrice.

This morning everything might have gone nicely. But then Beatrice rings up—three times in a row, because we keep getting disconnected. I tell her I'll call her. Now Beatrice no longer believes me, and I'm attacked on both fronts.

Biggi turns aggressive. She refuses to believe that Beatrice means more to me in bed than she does. She thinks there's only one reason why I can't stop seeing Beatrice: I no longer love Biggi.

"Tell me you don't love me anymore! Tell me you don't love me anymore!" She keeps screaming that sentence all day long until she nearly loses her voice and bursts into tears again. I can't tell her I no longer love her: I'd be lying.

For a week I keep running to the post office to call Beatrice because I can't do it from the apartment. Then I fly to Rome.

Beatrice has also changed. And as if she knew that Biggi wanted to prove that she's the better slut, Beatrice leaves no stone unturned as she tries to outdo Biggi. For the first time she asks me which positions I prefer and in which way she can give me the most intense orgasms. Every day she asks me what I'd like her to wear. Should she put on undies? How about garters? With or without panties, and if "with," which? She yanks out the drawers in her dressing room and pulls out a heap of sluttish panties, teensy butt floss she bought in Pigalle. There's a tiny satin pouch held together only by thin strings vanishing inside the ass crack, covering the pussy hole but not the vaginal lips, while the crotch hair spills out on all sides. Other thongs, in garish colors—yellow, orange, red, green, turquoise—with a slit over the pussy or totally open all the way from the twat lips to the asshole. She gets fucked in every panty she models—gets fucked standing, crouching, leaning over. . . . And she's thoroughly convinced that she outsluts Biggi with all her cunning.

She asks me whether I want her to get me other girls. Whether I want to fuck with her and another girl or watch while she does it with the girls. To turn me on she tells me about very young girls who are picked up in the street and seduced. She triumphantly asks me whether Biggi would do all that.

"Do you wanna marry me?" she asks, hesitant, almost anxious, as we sit down in an outdoor restaurant near Ponte Milvio. And as if I had already replied, she suddenly becomes sad. There's nothing corrupt or perverse about her now. None of the cynicism with which she usually tries to gloss over her innocent helplessness. Now she's just a lonely little girl who was born in a mountain village on the French-Italian border and who, like any other girl on this planet, simply yearns for love and security.

"I can't marry you, Beatrice. I'd like to, but I can't leave Biggi alone."

"Bourgeois," she replies, full of hate.

"Don't act stupid."

"All my life I've longed for the man I love. And now that I've found him, he's too chicken to marry me."

She cries.

"I'm not too chicken to marry you, Beatrice. It wouldn't take any courage. Let me tell you something I didn't realize till now: I love you."

"But you love Biggi too!"

"Yes. I love you both!"

I can't tell her that I love all women, but that doesn't mean I can marry all women. I dry her tears, which are dripping over her nose and into the minestrone. Then, canceling the trout entrées, I pay the check, and we leave.

That night, after fucking our brains out, we sleep on the terrace, entangled in each other. She's put a huge sofa out on the terrace because she knows I prefer sleeping outdoors.

The breakfast table is set on the terrace. And while her maid pours the steaming coffee, already up in arms because we always let everything get cold, we enjoy a final naked embrace, while far below, at our feet, Rome is starting its daily life and noise.

After breakfast we walk over to Via Nemea, to a luxury complex of ten palazzi, a tennis court, and a swimming pool, where a garret apartment has become vacant. I rent it, paying for an entire year in advance. I've decided to stay in Rome. The flat is large enough for three, if Biggi and Nasstja want to move here. At one o'clock Beatrice takes me to the airport.

Biggi wants to move in with me and Nasstja in Rome. We terminate our lease on the house in Berlin and temporarily rent a two-room pad in Wannsee. Biggi wants to keep a place in Berlin because of her mother.

The contract for the Fellini film reaches us belatedly. The fee is outrageously tiny. That Fellini keeps everything for himself. Instead of signing the contract, I wire him: "Fuck you!" The telegraph office calls me, saying that such a text cannot possibly be sent. But the telegram arrives in Rome all the same.

I have to go to London for a British flick. I rent a small two-story house opposite Hyde Park and summon Biggi and Nasstja. The house is clean and charmingly furnished—a true dollhouse. It's spring again. The house is surrounded by blossoming trees. Cats—and Biggi is crazy about cats—lounge on the roofs of the parked cars. In endless Hyde Park, where everyone can do anything he likes, Biggi and Nasstja can frolic about to their hearts' content.

I keep whoring. I fuck the red-haired production secretary so hard against the head of her bed that I'm worried I've broken her pelvis. Her fat twat gapes open like the jaws of a snake devouring an oversized prey, and she keeps shrieking: "Drain me! Drain me!"

I no longer come up with smart excuses. "I have to buy cigarettes," I simply say to Biggi, or "I have to get to the bank." Then I visit the production secretary or one of the actresses, or an extra, or the strippers in Soho, or I just hit on some broad in the street. In the middle of the night I may sneak out of bed and go to Piccadilly for the young hookers in Chinatown.

I bring one woman home. Biggi and Nasstja have gone to Brighton. The woman is an Israeli colonel in mufti. I explain that I'd like to see her papers because I've never fucked an officer and I want to make sure she's not putting me on. If Mary Magdalene was as big a turn-on as this colonel, I can understand why Jesus had the hots for her. Even though she's got black hair on her upper lip, something that totally excites me in a woman, I'm not quite with it. Beatrice has announced that she'll be spending half a day in London. I fuck the colonel and send her away.

Just when Beatrice arrives, I have to be shooting, and she has to get back to Rome that same evening. Wearing the costume of an eighteenth-century British lord, I dash into the Hotel Dorchester. For exactly thirty-five minutes Beatrice and I squat on one another. She goes to the airport alone.

David Lean's assistant comes to the Shepperton Studio and says that three characters are left in *Doctor Zhivago*. Lean, who's in Madrid, wants to know which I'd like to play. "Any of them," I reply.

At the end of November I shoot a Spanish movie in Barcelona, where MGM sends me the script and the contract for *Zhivago*.

Christmas Eve. I buy presents for Biggi and Nasstja and give the Barcelona hookers whatever's left over from my final installment, for nearly all of them have kids. On Christmas Day I'm back in our apartment in Wannsee, and Biggi and I go skating across the frozen lake.

In January I have to start shooting *Zhivago*. Biggi and Nasstja come along to Madrid because I'm contracted for four months even though I could shoot this garbage in a week. We rent a pad and stay until February. I've got four weeks off but I'm still on salary.

We stop off in Munich, where Sergio Leone is screening his Western *A Fistful of Dollars*. He wants to meet me. Then he hires me for his second Western, *For a Few Dollars More*.

Back in Berlin, I get the Jaguar out of the garage, race to Munich, get Pola, and dash with her to Rome for costume tryouts. This is the first time that we sleep in the new apartment on Via Nemea. I don't call

Beatrice. I stay alone with Pola. She's almost thirteen, and I'm absolutely nuts about her.

David Lean's crew scours the whole of Spain for the final remnants of unmelted snow. We drive almost two hundred miles from
Madrid, spending the night in some crummy village hotels. The
woman caring for the boy who has to be filmed (with Omar Sharif,
Geraldine Chaplin, Ralph Richardson, and myself) in the cattle car
heading toward Siberia accompanies him.

Her broad hips and heavy thighs contrast unbelievably with her
slender torso, as if Nature had whimsically joined the upper body of
one person to the lower body of another. Furthermore, her thighs are
hirsute all the way up to the hips. The hair makes her look like a female satyr. I fuck her only standing in front of a mirror so I can keep
this strange creature constantly in view with every thrust, especially
when I shoot inside her. I have to wear socks when I sneak across the
creaking floorboards of the motel hall, because you can hear every fart
in the rooms. We also fuck during lunch breaks. After midnight she
steals into my room, wearing only a teddy. If someone has to go to the
hallway toilet at night and runs into her, he'll know what she's doing.

In Madrid, the fucking ought to stop. Her husband comes to their
villa every evening and often during lunch breaks. But he's in the United
States now, and the villa is on our route. So first we stop off there. While
I look over the house, the driver brings in the suitcases, including mine.

"Herr Kinski will be taking a cab," the female satyr says over my
head to the driver. We fuck all night in her double bed.

David Lean has a red Rolls-Royce Cabriolet, which, aside from the
satyr, is what interests me most about making *Zhivago*. I keep gaping
at the car, just like when I was a little boy gawking at toy cars, pressing
my nose flat against the window of the toy store.

"Don't lose your mind," says David Lean with a smile. He's crazy about his red Rolls. All day long, he keeps it under a customized cover like a pair of rompers, molded right down to the shape of the hood ornament, like a condom to a boner. "In a couple of years you'll be sitting in a Rolls yourself."

I don't dare show Biggi the wire that's just arrived and that I automatically tore open because I thought it was addressed to me. But it's for Biggi, and it's from a friend of her mother's in Berlin. Her mother's dead. The situation is all the more hopeless since we were arguing and fistfighting until the telegraph boy rang the bell.

I lock myself in the bathroom and keep rereading the wire. And I still can't grasp the news, just as I couldn't grasp the news about my mother's death, about the journalist who killed herself, about Gislinde's sister, and about Jasmin. I have only one thought: Make up with Biggi and let her know that she's not defenseless. Her mother was the only person she had aside from me and Nastassja. When I go to Biggi, I forget the telegram in the bathrobe.

Biggi and I have reconciled—but then I hear her shriek in the bathroom. I dash over to her and find her collapsed on the floor, the crumpled telegram in her clenched hands. I pick her up in my arms and carry her to her room.

For the rest of the day she's unable to come out with a coherent sentence. She takes Nastassja into her bed, hugs her desperately, and covers her with kisses. Nasstja eyes me, quizzical and helpless. Pola, too, keeps quiet; she spends hours standing motionless on the threshold. I walk out on the balcony of our apartment on the twenty-second floor and stare at the brown ball of the sun, which is smeared over the stony desert of Madrid like coagulated blood.

Biggi stands next to me. I didn't hear her coming. She's stopped crying, and her voice is soft, yet impatient and absent, she speaks like someone who has to do a lot of preparing for something she can't remember.

"In any case I have to go to Berlin first thing tomorrow. I'll take Nastassja along."

"I'll get the tickets very early."

"Book the first flight out. Even if I have to change planes. Any flight. I mustn't be late for the funeral, no matter what. I may be the only mourner. I also have to order flowers. Lots of flowers, very, very, beautiful flowers. Or do you think I should order a wreath?"

"Bring your mother flowers."

"What about the coffin? My God! She probably doesn't have a coffin yet! What kind of coffin should I get? I want a zinc coffin. I don't want her eaten up by maggots. Is it true that corpses in the ground are eaten up by maggots?"

"Yes. It's natural. The maggots arose from the earth, from the decay of animals and plants. The animal eaten by the maggots also decomposes, and its decay produces new maggots. But it also produces plants and flowers. Decay produces new life."

"But I don't want my mother to decay. I want a zinc coffin."

"I'll give you enough money."

"She won't decay in a zinc coffin?"

"No."

"Then I'll buy a zinc coffin. And a gravestone. How will I manage?"

"We have time for the gravestone."

"But the grave. I have to pick a grave. And then plants for the grave."

"We have time for the plants."

"Do you think I'll get everything done in time?"

"Definitely."

"So get the tickets at the crack of dawn, okay?"

"I can drive to the airport right now."

"No, no. Tomorrow morning. Don't leave me alone now."

She goes back inside the dreary apartment. No one has turned on any light. Pola is still standing around and she's scared when I bump into her in the darkness. But then I find the light switch.

A swallow crashes against the large glass window and drops into the corner of the balcony, where it remains, twitching. It must have lost its sense of direction. I pick it up just as Biggi comes out on the balcony. She takes the swallow from my hand and gently strokes its head. I've never seen a swallow at such close range. Its body is so tender and frail. But its down and its flight feathers are weathered and tangled, and its roving eyes peer into the distance. The swallow has an indomitable urge for freedom. I feel as if it's trying to smell out freedom. Biggi, attempting to make it fly again, opens her hands. For a few seconds, nothing happens. Then, with a powerful thrust of its wings, the swallow zooms up from Biggi's palm and melts into the cool night sky. Biggi smiles. I put my arm around her shoulders.

"Does the swallow also decay when it's dead, and is it eaten by maggots?"

"Yes. It also decays and it's eaten by maggots."

"Then I won't buy a zinc coffin."

She snuggles very close to me, and we remain like that for a long time, not saying a word about her dead mother.

I've brought Biggi and Nasstja to the airport, and now I'm alone with Pola. Her vacation is ending. I'm afraid of being all alone; what if Biggi and Nasstja don't return before Pola's departure? Thank goodness, Biggi calls me from Berlin, saying she'll be back in two days. She only wants to order the headstone and also the plants for the grave and its tending.

At last we get away from the poisonous heat of Madrid and drive to Almería on the sea, where Sergio Leone is shooting his Western. We rent a dilapidated beach house with a terrace so huge that we can play tennis on it. The ocean roars day and night, and I can finally sleep again.

The Gypsies of Andalusia become my brothers. They regard me as one of their own and take me into their families. Soon I know all of them, from Almería to Granada, from Málaga to Seville. And also the Gypsy women, from the schoolgirls to the flamenco dancers and the hookers. Once a week I throw a party on my terrace, inviting only Gypsies. We wreathe our heads in flowers and dance and sing under the stars, which are immense and hang so low it's as if they're about to land on our heads. The flamenco of the Gypsy has nothing to do with the flamenco for tourists. Real flamenco is like sex.

Biggi, Nastassja, and I move into the Rome apartment. I've left the Jaguar in Germany and I buy a Maserati. To make things as nice as possible for Biggi and Nasstja, I put in the most expensive velvet carpets, I hang the walls with pure Italian silk, which I also use for the curtains and tablecloths, and I mount gilded doorknobs and window handles as well as gilded faucets in the bathrooms and toilets.

I agree to do a British flick in Morocco with Margareth Lee and Senta Berger. Biggi is taking care of the apartment on Via Nemea, which she loves, even though I bang my head a hundred times a day on the sloping walls.

Upon reaching the Hotel La Mamounia in Marrakesh I tell them to take my bags up to my room. I've got more important things to do.

My first woman is a veiled cyclist. She wears a black burnoose like a nun's habit, and all I see is her ringed fingers on the handlebars, her bare feet in her sandals, and her coal-black eyes. I call to her as if hailing a cab. She turns her head, narrowly missing a car. The drivers here must all be ex–camel drivers. I have her write the time and place on a scrap of paper. She's written "twelve midnight"—that much I can read. The address is in Arabic, and I can't possibly decipher it. I'll hand the scrap to a cabby. It's three P.M. Nine hours more to midnight. I spend them in the bazaars, where the street kids pull me around, offer me drugs, and ask if I wanna go to bed with them. Finally I join the hash smokers on the dusty ground and listen to the storyteller. I don't understand a word, but he nevertheless transports me to an Oriental fairy world.

Then I heave a little girl to my shoulders: She can't find her way through the teeming marketplace and so she can't see anything. She's not wearing panties under her torn little dress. I can tell because her naked twat sticks to the back of my neck, which gets wet. The girl rubbing her clit against me as I caress her skinny thighs; the evocative movement of the storyteller; the hash, which is extremely strong in Morocco; the numbing air, spiced with indefinable aromas and a sultry stench; the monotonous Oriental music seeping in from all nooks and crannies like a narcotic; the voices whispering, murmuring, calling, yelling, yelping, laughing in the most disparate Arabic dialects—all these things might have caused me to miss my appointment with the cyclist. But the half-naked girl on my shoulders points to the crumpled-up note that drops to the ground from my pants pocket.

It's shortly before midnight. The little girl clings to my hand and won't make a move without me. I give her all the cash I can spare, and with body language I make it clear that I'll be back in the market tomorrow, same time, same place.

The cabby apparently can't read the scrap either. At any rate, he drives up and down, asks directions of every muffled figure in the unlit, zigzagging alleys through which his car can barely squeeze. Eventually, at one A.M., he stops at an unlit, ramshackle house with a heavy, iron-fitted door.

The door is ajar. I light a match and grope my way through the corridor, which smells of mint and cinnamon. The match flickers out. I don't see the steps and so I plunge down them, banging my shin and cursing loudly.

A door opens a crack. From inside comes the dim glow of a kerosene lamp, and I can make out the silhouette of a veiled figure. She steps aside as if inviting me in. But I can't yet tell whether it's my biker. The eyes of veiled Moroccan women all look confusingly alike. She pulls me into the almost empty room, which contains nothing but a bare bed. So it must be my cyclist.

She slips out of her burnoose and veil, and she's naked. The trouble with veiled women is that you can't tell how old they are; their eyes still sparkle even when their bodies are long since withered, so you can't see whether they're beautiful or ugly. My cyclist isn't beautiful in the usual sense, not even pretty. But so far, I've never cared. Her pockmarked face and her entire body look like the face and body of a predatory beast that has fought a lot of fights. She has a protruding belly, with a shaved twat underneath. Her tits aren't big, but they're heavy. I strip naked, and she pulls me down to the mattress. Her hole is as hot as if she wanted to boil my dick. She moans very softly. But she clings tight to the brass rods of the bed over her head, twists her pock-marked face, and exposes her clenched predatory teeth. . . .

She's got a big scar on her left areola; she must have had a deep injury. When I finger the scar, she tells me in sign language that someone put out a cigarette on her breast. Kissing the scar, I glance at the clock: Daylight is pushing through the cracks of the ill-fitting shutters. It's seven. I dress and hunt for money in my pockets. But she doesn't want any.

The park of La Mamounia once belonged to a prince. It's got several acres jungle-dense with the rarest palms, orange trees, lemon trees, date trees, and fig trees, and fleshy plants and gigantic blossoms in between. A huge, bricked-in palm tree towers from the swimming pool. You can assume you'll find R and R here. Churchill and the slut queen of England may have managed to relax here, but not me. Since I can't sleep at night, I at least try to sleep during the day, when I'm not shooting. I stretch out on a chaise longue by the pool. A breeze wafts over from the shady park twenty-four hours a day.

But even in the daytime I'm haunted by a young Moroccan woman who works as a telephone operator at La Mamounia. She does the graveyard shift, like her husband, the head of personnel. During the day she sleeps with him. So at night she comes panting up the stairs and corridors for a quickie with me. She's skinny, and her bones are as hot as glowing coals. Her mouth is parched from the heat of her body, as if from a fever. It wouldn't surprise me if she spewed fire. We have to fuck fast, and she has to be super-careful.

Taking a shortcut to the Mamounia, I have to pass through dark streets and alleys. Two young Moroccans are tailing me. I noticed them long ago, when I first turned in to the unlit, unpaved alleys. They quicken their pace and are already at my sides. Now I know what they're after. Or at least I think I know.

Earliest known family photo of Klaus (on his mother's lap), taken in Sopot, Poland, 1928.

Kinski in the fifties, most likely in Germany.

Reciting poetry in Germany in the fifties.

Kinski in his famous solo performance of Jean
Cocteau's *La Voix humaine*, Germany, 1949.
*(Akademie der Künste/Freie Universität,
Berlin)*

The Idiot, by Dostoevsky, a performance of ballet, pantomime, and theater, International Theater Festival, Venice, 1952.

Kinski with O. W. Fischer in *Ludwig II of Bavaria*, Munich, 1954. *(Elan Film)*

Kinski, Nastassja, and Biggi. (Gamma)

Nastassja as a little girl, Berlin, about 1963.

The Idiot, by Dostoevsky, a performance of
ballet, pantomime, and theater, International
Theater Festival, Venice, 1952.

Kinski with O. W. Fischer in *Ludwig II of
Bavaria*, Munich, 1954. *(Elan Film)*

Kinder, Mütter und ein General,
Germany, 1954. *(Eric Pommer/*
Intercontinental Produktion)

Kinski *(far left)* talking with a director
on the set of one of his early movies in
Germany, sometime in the fifties.
(Deutsches Institut für Filmkunde)

Kinski on location of
*For a Few Dollars
More*, Spain, 1965.
*(Grimaldi/P.E.A.
Production)*

Kinski in *Iskender* (theater), Munich, 1954.
(Star Photo/München)

For a Few Dollars More, Italy, 1965.
(Grimaldi/P.E.A. Production)

Kinski, Nastassja, and Biggi. (Gamma)

Nastassja as a little girl, Berlin, about 1963.

Kinski and Nastassja in
Berlin, about 1964.

Kinski and Nastassja,
Bavaria, Germany, 1972.

Woyzeck, Germany (shot on location in Czechoslovakia), 1978. *(Werner Herzog Filmproduktion)*

Kinski in *Il Grande Silenzio*, Italy, 1967. *(Adelphia Cinematografica)*

Marquis de Sade: Justine, Italy, 1968. *(Associazione Nazionale Cinematografiche)*

L'Important c'est d'aimer, France, 1974. *(Albina Productions)*

Aguirre, the Wrath of God, Peru, 1971–72. *(Werner Herzog Filmproduktion)*

L'Important c'est d'aimer, Paris, 1974. *(Albina Productions)*

Fitzcarraldo, Iquitos, Peru, 1981.
(Beat Presser/Werner Herzog Filmproduktion)

La Chanson de Roland, France, 1977. *(Gaumont FR3 Productions)*

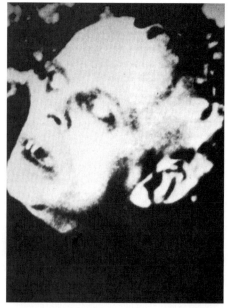

Nosferatu, Delft, Holland, 1978. *(Werner Herzog Filmproduktion)*

On a Chinese junk in the harbor of Hong Kong, 1972. *(Minhoï/Estate of Klaus Kinski)*

Opposite: Kinski and Minhoï on the grounds of their villa on the Via Appia Antica, Rome, 1969.

Wedding of Kinski and Minhoï, Rome, May 1971.

Portrait of Minhoï taken by Kinski, Rome, 1969.

Nanhoï as a little boy, Lagunitas, California, 1980.

Right: Kinski with five-day-old Nanhoï in Paris, August 5, 1976.

Kinski, Minhoï, and Nanhoï on the set of *La Chanson de Roland*, France, 1977.

Kinski as
Paganini, Rome,
1987.

Portrait of Nanhoï at age
seventeen, Paris, 1993. *(Fabian
Cevallos/Sygma)*

Kinski with puppy on his
property in Lagunitas,
California,1990. He is
clutching the typewritten
manuscript of his auto-
biography.
(Gérard Rancinan/GLMR)

Many Moroccans carry a knife, and you get stabbed without being able to emit a sound. But I'm not scared; I keep marching. The guy on my right comes so close that our shoulders touch.

"You're good-looking," he says mysteriously, without missing a beat in his cheerful march, which keeps step with mine. So that's it, I think.

"Yes, you're good-looking and I want you," he repeats.

The guy on my left must be deaf and dumb, or else he doesn't know French.

"If you say so . . . But I'm wiped out, I've gotta get some shut-eye."

We march in unison, forming a broad front like the Three Musketeers. The guy to my right slips his arm into mine. When the mute one sees this, he does likewise. If they've got knives, I muse, then my arms aren't free.

"You've got spunk," says the right-hand guy.

"Why?" I ask as innocently as possible, aware of what he's hinting at.

"Because you don't know if we've got knives. We're two against one, it's dark, and nobody would hear your screams."

"Why would you hurt me?"

"For instance, if you refuse to get fucked."

"Now look, I've got nothing against you. I'm just wiped out. I've been fucking all night and I'm totally drained. You wouldn't have much fun with me. By the way, I think I'm lost. Where's La Mamounia?"

"We're going in the right direction."

I don't believe him. There's no light anywhere to be seen, not even in the distance. Nothing. And I'm unfamiliar with these surroundings. The right-hand guy keeps whispering various declarations of love to me while the left-hand guy is content to squeeze my left arm.

Eventually we come to a dark, unpaved, semicircular street. A few yards later, lights flicker from very far away, like a coastline when you've swum out to sea at night.

"Head toward the lights. Hang a right at the next corner, and then keep going straight. You'll hit La Mamounia directly. You're a nice guy. Maybe we'll meet again someday."

"Who knows . . . ?"

I turn around—you can never be sure with these creeps.

When I piss against a palm, my dick burns like nettles: another dose of the clap.

I have no time to go to the doctor's office. He brings his shot to me. We're filming in a mosaicked palace. Between takes the doctor and I go up to the gallery above the tea salon. I drop my drawers, and just as the penicillin goes into my bare butt, they're calling me for the next take.

Maria Rohm is the steady girlfriend of the producer I'm doing the Marrakesh flick for. But that doesn't stop her from fooling around with Margareth and with me. And Margareth, who's married to my agent, fools around with me, and I with both of them. Their flesh remains snowy white despite the ruthless sun, and it's so soft and clean that I'm turned on by its contrast with that of the Moroccan women, who are neither light-skinned nor clean.

"You're lucky," Senta Berger tells me. "During my seven weeks here, I have to keep my thighs together."

"Then come to me," I say from my chaise longue. She's standing with her sweet, full pussy right in front of my mouth while pubic hair wells out of her tiny bikini.

"No way," she says. "I'm engaged." Then she frowns as if thinking how stupid her words are.

After Marrakesh two movies in London. Then one in Paris. Then one on Capri, with Martine Carol.

Every day Martine shows off one of her fur coats for me. She's got at least twenty, and there's one she's especially proud of: The unborn babies are cut out of their murdered mothers' bellies. Then the babies are skinned alive. This makes the fur shine unbelievably. A coat is made up of many skins of many babies cut from their wombs. Such a coat fetches several hundred thousand marks. They're very rare. Thank goodness!

Not only is she obsessed with fur, she also collects clothes, houses, land, islands, and, above all, diamonds. Lots of diamonds. Big ones. The biggest are the size of pigeon eggs, and she's already wearing them for breakfast. I feel sorry for her. She'd give it all up just to be a couple of years younger. She didn't have to confess it to me tearfully.

"As soon as you get to London again, you'll live in my villa in Hyde Park," she repeats several times a day, as if talking to a disobedient brat. "I'll pick you up at the airport in my Rolls-Royce."

Some asshole artistic director has the nerve to keep asking me if I'd be willing to perform at Berlin's Schiller Theater. His assistant keeps calling me, but I tell him: "You could offer me any amount of dough, but I'd rather do the lousiest movie than set even one foot in your graveyard!"

I can also afford to turn down the contemptible German movie projects. The Italians offers me a choice of thirty flicks a week. I accept the one that pays the most.

We've moved from Via Nemea to Cassia Antica, Beatrice's quarter. But I see her only twice more. The first time's in the home of Carla Gravina, the wife of the actor Gian Maria Volonté. Carla's in bed with the flu. I visit her with Beatrice.

Our house in the Cassia is a freestanding palazzo behind a high, rose-covered wall. It's got eight rooms, four baths, a garden terrace, a garage, a swimming pool, and one of the biggest and loveliest private parks in Rome. All year long, the most exquisite tropical plants and flowers grow and blossom here. Like half of Rome, the place is owned by a real estate office that belongs to the Vatican. Rent: eight thousand marks a month. Our staff consists of two maids and a cook.

I get a warning from fate. But I pay no attention. I'm doing a Western at Cinecittà. On the first day of shooting, the horse I'm dozing on does half a backflip, squeezes me against a wall, and falls on top of me with its entire body weight. I manage to kick it to avoid getting trampled to death. But now I can't stand up; I can't even sit up or kneel. My pants have burst open at the crotch and the inner thighs. The glands at the right of my genitals have swollen up into a black-and-blue mound.

I absolutely refuse to go to the hospital. Two members of the crew lug me to my dressing room. They lay me out on the couch, and I ask them to leave me alone. I just want to rest up a little. The pain is so bad that I try to call them back and ask for a painkiller. But they can't hear me.

As soon as I attempt to sit up, I collapse like Jell-O, as if my spine were gone. Rolling off the couch, I crawl to the door. I throw my belt over the door handle and succeed in pulling it down. Then I crawl down the corridor to the fitting room.

The dresser gets a crew member, and I'm taken to a hospital. After X-raying me, the doctor says that my backbone is fractured. "Cracked," he corrects himself—that is, the spinal cord isn't injured. Another half inch, and I'd've been paralyzed for life. I have to stay at the hospital.

Biggi, whom we've called up, weeps and yells in fear. I can't move my body. All I can do is press the buzzer at the head of my bed and, with utmost effort, use the telephone. I have to make do with a bedpan that the nurse shoves under me.

I tell the night nurse to come back when everyone else is asleep.

In my state sex is pretty tricky. But she straddles me so skillfully that my dick stands up despite everything, and she rides me so cautiously that neither her butt nor her vaginal lips so much as graze my abdomen even once. The climax is very painful, so we can do it only once. But from night to night, the nurse's positions get more and more inventive.

After twelve days I'm fed up with being a cripple.

With a customized corset I make my first attempts to stand and walk, and I let the nurse lead me shuffling to the toilet.

The Western is down the drain for me. I get neither my salary nor insurance because the producer turns out not to have carried a policy. Furthermore, for the time being I can't accept any role in which I ride a horse or have to strain myself physically in any other way. I can't even ride in a car. "Except a Rolls-Royce," the doctor says laconically. I take him at his word and buy my first Silver Cloud. Three weeks later I toss my corset through the window of the rolling Rolls-Royce and sign a contract for *Carmen, Baby* in Spain, where, despite a strict prohibition by the doctor, I gallop around from dawn to dusk and fight an eight-hour duel with knives.

Biggi and Nasstja have come along to Spain. At night the pain makes me shriek in bed, and in the morning Biggi and the bellboy have to pull me to a sitting position because I'm as stiff as a log.

After Spain, Brazil. Again I fly alone. A rainstorm has washed away the slum shacks of the favelas, claiming thousands of lives. When I arrive in Rio, the water is three feet deep. But it's neither the natural disaster nor the cholera epidemic that prevents me from doing very much.

Day and night the pain is unbearable, and the awful weather—120 degrees Fahrenheit, with 80 percent humidity—drains me so thoroughly that I'm afraid I won't get to enjoy the pre-Carnival season.

The pre-Carnival is a lot more exciting than the Mardi Gras itself because it's done without silly costumes, and you can smell and grab the sweaty, barely clad bodies of the women. The Brazilians, from youngsters to oldsters, move to a samba beat wherever they're walking or standing, and the drums never stop playing. When one stops, another starts. With these samba steps, the girls of Rio, whose swinging hips and whirling butts get you so drunk even when they walk normally, can give you the boner of a lifetime without touching you.

I move out of the senile Copacabana Palace Hotel. The modern Leme Palace Hotel, where I'm now staying, lies right on the long beach of Rio de Janiero. Nevertheless I usually sleep outdoors. The nights are so mild that the sand is covered with tangled bodies even after twilight. No one cares what anyone else is doing, because they're all fucking.

The girls of Rio, rich and poor, were made for love. The paupers go streetwalking to earn some money on the side even if they're married. They lean against the parked cars in the Copacabana, lifting their skirts, under which they wear no panties.

"Grab it," says one. "If you like, you can fuck me right here."

The rich girls differ only in being rich and not necessarily having to walk the streets—at least, not to survive.

The Brazilian climate is good for my spine. The pain is gone. My next stop is Hong Kong.

By the time we get there after a twenty-six-hour flight, the only one of us who isn't wiped out is Nasstja; she's been running through the plane, perking up even the grouchiest passenger. Biggi is furious at me because I disappeared with the Lufthansa stewardess for such a long time and because the girl even tried to write down her Hong Kong address for me.

During the ferry crossing from Kowloon, Biggi slaps my face. Then, at the Hilton, she has a nervous breakdown. There's nothing I can do. She doesn't even want me to touch her. Nasty as it may sound, all I can think about is the Chinese women, and my pulse beats like crazy.

I stroll through the teeming streets until I find a ricksha, which takes me to a Chinese hooker. When my initial thirst is slaked, I sit down with the Chinese on the street in front of her house and eat with them, among steaming kettles and crackling, smoking fires on which crabs and octopuses are roasting. I've got two movies to do in Hong Kong . They're gonna take ten weeks. I'll stick to a sound, regular diet to keep up my strength. All I have to do is think of the hooker I just went to.

Margareth Lee and Maria Rohm are also in the cast; they fuck each other like mad because the producer, who flies to Europe once a week, is practically never around.

There's no hotel nearby in Kowloon, so Margareth, Maria, and I are in a real pigsty of a room, waiting to shoot. We're joined by the British makeup woman and her daughter. But Margareth and Maria aren't in the mood. They and the daughter sit down on my bed, deciding which of them should remove which of my clothes, and which one can use which of my body parts first. No one asks me.

Nastassja has to have her appendix removed. When she's up and around again, we go to the Tiger Balm Garden and to Aberdeen, where junks soundlessly glide past us like phantom ships, floating above the surface like patches of fogs. People offer us cuttlefish and crabs and shrimps, which are roasted alive before us on charcoal fires.

During the nights we sail out on the China Sea.

The months in Hong Kong are drawing to a close, and I dash from one hotel room to the next, from the girls in Kowloon to the girls in Aberdeen to the Filipino models demonstrating their national costumes at the Hilton From Margareth to Maria. From Hong Kong to Taipei, Beijing, and Shanghai.

In Rome I trade in the Rolls-Royce for another. When I'm sick of this one, I again buy a Maserati, then a Ferrari, and then a Rolls-Royce Cabriolet again, for a hundred thousand bucks. I trade in cars because a door is rattling, or because I can't get the window down fast enough when a girl strolls by, or because I've had the car for over a week and I'm fed up with the color.

Our first stop is New York, where I have to shoot for a week with Edward G. Robinson. After screwing a couple of clapped-out Broadway hookers, I go hunting in Greenwich Village, where at night the girls wait outside the Beat dives for someone who'll pay them a couple of bucks with which to buy grass. They'll do anything for grass. You can't loiter in groups on the street because the cops yell, "Keep moving!" So I bring as many of these Lolitas as possible back to my hotel. Even in winter they only wear skimpy rags on their bodies, which are scrawny from drugs, and so I first buy clothes for them. They ask for cash so they can buy their winter clothes themselves. But I don't fall for that.

In Cortina d'Ampezzo, I make the first snowbound Western. Biggi and Nasstja are happy and cheerful; they frolic in the snow, go sledding all day, skating, and ride jingly, horse-drawn sleighs to the mountains. But the instant I'm alone with Biggi, we argue and hit one another.

This time the reason is the black American actress Sherene Miller, who's also starring in the movie. She's got a boyish body, boyish haircut, boyish ass, and almost no tits. Her room lies directly over our apartment.

In the morning, when I come back after fucking Sherene half the night, I sneak past a sleeping Biggi to get my toothbrush, razor, and fresh underwear. This way, we can't fight. I kiss her and Nasstja cautiously, to avoid waking them.

Does Nasstja have any inkling of my lifestyle? She adores her mother more than anything in the world, but she also loves me more and more every day, and I'm crazy about her. I just can't imagine that we could be separated someday.

In Rome Marlon Brando bangs away at Sherene's door every night. He's filming some piece of garbage and lives in the same *pensione* as Sherene. I hope she finally opens the door and lets him in so I can attend to other twats. But she never does open the door, and the next day I have to fuck her in her dressing room at Helios Studio. Sherene is very jealous and can't take jokes in this department. Leaving the *pensione,* where Brando won't give her a moment's peace, she switches to the Hôtel de la Ville, near the Piazza di Spagna. She orders me to visit her. The little sister of Jean-Louis Trintignant's wife is also here. She wants to drag me to an LSD party, but I prefer to stay with Sherene's friend, a black American singer, who hasn't dressed yet. Sherene is furious and cusses me out in front of all the people in the hotel lobby. But if she doesn't like my habits, why did she tell me that her friend was still in the room and had to get dressed? Sherene ought to know me by now.

Visconti has his people inquire if I want to do a movie with him. They keep ringing me up at the studio, asking me to be patient until the dates are decided on and the contract can be worked out.

"Who is this Visconti?" I ask my agent, Gino.

"You'd be better off doing your next Western," he replies.

"Esso," says Rinaldo Geladi, a PR man, pointing his thumb over his shoulder. He's referring to the girl who's vanished in the toilet. I met her half an hour ago. Rinaldo brought her to our location in Magliana, outside Rome. The girl had asked him to take her along because she wanted to meet me. I greeted her, got behind the wheel of her Ferrari, and drove her to the restaurant, where we're still sitting during the lunch break. She couldn't lift a forkful of spaghetti to her red lips without first looking up with her gorgeous Italian eyes and smiling at me. Now I see that she's only picking at the spaghetti and hasn't eaten a bite.

"What does 'esso' mean?" I ask Rinaldo.

"Moratti."

"Oh, the cigarette maker."

"Hell, no. Not Muratti, Moratti. Her name is Susanne Moratti. Her father is the richest man in Italy."

"Interesting," I say.

Susanne returns from the toilet. She's put on more lipstick and smiles even more lovingly than before. I now take a much closer look at her. Not because her father is the richest man in Italy, but because I previously looked at her in a purely mechanical way.

She has long, silky hair, super-healthy teeth, fine, sensual lips, and dreamy, yearning eyes. Her body is thin and frail, like a porcelain figure. But as absent and mournful as her expression may be, and as elflike as her body is, she must be incredibly tough and energetic. After all, she drives the fastest racing car in the world. She wears a lightweight, flowery summer frock and a diamond of at least ten carats.

Rinaldo slaps me on the back. I was so absorbed in Susanne, who likewise seemed to have forgotten everything and everyone around her—forgotten even to smile at me—that I didn't notice the director, who came to our table ten minutes ago to get me back before the camera. I give Susanne my phone number, she gives me hers, and we promise to meet again.

She rings me up that very same evening. It didn't occur to her that Biggi might answer. Nor did I reckon with the possibility—Biggi never answers the phone.

"For you. Some woman," she says nastily.

I can't talk to Susanne for long. Biggi has gone to her room and can't hear me, but I don't want a repeat of what happened in Yugoslavia. I tell Susanne not to call me up anymore, and I'll meet her at Rinaldo's studio.

Some Russian princess offers me a house on the Via Appia, one of the oldest and most beautiful roads in the world. The house, owned by Countess Vassarotti, is for rent.

Together with the princess, whose dog pisses in my Rolls-Royce, I drive over to have a look at the place. It's next door to Gina Lollobrigida's villa. The house is completely isolated, on a gigantic lot filled with pines, cypresses, centuries-old Japanese cherry trees, roses, oleanders, orange trees, and lemon trees, with scattered

Roman ruins. The entire property is surrounded by an ancient wall seven feet high.

The house itself is nine centuries old and is included in books on historic Italian landmarks. It's got four stories, fourteen rooms, seven baths, five fireplaces, and an elevator going up to the tower. The second-floor salon is sixty-six feet long and has a thirty-three-foot ceiling. There's also a separate wing for the staff and, in the orchard, a guest cottage with its own salon, two baths, and four rooms on the second story. Under the heavy, luxuriant branches of almond and walnut trees is a hothouse containing rare orchids.

In the Middle Ages the *castello* was transformed into a church. No one knows what it was before that. The foundation walls were built on granite before the Christian era, and the sign of the Vatican is carved into the ashlar staircase. Indeed, the Vatican leaves its brand on all sorts of property, the way ranches mark the butts of their cows.

Countess Vassarotti lives alone in the *castello*. Her husband, a movie producer, committed suicide. She's surrounded by worm-eaten antiques that collapse when you lean against them. The place is a jungle of decaying straw flowers, hundreds of tasteless and rotting paintings, Chinese rugs endlessly pissed on by the dogs and cats, and mountains of valuable but chipped porcelain.

The electric lights don't work, and neither does the elevator, whose shaft lies in two feet of water under the main floor. While making a dreadful movie in Rome, Jane Fonda stayed here for six months, and during a cloudburst she was stuck in the elevator for hours. Roger Vadim dealt the coup de grâce, turning the place into a complete pigsty.

If I throw out most of the junk and bring the house up to par, I can turn it into the fairy-tale castle I need.

When I tell Biggi about the house, she wants to see it right away. And once she sees it, she doesn't want to leave. Gino tears his hair:

"Don't you realize the entire Via Appia is infested with snakes and rats? The poisonous lizards creep into your bed! The mosquitoes eat you alive! The ants and spiders crawl into your soup! The house is so old that you'll still be trying to save it from dry rot when you're an old man! You'll be coming back to me three months from now, cursing me for not keeping you from renting it!"

I let him talk. Biggi and Nasstja are gonna have their dream castle. Nasstja is attending school in Rome, and both of them absolutely want to remain in Italy.

I've known for weeks that I have to get back to Almería. Biggi knows it too, but we haven't talked about it. Now, all at once, she wants to come along. I tell her it would be better if we separated for a couple of weeks.

The reason is Susanne. I see her more and more often. She accompanies me wherever I go, waiting patiently while I shoot in the suffocating studios, though I have barely any time for her. She endures the broiling heat during outdoor filming, when there's often no vacant chair, much less an umbrella. She dogs my every step and grows sadder and sadder as the day of my departure comes nearer. For I haven't told her whether she can come with me or how I feel about her. I myself don't know. She sits silently next to me, not eating a bite of food, when I dine in a Japanese restaurant or when I'm with architects and designers to discuss silk for walls and curtains, gilded faucets and doorknobs, moquette and color samples for the *castello*. And Susanne offers to chauffeur me around in her Ferrari at every opportunity.

This morning I'm taking my Rolls-Royce Cabriolet after commissioning the work for the *castello*. Susanne has arrived at the Piazza di Spagna at six A.M. to see me one last time. I hug her on the Spanish Steps, kissing her on the mouth for the first time. As I turn into Via del

Babuino toward the Piazza del Popolo, she's still standing there, just as I left her after the kiss.

On the first day I drive all the way to Marseilles. At three A.M. I go to the hookers. I pick one who's huddling in the gutter, and we go to a seedy hotel. But it's no fun. I return to my hotel and call up Susanne in Rome.

From Marseilles I head for Barcelona. But this time none of the hookers can turn me on. Not even the flamenco dancers. Not even the Gypsy girls, whom I truly love.

When I arrive in Almería, a wire from Susanne is waiting at the hotel desk. She's joining me tomorrow night. I'm so happy that I throw a party with my Gypsies in a flamenco restaurant. The girls dance in front of me on the tables, and I can see their pussy lips rubbing together.

One of the girls is the owner of the restaurant. I fuck her standing in the tiny john behind the kitchen. Before driving back to the hotel, I jump into the sea.

Susanne has already asked for me and is standing at the desk, pale and tired. She has no valise, only a makeup kit. Instead of taking a commercial airline, she flew in a private jet. She had to land in Málaga because there's no airfield in Almería. She took a cab to cover the winding hundred and twenty miles from Málaga. Her father alerted bloodhounds in all airports: They're supposed to catch Susanne and bring her home. At four A.M. she has to get back to Málaga, where her plane is taking off at seven. It's ten P.M. We've got six hours.

Susanne is inhibited and awkward, as if she's worried about satisfying me. I fuck her seriously, with all my devotion: I'm tender, brutal, and ruthless. She glows and smells and kicks and foams at the mouth. We fall asleep, intoxicated and satisfied. . . .

I don't notice when Susanne slides quietly out of bed, dresses, and vanishes. The second time the desk clerk wakes me up, I find Susanne's letter, which she wrote in the bathroom to avoid making any noise. I get a hard-on when I read the sentence "I hope I wasn't too clumsy in bed. . . ."

I get dressed because the phone's ringing a third time.

In the streets of Almería the shoeshine boys, who are all Gypsies, spit on their customers' shoes and clap their hands when they toss their brushes aloft like jugglers. Spotting me, they abandon the stunned tourists and shout at me across the street. They know I love it when they do a few flamenco steps for me in the middle of the roadway, in the heart of the traffic; they fanatically puff out their chests, and their faces take on an earnest, painful expression.

Susanne comes again. I've got time off, so we drive to Málaga. She has to leave in two days. I have to go to Barcelona. Susanne joins me and remains for one night. Comes again. Leaves again. And comes again, wherever I am.

Meanwhile Biggi and Nasstja have moved into the *castello* because the remodeling is as good as finished. When I return from Spain, Biggi yells that she's gonna pack her things and leave me forever. During those ten weeks in Spain I never once called, wired, or wrote—which I have always done, despite all my whoring, except from Prague. I know that our marriage is totally on the rocks, but I love Biggi and try to talk her into staying in Rome. It's no use.

"You'd go to bed with your own daughter!" she shrieks, beside herself, and storms out of the house.

I can't find her that day, nor does Nasstja know where she has gone. Nasstja looks for her.

I find Biggi in a corner of the hothouse: She's sitting on the floor among flowerpots that hang overhead or stand on long tables. They're filled with orchids that are spotted like wildcats; this is the first time that I'm aware of how beautiful they are. Biggi refuses to look at me. Touching a flower, she is as amazed as a child: "I was firmly convinced that Nasstja and I would be living in this paradise. And now you've destroyed everything."

"But I rented the place only for your sakes!"

"That may be. I actually believe that you were sincere. But we can't stay on with you. We can't live in a house to which you return after your bouts of whoring. Tomorrow I'm flying to Berlin with Nasstja, and I'll be looking for a new apartment."

I drive Biggi and Nasstja to the airport. Before passing through the checkpoint, Biggi starts crying. She feels, as I do, that it's all over. Nasstja throws her arms around Biggi's legs and buries her face in her mother's lap.

"Why are you sending us away . . . ?"

"I'm not sending you away, Biggi. You don't want to stay with me."

Everything I say sounds meaningless. For Biggi is right. Basically, I'm the one who's been sending her away for years without meaning to. She's still crying on the other side of the barrier. Nasstja keeps looking back at me as she stumbles along, holding Biggi's hand. Tears come to my eyes.

I ring up Susanne from the airport. I want to go to the seashore with her and not think of anything. In Fiumicino we board her father's yacht and sail to Sardinia, where her parents own a mammoth hotel. That's where her brothers' yachts are anchored, as is her mother's luxury ship, which is the size of a small ocean liner.

Susanne moves in with me on Via Appia, bringing along a portion of her wardrobe. Wherever we go in Rome, we're hounded by paparazzi, and the gossips have a field day.

Pasolini shows up at the *castello* with a horde of young men after sending me the script of his next movie, *Porcile*. He wants to talk to me. Pola is visiting because Susanne has to spend some time with her family. I don't feel like going down to the salon. I call up Susanne, who's called from Milan, and I tell Pola that she should entertain Pasolini and his coterie while I'm on the phone. Gino is also here.

One hour later I go downstairs. An awkward atmosphere has developed because I've made Pasolini cool his heels all that time.

I apologize for my behavior and say that I've been reading the script but that I don't understand it. Actually, Gino outlined the crap for me.

It's true that the plot's a little weird. The lead, whom I'm supposed to play, is a guy who's so hungry that he mugs a well-built soldier and eats him up. He's also turned on by the muscular body parts of his food. After all the garbage I've had to be in, this'll pass. But not the salary. Doria, the producer, is one of the best in Italy, but if I always got the starvation wages he offers me I'd be hungry enough to gobble up Doria. Or Pasolini. Gino and I have agreed to raise my price with every new film. That's why he isn't disappointed when the contract doesn't materialize.

I Bastardi (Sons of Satan) with Margareth Lee and Rita Hayworth, in Spain. Susanne wanted to fly with me but ultimately doesn't join me till later on. Margareth is friends with a hairstylist, whom she brings along to Madrid. I want to seduce the hairstylist, who's such an inveterate lesbian that she smacks my hand whenever I feel up Margareth.

I invite them to my suite at the Palace Hotel and dance with the hairstylist while Margareth jerks off on the bed. I've already got my finger inside the hairdresser's little pussy—but then the doorbell rings. When I open the door, ready to yell at the party-pooper, I find Susanne, who hugs me passionately. She could have called or wired! I draw out our greeting in the vestibule as long as possible so that the two women inside can straighten up their clothes. Before introducing Susanne, I whisper to her: "They're two dykes. They were about to leave."

I've switched cars again. Out of seven Ferraris I've ruined four, and now I'm trading in my sixth Rolls for another Ferrari. With the last trade-in I lost about 40,000 marks. During these four years in Rome, I've bought and traded in sixteen cars. Three Maseratis, seven Ferraris, and six Rolls-Royces. I've poured 300,000 marks into the house even though it doesn't belong to me. I've got a staff of seven: a chauffeur, a gardener, two maids, a butler, a cook, and a secretary. My secretary alone costs me over 7,000 marks a month. Living expenses run to some 8,500 a month. Russian caviar and champagne, which any jerk gets from me, cost about 10,000 marks. Mailmen and gas men likewise often get a glass. Even the firemen who hooked their hoses up to my water when they had to put out a gas fire next door.

It's mainly journalists who booze and chow down in the *castello*. A German newspaperwoman pukes on a Chinese rug because her googly eyes were bigger than her stomach. She then writes in a glossy mag that I gobble caviar by the spoonful.

Further expenses include clothes, travel, gasoline, telephone bills of 8,000 to 10,000 marks, and my constant parade of cars, which eat up a fortune. Though I race from one film to another—as many as eleven a year, once even three simultaneously—and my daily salary has shot up to 50,000 marks, I constantly need money. Since the days of the pawnbroker who took my mother's wedding ring, only the numbers have changed.

The next two projects are a war movie in northwest Italy and a gangster flick in Genoa. Susanne races her Ferrari through fog and snow flurries along the icy thruway from Milan to Montecatini, Livorno, and Genoa. For a night. For a day. For a couple of hours. If Susanne can't get away, I dash off to Milan in my Ferrari when the shooting's done. For a night. For a couple of hours. We meet at the Principe e Savoia, where Susanne keeps a suite aside from her pad in Milan and Moratti's houses.

Susanne is at the end of her rope. The nine and a half months with me have wiped her out. She has a physical and mental breakdown and has to be hospitalized in Switzerland.

Outside a tiny hamlet in the mountain jungles of South Vietnam, near Dâlat, where the Moi nation lives, a four-year-old child is crying. The little girl knows nothing about the filthy war that has been exterminating her people for over ten years now. She knows nothing about the patrols of invaders or the Vietcong stealing through the jungle. And she knows nothing about the tiger pit into which she plunged that afternoon. She didn't see it because the villagers camouflage the traps with bamboo reeds.

The little girl is screaming because she tore her lower thigh when she fell in. She screams and screams. But no one hears her. The pit, thirteen feet deep, swallows up the slightest noise and doesn't let any sound get out.

When darkness fell—suddenly, as it does in the jungle—the villagers stopped searching for the little girl, who hadn't come home from playing.

Eventually the little girl's screams grow weaker and weaker and then die out altogether. Only the pig in the bamboo cage, whose smell is meant to attract a tiger, squeals in fear.

The little girl has fallen asleep; she hears neither the squealing of the pig nor the soft snarling of the tiger. The predator, drawn by the scent of the pig, is stealing around the edge of the pit, which is three feet by seven feet wide.

At daybreak the villagers resume their search for the little girl. They discover the spoor of the tiger, whose pawprints are clear in the damp soil. The trail leads to the tiger trap. When the villagers, armed with bamboo spears, creep up to the pit, the most courageous man cautiously peeps over the edge in order to tell the others how big the tiger is. But no tiger snarls at him. Instead the little girl smiles up at him. She's stuck her tiny fingers through the dense bars of the bamboo cage and is petting the sleeping pig.

Minhoï, the four-year-old from the tiger trap, is nineteen today and standing across from me. I hug her and try to kiss her, as if I already knew her story and had been waiting all these fifteen years for this very moment, waiting to hug and kiss this girl whom I've never set eyes on before and who seems to be the fulfillment of my yearning for love.

The mysterious, shocking beauty of her exotic face is further emphasized by her aggressive look, that of a captured animal that has been dragged to civilization and is as out of place here, on Rome's Via Appia Antica, as in the rest of the so-called civilized world. Annoyed and indignant at my pushiness, she brusquely extricates herself from my arms.

Her long, full hair, which is the color of sharply roasted chestnuts, falls heavily down. Her eyebrows form two sickle moons over

the dark, remote eyes. The regularity of her oval face balances her fe-
line cheekbones. Her ocher skin has no creases, not even under her
eyes. The upper and lower lips of her shimmering violet mouth are
evenly arched and so silently earnest that the noisy chatter of the other
guests vanishes from my ears.

Her figure is as childlike as that of most Vietnamese women. Her
breasts are barely hinted at by her white trapeze-shaped minidress under the open leopardskin coat, which, like her body, emanates an intoxicating Oriental perfume. Her slender, childlike hands are hot and
soft, and her black fingernails are as long as those of a Chinese
princess.

I'm throwing a party at my *castello*. I've invited all my friends,
telling them to bring along whomever they like. But none of the guests
knows this Vietnamese woman. She didn't arrive with anyone, and no
one saw her come in.

The tables are groaning with caviar and champagne and all kinds
of goodies. Rock music is booming from the loudspeakers. The guests
are eating, drinking, chatting, laughing, dancing. Everyone can do
whatever he likes, and I don't worry about anybody.

I'm not angry at her for reprimanding me so sharply. It was my
fault. But what can I do to get her to love me? I am certain that I have
found my true love.

My brain is working feverishly. First I have to get her out of this
hubbub. But how? On what pretext? Chance comes to my rescue:
She's hungry—at least a little—for she tries to make her way toward
the table with the caviar, on which the guests have descended like piranhas. I struggle through the gluttonous crowd, shovel three ladle-
fuls of caviar onto a gold plate, pile up mountains of Nova Scotia
salmon, thinny-thin slices of ham, and white truffle shavings on another plate, wedge an open bottle of Dom Pérignon under my arm,
and look for Minhoï.

She's standing at the ten-foot-high baroque fireplace, warming herself on the blazing flames, which, together with hundreds of flickering candles, illuminate the salon. But she still seems to be freezing, despite the leopardskin coat.

There's no chair anywhere in the salon, no armchair, no vacant place on a couch for Minhoï to sit. This is my chance. I tell her that she can eat and drink in my blue room, and I lead her down half a flight. The footmen in their white gloves and livery try to kindle a fire in the blue room, but I send them away and start the fire myself.

In the blue room, with heavy blue Italian silk on the walls, floor-length silk curtains at the windows, and a blue-patterned Chinese rug on the floor, there is no furniture but a French bed covered with blue silk. Light is provided by a candlestick on the fireplace mantel.

I set the plates on the silk bedcover and ask Minhoï to sit on the bed. But she eats standing.

"Do you have any cocaine?" she suddenly asks, like a child looking forward to chocolate pudding after eating its veggies.

"No. None. And I don't want you to sniff any, either."

"Hash?"

"Nope. Anyway, sit down when you eat, otherwise you won't digest it."

"If you don't have something, then it's unbearable."

"What?"

"Life."

"That's not true. But if you eat nicely, I'll get you some."

As fast as I can without falling, I tear up the steps to the salon and ask everyone I meet whether he's got any hash. A girl hands me a joint, I light it on the spot. When I try to storm down the steps to the blue room, some chick gets in my way.

"Do it! Fuck me! I want you to fuck me! Now!"

I shove her aside and jump down the seven steps to the blue room in one fell swoop, tortured by the fear that Minhoï might have left. She emerges from the toilet as I push open the door to the blue room. I hand her the joint, and she inhales the blue smoke, drawing deeply. After finishing the joint, she stretches out on the bed. She's relaxed. . . .

The final guests have left. It's growing light outside. The first larks are chirping. . . . The day is coming, full of sweetness, just as Minhoï has come into my life.

Out in the garden Enrico is washing the Rolls-Royce or the Ferrari while the gardener is raking the gravel. The splashing of the water and the crunching of the gravel are driving me up the wall. I buzz the kitchen on the house telephone and tell Clara, my housekeeper, to have them all get the hell out of here, even the cook. I want to be alone with Minhoï.

Minhoï's belongings are still in Paris, where she's been living till now and where she attended school from the time she was seven. I loot the Roman boutiques for her, buying anything she likes. If she can't find her gloves because she forgot them in Paris, I buy her twenty pairs. If her leotard has a run, I buy her fifty new ones of all sorts and colors. If it's too cold for her leopardskin, I buy her an ankle-length sable. If her shoe is too tight, I buy her piles of new shoes. And if she needs lipstick or nail polish, I blow a couple of thousand marks on new makeup. I give away the Rolls-Royce Cabriolet and buy a Rolls-Royce Phantom with a built-in bar.

I order a dark-blue thirty-foot trailer that looks like a Pullman car. The wall coverings, tablecloths, bedclothes, curtains, pillows, and cushions are pure silk. The floor is carpeted with velour. The doors and closets are teak. The handles, faucets, and doorknobs are gilded. The silk window shades have pictures of clouds. Vestibule, living room, dressing room, and bedroom are separated by sliding doors. Air-conditioning, heating, TV, radio, tape recorder, cassette player, stereo, and radio telephone are installed in the wall cabinets. Soft light is provided by wall brackets with frosted-glass globes. Bulbs are mounted in the two high crystal mirrors. We eat by candlelight. A special unit supplies power for the trailer, and the staff consists of a chauffeur, a servant, and a cook.

The trailer is for Minhoï, who accompanies me to all countries, even at night, whenever I'm shooting. No luxury is too expensive for her. Minhoï is delighted at everything I do for her. But she's always so speechless and incredulous, as if I've done something wrong. I still don't understand that all this extravagance is totally useless.

Though I don't have the least grounds, I'm so jealous that I can barely stand it if Minhoï so much as calls up a girlfriend in Paris. When she writes letters, I throw them away. Likewise any mail she receives. If someone calls up, I say she's out. I don't want Minhoï to take even one step alone. I'm constantly worried about her.

When she strolls through our garden and I lose sight of her for even an instant, I look for her desperately, as if I've lost her. I wade through the man-high grass of the endless grounds, I scour the overgrown bushes and tangled blackberry brambles, and I crawl through the ruins of the ancient catacombs, which abut the thorn-covered wall several hundred yards from the house. If she's not where I think she is in the gigantic *castello*, I comb all the floors until I find her. I even wake up with a start if she's rolled over and I don't feel her body or at least her hand.

I don't want to crowd Minhoï, and I know that I myself can't live in this constant tension. If my imagination bolts in my dreams even though Minhoï is lying next to me, then what's going to happen if I ever really have to spend a day without her? I shoo away these thoughts because I can't even picture such a situation.

It takes Minhoï's Asian soul a long time to adjust to the dreadful extremes in my character. On the one hand, I'm irritable, I fly off the handle too easily, I react too quickly. My French is bad, but I'm impatient if Minhoï doesn't understand me right away, and these misunderstandings, behind which I suspect the most subtle schemes, poison my mind and my soul. I'm desperate. I have a low frustration tolerance, and my outbursts are unlimited. On the other hand, I'm considerate to the point of self-sacrifice, and my love is so immense that it terrifies Minhoï.

Yet the more Minhoï comprehends my anxiety about her, the more she gradually takes in my love (which originally terrified her), the more sensitive she becomes and the less often she leaves my side. To keep me calm, she never answers the phone. And she doesn't call people anymore. Nor does she write to her friends. She tosses her address book into the burning fireplace before my very eyes.

One has to love me the way Minhoï loves me to understand me and put up with me. I soon improve my French, which I used to "speak like a Spanish cow," as Minhoï lovingly teases me. And from her I learn patience and self-control. In this way the little girl from the tiger trap in Vietnam has become my teacher and is transforming my entire life.

Today I look for Minhoï everywhere—in the house, the garden, the most remote corners of our property. I cussed her out in a jealous fit and told her I can't stand living with her anymore. Which is the biggest paradox, since Minhoï is my life.

As darkness sets in, I find her in the tower room. I've never looked for her there because she normally wouldn't climb up the stairs—she's afraid of the bats that fly in and out. She hasn't switched on the light. It's dark. I almost trip over her. I touch her face, which is drenched with tears. I kiss her and beg her to forgive me. Then I go to the kitchen to rustle up something to eat. It's Sunday and the staff is gone.

When I return to the tower, Minhoï is slumped over. An empty vial of sleeping pills is on the floor. I wrench her to her feet and try forcing her to walk up and down. I've heard that this helps in an overdose case: The blood circulation, the nervous system, and the entire organism are yanked away from the narcotic, which is starting to paralyze them. Minhoï can't walk; I have to support her. Nor can she speak; she can only babble. She embraces me lovingly and kisses me on the mouth when I shake her in my panic, and her face falls on my face.

I feel I'm losing my mind. I have to take her out to the fresh air! I carry her down the spiral staircase to the fourth floor. The elevator has a short circuit. On the stairway to the salon, she collapses in my arms. I carry her to the blue room. Her pulse is racing so wildly that I can't feel individual beats. She moans, rattles, reaches for her throat, gasps for air. I tear open the windows, dash down the steps to the kitchen, and grab a bottle of cold milk. On the way, I kneel on the steps.

"God! Please don't let Minhoï die—she's just taught me how to live!"

When I return to the blue room, Minhoï has tumbled from the bed and is writhing convulsively on the floor. If the milk doesn't counteract the pills, it'll at least make her throw up. But after I've poured most of the milk down her throat, Minhoï neither improves nor vomits.

I call up all the doctors I know. No one answers. They're all out in this beautiful weather. Minhoï can't breathe. Her face turns blue. I massage her heart, press my mouth on hers, and squeeze my breath into her throat. Then I drag her to the bathroom and run cold water over her face, the back of her neck, her heart, and her pulses. . .

Minhoï has thrown up, she's weathered the crisis. I don't let her out of my arms for three days. She tells me about her past life for the first time.

The night I met her, Minhoï asked me for coke and hash. Now I see why. She's no addict. Nor does she drink—not even wine—and she doesn't smoke.

In Paris she tried drugs, including LSD, a couple of times, because she can't stand life. Life in Paris. Life in Europe. Life anywhere in the world, ever since they pulled her up like a plant from the Vietnamese jungle of her childhood. At seven she began to realize that her nation and her world were being systematically exterminated, and that she couldn't go back because her relatives had all been wiped out. She could no longer endure life without drugging herself.

Now that Minhoï is certain of my love and knows that I can't live without her, and now that I'm beginning to understand her and we both realize that we've lived solely to meet each other, she starts regaining confidence in her own life. She becomes the yardstick by which I measure myself from now on.

She makes me conscious of what I'm living for. She manages to do something that no one has succeeded in doing all these years: She teaches me how to handle money. She convinces me that I don't have to treat every Tom, Dick, and Harry to caviar and champagne and that no one has the right to throw ten million lire a month out the window. We don't need a driver, who merely stands around and is never satisfied. We don't need a gardener who does nothing but continuously rake gravel in one and the same place. Minhoï tells me to dismiss my secretary, who keeps handing me the same unpaid bills, which I keep paying because I never check them. We don't need a cook who lugs my food to her home every month while serving us yesterday's leftovers. We don't need a butler and two maids. We don't have to have a Rolls-Royce or a Ferrari. And we can do without the *castello*. She asks me if I've forgotten what I really want. Have I forgotten my sailboat? My freedom?

I once agreed to buy the house from Count Marcello, a Venetian who owns the property on Via Appia Antica. But now I don't sign the sales contract. Minhoï is right. It's all bullshit. In a couple of years I'll be at the seashore, and in my "roaring forties" I'll forget all about the human ghettos and their prisons and lunatic asylums. The sums I demanded for my work and then squandered were tranquilizers for a life in which I felt hopelessly trapped.

We move out of the *castello*. I don't get back a penny of the money I put into it. I dismiss the servants. I keep only Clara, who's going to take care of our apartment on Flaminia Vecchia.

I'm still not completely cured when I give up the Rolls-Royce: I buy a Maserati instead.

Westerns. One after another. They get shittier and shittier, and the so-called directors get lousier and lousier. And the more incompetent they are, the more hostile they act. One of them is named Mario Costa. When I refuse to follow his orders, he threatens me: "I'll make sure you get kicked out of Italy!"

"Why? I haven't broken any law and I have a right to be here."

"In any case you'll never do another movie."

"You shouldn't have said that, you pathetic jerk. No one, aside from God and myself—and certainly not a worm like you—is going to decide when I stop making movies. And by then you'll be moldering in your grave!"

Biggi and Nastassja live in Munich. During the past year and a half, Biggi's never stopped hoping that we would get together again. I have to make it clear to her that I can never return. She doesn't know what Minhoï means to me.

In letters and endless phone conversations I try to explain it to Biggi. And eventually she agrees to the divorce.

Minhoï and I dash around to get a marriage license. When the registration official asks for the names of her parents, Minhoï starts trembling. She gets so choked up that she can't speak, and she clings to me. I take her into my arms. She tearfully whispers to me that she's an orphan and never knew her parents. I signal to the official to ask no more questions. The man has a heart and leaves the questions unanswered on the form. It's only when we reach the stairs that I get the full impact of what Minhoï has told me.

On May 2, a radiant spring Sunday, Minhoï and I get married in Rome. The ceremony at the Capitol has to be delayed for hours. The civil magistrate is rattled by the photographers' flashlights and the whirring TV and newsreel cameras.

"When do we start?" he shouts, feeling superfluous.

"When I say so," I retort. "This is my wedding!"

But the clicking and popping soon get too much for us. I take a long swig from the champagne bottle.

"Quick!" I shout to the magistrate.

The magistrate, a retired colonel with a sash, begins spouting his horrible formula.

"It's no use reeling all that off," I break in. "My wife speaks only French."

"I know French," says the former colonel, and his bloodless lips purse voluptuously to pour out his crap in French.

"Oh, no, not French," I correct myself. "She speaks only Chinese. Do you know Chinese too?"

The whole mob cracks up. Photographers and cameramen seize the opportunity and they click and whir like crazy.

"No, I don't," says the colonel, his face a bright crimson.

"Well, then you'd best hold your tongue," I say, reaching for the champagne bottle, which I've left with one of the photographers.

"If you don't behave as is suitable for such a dignified place, then I will refuse to perform the wedding," the insolent jerk snaps, removing his sash, without which he apparently can't say his bit.

"Keep your girdle on and finish up!" I scream, beside myself because I've finally lost patience with this matchmaker.

It must have dawned on him that he's gone too far, for he slips back into his sash, from which he'd crept halfway out like a Houdini. He limits himself to our names, dates of birth, nationality, date of wedding, and so forth.

Then he asks us if we agree to enter into the marriage. I burst out laughing.

"Why do you think we've put up with all this?!"

We sign the scrap of paper and, with the two girls who acted as our witnesses, we hop into our Maserati and dash over to George's, the most expensive restaurant in Rome. After the meal I smash all the plates and glasses and pay for the damage—it's worth it. I feel as if I've shattered the past.

Mario Costa is dead. Just as I prophesied, because he couldn't keep his damn trap shut. We sell off the Maserati and the trailer and buy a Land Rover. We pack in our haversacks and leave Rome before daybreak.

First we drive to Munich, where Werner Herzog is waiting for me. He's offered me the lead in a movie to be shot in Peru: *Aguirre: The Wrath of God.*

Biggi gives us the apartment because she's going to spend a year in Venezuela, where Nastassja is attending school.

Back in Munich I bump into Helmut von Gaza in the street. He's just back from an Italian prison, where he was locked up for seducing minor boys.

"What's become of the others?" I ask, trying to pep him up.

"They found Prince Kropotkin dead on a Spanish island. He'd been suffocated with a pillow."

"What about Gustl?"

"I married Gustl. So she did become an aristocrat after all before she died of cancer."

Herzog, who's producing the film, also wrote the script—and he wants to direct it, too. I promptly ask him how much money he's got.

When he visits me in my pad, he's so shy that he barely has the nerve to come in. Maybe it's just a ploy. In any case, he lingers at the threshold for such an idiotically long time that I practically have to drag him inside. Once he's here, he starts explaining the movie without even being asked. I tell him that I've read the script and I know the story. But he turns a deaf ear and just keeps talking and talking and talking. I start thinking that he'll never be able to stop talking even if he tries. Not that he talks quickly, "like a waterfall," as people say when someone talks fast and furious, pouring out the words. Quite the contrary: His speech is clumsy, with a toadlike indolence, long-winded, pedantic, choppy. The words tumble from his mouth in sentence fragments, which he holds back as much as possible, as if they were earning interest. It takes forever and a day for him to push out a clump of hardened brain snot. Then he writhes in painful ecstasy, as if he had sugar on his rotten teeth. A very slow blab machine. An obsolete model with a nonworking switch—it can't be turned off unless you cut off the electric power altogether. So I'd have to smash him in the kisser. No, I'd have to knock him unconscious. But even if he were unconscious, he'd keep talking. Even if his vocal cords were sliced through, he'd keep talking like a ventriloquist. Even if his throat were cut and his head were chopped off, speech balloons would still dangle from his mouth like gases emitted by internal decay.

I haven't the foggiest idea what he's talking about, except that he's high as a kite on himself for no visible reason, and he's enthralled by his own daring, which is nothing but dilettantish innocence. When he thinks I finally see what a great guy he is, he blurts out the bad news, explaining in a hardboiled tone about the shitty living and working conditions that lie ahead. He sounds like a judge handing down a well-deserved sentence. And, licking his lips as if he were talking about some culinary delicacy, he crudely and brazenly claims that all the participants are delighted to endure the unimaginable stress and deprivation in order to follow him, Herzog. Why, they would all risk their lives for him without batting an eyelash. He, in any case, will put all his eggs in one basket in order to attain his goal, no matter what it may cost, "do or die," as he puts it in his foolhardy way. And he tolerantly closes his eyes to the spawn of his megalomania, which he mistakes for genius. Granted, he sincerely confesses, he sometimes gets dizzy thinking about his own insane ideas—by which, however, he is simply carried away.

Then suddenly, out of a clear blue sky, he knocks me for a loop: He tries to make me believe that he's got a sense of humor. That is, he almost unintentionally, sort of carelessly hints at it—and, half in jest, he's embarrassed, as if caught with his pants down.

If he initially applied some cheap tricks to get me drunk, he now throws caution to the winds and starts lying through his teeth. He says he enjoys playing pranks; you can go and steal horses with him, and so forth. And since he's already confessed all that, he doesn't want to hide the fact that he can now laugh his head off at his own roguishness. While it's quite obvious that I've never in my life met anybody so dull, humorless, uptight, inhibited, mindless, depressing, boring, and swaggering, he blithely basks in the glory of the most pointless and most uninteresting punch lines of his braggadocio. Eventually he kneels before himself like a worshipper in front of his idol, and he remains in that position until somebody bends down and raises him from his humble self-worship. After dumping these tons of garbage (which stinks so horribly that I felt like puking), he actually pretends to be a naive, innocent, almost rustic hick—a poetic dreamer, or so he emphasizes, as if he were living in his own little world and didn't have the slightest notion of the brutal material side of things. But I can very easily tell that he considers himself ever so cunning, that he's waiting in ambush, dogging my every step and desperately trying to read my mind. He's racking his brain, trying to determine how he can outfox me in every clause of the contract. In short, he has every intention of outwitting me.

Still and all, I agree to do the movie—but only because of Peru. I don't even know where it is. Somewhere in South America, between the Pacific, the desert, and the glaciers, and in the most gigantic jungle on earth.

The script is illiterate and primitive. That's my big chance. The jungle smolders in it like something that infects you when you see it, a virus that invades you through your eyes and enters your bloodstream. I feel as if I knew this land with the magical name in some other lifetime. An imprisoned beast can never forget the reality of freedom. The caged bird cranes its neck through the bars to peer at the clouds racing by.

I tell Herzog that Aguirre has to be crippled because his power must not be contingent on his appearance. I'll have a hump. My right arm will be longer than my left, as long as an ape's. My left arm will be shortened so that since I'm a southpaw I have to carry my sword on the right side of my chest, and not in the normal way, on my hip. My left leg will be longer than my right, so that I have to drag it along. I'll advance sideways, like a crab. I'll have long hair—down to my shoulders by the time we start shooting. I won't need a phony hump, or a costumer or a makeup man smearing me up. I will *be* crippled because I *want* to be. I'll get my spine used to my crippling. Just as I'm beautiful when I want to be. Ugly. Strong. Feeble. Short or tall. Old or young. When I want to be. The way I hold myself will lift the cartilage from my joints and use up their gelatin. I will be crippled—today, now, on the spot, this very instant. Henceforth everything will be geared to my condition: costumes, cuirasses, scabbards, weapons, helmets, boots, and so on.

I determine the costume: I tear a couple of pages out of books showing Old Master paintings. I explain the changes I want, and I fly to Madrid with Herzog to find armor and weapons. After days of rummaging through mountains of rusty scrap metal, I fish out a sword, a dagger, a helmet, and a cuirass, which has to be trimmed because I'm a cripple.

Traveling all the way to the jungle is the worst kind of agony. Penned up in old-fashioned trains, wrecks of trucks, and cagelike buses, we eat and camp out like pigs. Sometimes in Quonset huts or other torture chambers. We can't even think about getting any sleep. We can barely breathe. No toilets, no way to wash. Many days and nights. I stay dressed day and night; otherwise the mosquitoes would eat me alive. I feel as if I'm standing under a nonstop jet of boiling water. Indoors the heat is lethal. But outdoors it's just as venomously hot. Whole mountains of garbage, inundated by a cesspool of human piss and shit. The populace tosses the ripped-out eyes and innards of slaughtered animals into this sewage from hell. Huge carrion birds the size of great Danes strut and squat on this horror as if it were their private playground.

Wherever I go I see these disgusting Quonset huts. If only I didn't have to lay eyes on these half-finished cement barracks with corrugated-iron roofs. Nothing is completed. Everything is abandoned halfway through, as if it had been surprised by the decay. Iron window shades and fences jeer at you. Why?

Garbage heaps, sewage, eyes, innards, breeding grounds, carrion birds and—TV antennas. Just like in New York, Paris, London, Tokyo, or Hong Kong, but more loathsome.

The road into the wilderness is long and tortuous—but no abomination is too unbearable to escape this hell on earth.

And as if Minhoï and I were to be rewarded for our getaway, we feel that our hair is becoming silkier, our skin softer, like the fur of wild beasts that have been set free; our bodies are lither and suppler, our muscles are tensing for a leap, our senses are more alert and receptive. Minhoï has never been more beautiful since the tiger trap in Vietnam.

Swelling up from mosquito bites without having eaten or drunk anything, we reel toward the next leg of our journey.

A little Inca girl stands on the runway for military aircraft. She's got a small monkey on her arm and she wants to sell it. But the terrified monkey clings to the girl, afraid that the buyer might take it away.

Here we clamber into ancient, battered transport planes for paratroopers, and the propellers rage in my temples like pneumatic hammers. A pungent stench, the odor of gasoline, hunger, thirst, headaches, and stomach cramps, and no toilet here either. Pent up and huddling together on the hot steel floor of the windowless plane. Hour after hour. During the flight each passenger in turn can spend one moment climbing from the plane's tomblike rear into the cockpit and peering out through a tiny window. Far below, the green ocean, thousands of miles of jungle, with a yellow tangle of vipers winding through it—the biggest river network in the world.

Next, single-engine amphibians that have to nose-dive to avoid missing that slim chance when the jungle opens—and promptly closes again.

Then more trucks and bus cages. Indian canoes. And finally the rafts, on which we stand, chained to one another, to the cargo, and to the raft, as we shoot over raging rapids. Our fists clutching ropes, as if we were making a laughable effort to halt runaway horses by clasping their reins even though the horses have already plunged off a cliff. The raft is too heavily loaded; the Indians warned us. But blowhard Herzog, arrogant and ignorant as he is, mocked their warnings and called them ridiculous. We're all in costume and fully equipped, because we wanted to shoot while riding the rapids. Herzog misses out on the grandest and most incomprehensible things because he doesn't even notice them. I keep yelling at the stupid cameraman through the thunder of our nose-dive, telling him to at least roll the camera because we're risking our lives. But all he says is that Herzog ordered him not to press the button without his, Herzog's, say-so.

I'm disgusted by this whole movie mob—they act as if you're supposed to shoot a flick in a pigpen.

My heavy leather costume, my long boots, helmet, cuirass, sword, and dagger weigh over thirty pounds. If the raft were to capsize because of Herzog's delusions of grandeur, I'd be doomed. I'd be unable to get out of my cuirass and leather doublet, which are buckled in back. Besides, the rapids are cut through with a chain of jagged reefs, and their razorlike tips lurk under the spume like piranhas, sometimes even looming out of the lashed waters.

And so, like a fired missile, we hurtle downstream while the steep waves attack our raft like hysterical bulls and clap together way over our heads. The air is filled with foam like white drool.

Suddenly, as if the plunging water had furiously spat us out, we glide almost soundlessly along a calm and powerful branch of the river in the middle of the jungle and deeper and deeper into its interior. There it lies: the wilderness. It seizes me. Sucks me in—hot and naked like the sweaty, sticky, naked body of a lovesick woman with all her mysteries and wonders. I gape at the jungle and can't stop marveling and worshipping. . . .

Animals as graceful as in fairy tales . . . Plants strangling one another in their embraces . . . Orchids stretched on stumps of rotten trees like young girls on the laps of dirty old men . . . Radiant metallic-blue butterflies as big as my head . . . Pearly floods of butterflies alighting on my mouth and my hands—the panther's eye blending into the flowers . . . Frothy streams of flowers; green, red, and yellow clouds of birds . . . Silver suns . . . Violet fogs . . . The kissing lips of the fish . . . The golden song of the fish . . .

We're going to be living exclusively on rafts for the next two months. Drifting downstream toward the Amazon. Minhoï and I have a raft to ourselves. We either float way ahead of the other rafts or lag behind as far as possible. When night falls, we moor our raft to lianas. Then I lie awake, diving into the galaxies and starry archipelagoes, which hang down so low that I can reach out and feel them.

We have a small Indian canoe that we tie to the raft, towing it along. If I don't have to shoot, we sneak away in the canoe, searching for cracks in the jungle wall. Sometimes we penetrate a tight slit that may have never existed before and that will instantly close up again. The water inside the flooded forest is so still that it barely seems affected by our paddles, which we dip cautiously to avoid making any noise.

Perhaps no boat has ever glided across these waters, perhaps no man has set foot here in millions of years. Not even a native. We wait without speaking. For hours on end. I feel the jungle coming nearer, the animals, the plants, which have been watching us for a long while without showing themselves. For the first time in my life I have no past. The present is so powerful that it snuffs out all bygones. I know that I'm free, truly free. I am the bird that has managed to break out of its cage—that spreads its wings and soars into the sky. I take part in the universe.

Although I constantly try to keep out of his way, Herzog sticks to me like a shithouse fly. The mere thought of his existence here in the wilderness turns my stomach. When I see him approaching in the distance, I yell at him to halt. I shout that he stinks. That he disgusts me. That I don't want to listen to his bullshit. That I can't stand him!

I keep hoping he'll attack me. Then I'll shove him into a side branch of the river, where the still waters teem with murderous piranhas, and I'll watch them shred him to bits. But he doesn't do it; he doesn't attack me. He seems unfazed when I treat him like a piece of shit. Besides, he's too chicken. He attacks only when he thinks he'll keep the upper hand. Herzog pounces on a native, an Indian who's taken the job to keep his family from starving and puts up with anything for fear of being kicked out. Or else he assails a stupid, untalented actor or a helpless animal. Today he ties up a llama in a canoe and sends it tearing down the rapids—supposedly because this is required by the plot of the movie, which he wrote himself! I find out about the llama only when it's too late. The animal is already drifting toward the whirlpool, and no one can save it. I spot it rearing in its mortal fear and yanking at its fetters, struggling to escape its gruesome execution. Then it vanishes behind a bend of the river, shattering against the jagged reefs and dying a torturous death by drowning.

Now I hate that killer's guts. I shriek into his face that I want to see him croak like the llama that he executed. He should be thrown alive to the crocodiles! An anaconda should strangle him slowly! A poisonous spider should sting him and paralyze his lungs! The most venomous serpent should bite him and make his brain explode! No panther claws should rip open his throat—that would be much too good for him! No! The huge red ants should piss into his lying eyes and gobble up his balls and his guts! He should catch the plague! Syphilis! Malaria! Yellow fever! Leprosy! It's no use; the more I wish him the most gruesome deaths, the more he haunts me.

We drift down the river all day long, shooting endlessly. Night falls. Nevertheless we all gather ashore, where a night scene is to be filmed. Herzog and his production morons haven't even supplied illumination—no flashlight, nothing. The night is pitch-black and we keep falling on our faces, one after another. We tumble into swampy holes, stumble over roots and tree trunks, run into the knives of thorny palms, get our feet caught in lianas, and almost drown. The area is teeming with snakes, which kill at night after storing up their reserves of poison throughout the day. We're completely exhausted, and once again it's been an eternity since we ate or drank anything, including water. No one has a clue as to what, where, and why we're supposed to shoot in this garbage dump, which stinks to high heaven.

Suddenly, in full armor, I plunge into a swamp hole. The harder I try to get my body out of the mud, the deeper I sink. Finally, in a blind fury, I yell, "I'm splitting! Even if I have to paddle all the way to the Atlantic!"

"If you split, I'll ruin you!" says that wimp Herzog, looking scared of the chance he's taking.

"Ruin me how, you bigmouth?" I ask him, hoping he'll attack me so I can kill him in self-defense.

"I'll shoot you," he babbles, like a paralytic whose brain has softened. "Eight bullets are for you, and the ninth is for me!"

Whoever heard of a pistol or a rifle with nine bullets? There's no such thing! Besides, he has no firearm; I know it for a fact. He's got no rifle or pistol, not even a machete. Not even a penknife. Not even a bottle opener. I'm the only one with a rifle: a Winchester. I have a special permit from the Peruvian government. To buy bullets I had to spend days on end running my legs off from one police station to the next for signatures, stamps, all that shit.

"I'm waiting, you vermin," I say, truly glad that things have reached this pass. "I'm going back to my raft now and I'll be waiting for you. If you come, I'll shoot you down."

Then I stride back to our raft, where Minhoï has fallen asleep in her hammock; I load my Winchester and I wait.

At around four A.M. Herzog comes paddling up to our raft and apologizes.

Herzog is a miserable, hateful, malevolent, avaricious, money-hungry, nasty, sadistic, treacherous, cowardly creep. His so-called "talent" consists of nothing but tormenting helpless creatures and, if necessary, torturing them to death or simply murdering them. He doesn't care about anyone or anything except his wretched career as a so-called filmmaker. Driven by a pathological addiction to sensationalism, he creates the most senseless difficulties and dangers, risking other people's safety and even their lives—just so he can eventually say that he, Herzog, has beaten seemingly unbeatable odds. For his movies he hires retards and amateurs whom he can push around (and allegedly hypnotize!), and he pays them starvation wages or zilch. He also uses freaks and cripples of every conceivable size and shape, merely to look interesting. He doesn't have the foggiest inkling of how to make movies. He doesn't even try to direct the actors anymore. Long ago, when I ordered him to keep his trap shut, he gave up asking me whether I'm willing to carry out his stupid and boring ideas.

If he wants to shoot another take because he, like most directors, is insecure, I tell him to go fuck himself. Usually the first take is okay, and I won't repeat anything—certainly not on his say-so. Every scene, every angle, every shot is determined by me, and I refuse to do anything unless I consider it right. So I can at least partly save the movie from being wrecked by Herzog's lack of talent.

After eight weeks most of the crew are still living like pigs. Penned together on rafts like cattle going to slaughter, they eat garbage fried in lard, and, most dangerous of all, they guzzle the river water, which can give them all kinds of diseases, even leprosy. None of them is vaccinated against any of these deadly scourges.

Minhoï and I cook alone on our raft. We dump soil on the wooden floor and start a fire. If either of us dives into the river to swim or wash, the other watches out for piranhas. Normally we have nothing to cook, and we feed on fantastic jungle fruits, which contain enough liquid. But these heavenly fruits are hard to get since we float downstream almost nonstop, and often there are long stretches when we can't go ashore to look for produce.

Eventually we start feeling our malnutrition. We grow weaker; my belly swells up, and I'm all skin and bones. The others are even worse off.

The wilderness isn't interested in arrogant bigmouth movie makers. It has no pity for those who flout its laws.

At three in the morning we're violently awakened on our rafts. We're told there's no time for breakfast, even coffee. We'll only be traveling for twenty minutes, up to the next Indian village on the river. There we'll get everything. The alleged twenty minutes turn into eighteen hours. Herzog has exaggerated again.

With our heads in heavy steel helmets that get so hot from the pounding sun that they burn us, we're exposed to the ruthless heat for days on end, without shelter, without the slightest shade, without food or drink. People drop like flies. First the girls, then the men, one after another. Almost everyone's legs are festering from mosquito bites and distorted by swelling.

Toward evening, we finally reach an Indian village, but it's blazing away. Herzog set it on fire, and even though we're starving and dying of thirst, reeling, exhausted after eighteen hours of infernal heat, we have to attack the village—just as it says in the mindless script.

We spend the night in the village, camping in the miserable barracks that haven't burned down. Giant rats insolently frolic about, circling closer and closer, drawing nearer and nearer to our bodies. They probably sense how feeble we are, and they're waiting for the right time to pounce on us. More and more of them appear.

Someone tells Herzog that his people can't continue if we don't get better food and especially water. Herzog answers that they can drink from the river. Besides, he goes on, they ought to collapse from exhaustion and starvation: That's what's called for in the script. Herzog and his head producer have their own secret cache of fresh vegetables, fruit, French camembert, olive oil, and beverages.

As we drift along, one of the Americans falls dangerously ill; he's got yellow fever and a high temperature, and he's writhing on the raft. Herzog claims that the American is malingering; he refuses to let him be brought ashore at Iquitos, which is getting closer and closer.

When we're near Iquitos and our rafts drift into the Amazon, we ignore Herzog and carry our patient ashore, to a hospital. We take the day off in order to buy the most necessary food, mineral water, bandages, medicines, and salves for mosquito bites.

Ten weeks later the final scene of the movie is shot: Aguirre, the sole survivor, his mind gone, is on his raft with several hundred monkeys, floating downstream toward the Atlantic. Most of the monkeys on the raft jump into the water and swim back to the jungle. A gang of trappers plans to sell them to American laboratories for experiments. Herzog has borrowed them. When only some hundred monkeys are left, waiting to dive into the waves and regain their freedom, I order Herzog to film right away. I know that this opportunity won't knock twice. When the take is done, the last monkeys spring into the river and swim toward the jungle, which receives them.

Minhoï and I have to spend three days in the Iquitos hospital getting vitamin transfusions.

When the jet plane, amid the murderous booming of its turbines, rises steeply, leaving the green sea of the jungle far below me, I launch into a crying jag. My soul is so deeply shaken and my body so violently convulsed that I think my heart is about to rip open. I hide my face from the other passengers, pressing it against the window and trying to stifle my sobs. Imagine someone weeping because he has to leave the wilderness, and because he's not happy and grateful to be back in the civilization ghettos, which are haunted by madness! If it's a human being, he'll be locked up in a nuthouse, and if it's an animal, it'll be put to sleep.

On the way back, Minhoï and I fly around the globe again. When we finally reach Vietnam, Minhoï is happy. In Saigon a Vietnamese teenager spits at me in the ricksha because he thinks I'm an American.

Once again, someone spitting at me! First it was the Belgians because I wasn't American. Then American strafers shoot my mother down. And now here in Vietnam, where Minhoï was orphaned by the dirtiest of all wars, someone spits at me because he thinks I'm American! Maybe the boy thinks that I'm one of those men who at Christmas sent home color Polaroids showing the corpses of massacred women and children. Minhoï, next to me, cries. I jump out of the ricksha to chase after the teenager, who scurries away—but then a Vietnamese soldier sticks a pistol into my chest, releasing the safety catch. I have to pull myself together, choke back tears of rage, at this glaring injustice. Nevertheless I love this nation more than any other in the world.

The streets are filled with barricades of sandbags. A little boy, at most seven or eight years old, stands there with gaping mouth and eyes, performing a pantomime. I don't understand what he means! Minhoï's caught on. His body language says that he's seen me in a movie in which I play an American soldier who, with gaping mouth and eyes, croaks in the hatch of a tank.

So we're back in the human hell, the hell of adults.

Since we're broke, I accept the very next offer that comes down the pike. Like a streetwalker who takes any john. We have to go to Holland, where the crap is being shot.

The American director (the word makes me sick) has been dumped by his girlfriend, Joan, who's run off with Maria Schneider. Now the two girls are fucking their brains out. Maria has just finished shooting that mindless flick *Last Tango in Paris*, and thinks she's hot stuff because Marlon Brando fucked her up the ass with butter. She drags around books containing photos of Bedouins, which she shows everyone, and she hands out cocaine. She shows me the books too. These junkies always think that freedom has something to do with their fucking drugs. Why does she show everyone these pictures of desert Bedouins? I've lived with Bedouins, and they don't need to trip on drugs. That sleazy bitch gives Minhoï some coke behind my back.

In Amsterdam the Dutch have set up an entire museum for Van Gogh, squeezing his paintings together like convicts in an overcrowded prison, like animals trapped in a zoo. Five paces to the left. Five to the right. Five in a circle. Here Van Gogh is spotlighted by electric lights behind steel doors and secured with electric alarm systems, like a man condemned to death. Every painting has a government stamp on it, like a prison number.

The visitors line up as if they're in a fast-food joint. They shuffle forward in fits and starts. Next! They clutch information leaflets about why Van Gogh sliced off his ear. Some visitors look battered. Others gape blankly, irritated, embarrassed. Some whisper jokes, giggling hysterically. A girl trembles. A man has tears in his eyes. Many hunt for the exit from this stuffy museum, where probably no window is ever opened. For lack of space the bleeding suns are squeezed one on top of another like dying corpses in a mass grave. The smoldering sunflowers. These hearts aching so dreadfully with passion and yearning. Yes, dying corpses of executed men! They're still alive! Like lambs in slaughterhouses, piled up on other dying lambs after their throats have been cut—then a slaughterer treads on the artery to make sure they bleed properly.

I dash out of Amsterdam's Van Gogh Museum. I have to puke in the street.

I mustn't end up like that!

I love Minhoï more than anything else in the world. I love her more than my life. I love the magical beauty of her face and body. I love her enchanting soul, which is full of wonders and full of mysteries. She is my wife and my beloved and the future mother of my son, whom she will bear. And yet our life together grows more and more painful. She's not to blame for our horrible fights—they're all my fault. I'm so hypersensitive, my imagination is so immense, and my reactions are so violent, a natural catastrophe that tears everything along, leaving only devastation behind. The contradictory forces in me fight to the death and threaten to rip me apart. I feel as if I have to jump off a tower!

Often Minhoï is so scared that she can't do anything but weep. Then she throws her arms out to me as if trying to stop the rage that's destroying me, to stop it with her delicate, beautiful hands.

Minhoï likewise loves me more than anything else in the world. But she can't stand my wild mood swings anymore. Everything about me is gigantic and measureless. Even my concern for her. Even my tenderness. Even my love. In any case, Minhoï says so. The violence of my feelings brutalizes and bewilders her soul.

"Help me!" we sometimes scream at the same time, clinging to one another as if we both were drowning.

We often talk about our son. Then everything is fine, and we're happy. We wonder what continent he'll be born on. We make plans and we dream about where our son will grow up. Maybe we'll go to the mountainous jungles of Vietnam; Minhoï is so homesick for them. Or we'll go to the Himalayas, directly to the Ama Dablam. Or we'll live in Tierra del Fuego, where the glaciers float in the raging waters of Cape Horn. Or should we sail across the oceans and never again set foot on shore?

Making films means money. With money we can buy our freedom from slavery. So I'll keep making flicks. First two in Athens and on Crete. One in Paris. One in Barcelona. Minhoï accompanies me everywhere. I can't take a step or draw a breath without her. But our life together has become impossible. It's a relentlessly vicious circle from which there seems to be no escape—unless we split up. I refuse to think that horrible thought. But both Minhoï and I know that a split is racing toward us like a monstrous wave, faster and faster, and that nothing can stop it. Separation is the only thing that can keep us from destroying ourselves.

We're back in Rome, where we rent a penthouse apartment opposite Visconti's and catercorner from the Villa Ada Park, which used to be Mussolini's residence. If a photographer's calls become unbearable, I agree to meet him at the entrance to the park. He doesn't realize that I can watch him from the roof of our building—all I have to do is climb the fire escape from our terrace. If he looks all around because I haven't shown up, and he happens to glance in my direction, I duck behind the chimney. After a while I cautiously emerge. I do that until the photographer gets fed up and leaves. For a long time I haven't wanted to be photographed by anyone. I don't want anyone to photograph my soul, which is being etched more and more deeply in my face. Besides, a photograph is a kind of prison, where my feelings will be tortured to death.

I've fallen asleep on the deck chair on our terrace and when I awake, Minhoï is gone. It won't sink in; it's so awful that I don't get it. I feel as if someone had knocked both my legs off with one stroke. I feel as if I've been shoved back into the horror, the grave I've been trying to dig my way out of all my life, always scared to death. It takes me a long time—then the truth suddenly shoots through my head as if someone had fired a bullet into my temple. Everything inside me is shrill. Tattered. Bloody. Everything shrieks. An alarm goes off. Shrieks, shrieks, shrieks for Minhoï. I dash out of the apartment. She left the door ajar—probably to avoid making any noise. I keep yelling, "Minhoï!" I break into a run; it has to be a joke! Maybe she's playing hide-and-seek. I laugh. But my laughter isn't genuine. The alarm in my head signals something that I've been fearing for a long time.

I dash into the bathroom and yank the shower curtain aside as if I were sure that I've discovered her hiding place. I peer into the tub. Into the niche containing the toilet and the bidet. I crawl under the bed—then jump up, as if I'd heard a noise that she has made while changing her hiding place. I yank all the closet doors open. I whirl around as if to surprise her, in case she tries to sneak into a new hiding place. I sprint back to the terrace. I climb up to the roof. Back into the apartment: shower, tub, commode, bidet, under the bed, in closets, even in drawers. Yes, even drawers and bookcases, behind the books, in the kitchen, in the icebox, in the kitchen cabinets, in the oven . . . My head is spinning. . . . I bump my forehead. . . . I grab the receiver . . . unable to dial a single digit. What for? No one'll know where she is. I dash down the five flights—the elevator is too slow for me. She's not in the garage. I race back up the five flights. Again the terrace, the roof, the kitchen, the bed, the closets, the bathroom, the shower, the tub, the commode, the bidet . . . And once again down the five flights, this time out into the street.

It's almost dark. Where should I go? Where should I look for her? My paralyzing numbness slowly settles, like gaseous fumes, as if I were getting on my feet again after being clubbed to the ground. As if hard on her heels, I tear off haphazardly in one direction for miles on end. Then in the opposite direction. Then I hang a sharp right. A sharp left. I must have stepped on broken glass—I'm bleeding like a pig. I didn't notice; I haven't even noticed that I'm barefoot. I run back. Once again up the five flights . . . this time directly from the street entrance, without passing through the courtyard and the garage. I couldn't bear to run into the concierge. . . . Who knows— maybe Minhoï is back again? Once I'm back in our apartment, I feel so dizzy that I can't stay on my feet. My knees buckle; I cry, begging for Minhoï's return! I don't know who I'm praying to. My prayer is aimed at the universe. At life! At love! I pray that I may be tortured, that I may be hurt—as long as I get Minhoï back. Yes! Let them pour all pains and torments on me, all the disgusting garbage that people are capable of inflicting on one another. So long as I don't have to live without my Minhoï! I also pray to Minhoï. I pray to our son: "You are the light that shines for me in my darkness. Never lose your faith in me, just as I can never lose my faith in you!"

The doorbell rings. I'm so startled, my body feels as if I'd had an electric shock. When I open the door, Minhoï is standing on the threshold. Her childlike hands are clutching a small floral wreath that she holds out to me. My God! Do you first have to go through hell in order to be as happy as I am now?

From now on I'm obsessively haunted by the fear that Minhoï could leave me at any moment. What should I do? How should I act in the future? (As if I could be any way other than as Nature has created me!)

Maybe she can't stand the way I dress? Should I throw all my clothes away? What should I put on? Maybe she wants me to restyle my hair? Shorter? Or a lot longer? Maybe she doesn't like my being blond? Or having blue eyes? Maybe I don't tell her often enough how beautiful she is? That's not possible; no one in the world can tell a woman how beautiful she is more often than I tell Minhoï. Don't I tell her often enough that I love her? I say it so often that I think she doesn't want to hear it so often! Why shouldn't I keep saying it over and over again, a thousand times, a million times! The words "I love you" are so beautiful when you really mean them. Have I never told her how intelligent she is, or have I not told her often enough? My God, how often have I done the wrong thing, said the wrong thing? Am I incapable of treating her right? Haven't I told her often enough how much I like the things she cooks for me? Don't I say it several times a day, whenever I eat? Have I unwittingly forgotten to say so? Don't I thank her enough for everything she does for me? When she washes or fixes something for me? Should I buy her more clothes? Or rings and necklaces? Does she resent me for not earning enough at the moment because I've alienated everyone? Doesn't she know that it's only a question of time before I'm back making as many pictures as I want, and that no one can stop me? Is it taking too long for her? Should I accept any movie, no matter how far away, just so that we can get out of here, now, instantly?

I can achieve anything I like. I'm capable of doing anything that's asked of me.

I know it's all absurd. Among people, I would only get more emotionally deformed than I already am. *I'm* to blame! *I!* I'm the only reason she'll leave me. Not only *as* I am, but the very fact *that* I am! All my love, all my good resolutions and efforts, can't hold out against the burning lava that comes pouring out of the volcano of my innards and often has such devastating effects. And it may be too late each time. Each time. I'm not afraid of anything. Only that Minhoï may leave me—at any moment. Daytime, nighttime—I don't have the nerve to step from one room to another without leaving the door wide open, even the bathroom door. Meanwhile, Minhoï says she doesn't want to leave the bathroom door open! I'm scared she might climb out the bathroom window: The fire escape leads to the roof, and from there you can flee across other terraces. I don't dare shower, much less wash my hair, because I might not hear the apartment door opening. Sometimes I race out of the shower to see whether Minhoï is still here. At night I often sit up and reach for her. At times I scream because I don't feel her there. The bed is empty. I switch on the light and look for her everywhere. She's sitting on the commode, half asleep. I never leave the house without her. I don't even let her go shopping alone. I make no appointments with anybody. Not without Minhoï. In this way we're gonna starve to death, for I never have money if I'm not working. It's worst when I have to shoot. Minhoï doesn't want to come along because it's strenuous and mind-numbing. Besides, I wouldn't have a calm minute if I was standing in front of the camera and not seeing her uninterruptedly.

If I'm filming, or if I just have to talk to someone, all I can think about is Minhoï and getting back to her. The instant I'm done with work, I yell for the car, and every passing second is a stab in my heart, and I think I'm losing it. Once I'm at the apartment door, I first listen. If there's only silence, I'm terrified that Minhoï is gone. If I hear a noise, I know she's home.

This is my living hell. And there's no end in sight.

Whenever we go to the park of the Villa Ada, we feel as if we're far away, in our future. We meet a friend of Minhoï's, a girl she went to school with in Paris. She's got her newborn baby and she lets Minhoï hold it so that Minhoï can feel what it's like to hold a baby. But Minhoï looks bewildered and tries to return the baby swiftly, like a mother who's accidentally being given the wrong child. When her friend doesn't take the baby back right away because she's preparing a fresh diaper, Minhoï hands it to me. But I don't want to keep it either. When I feel the weight of the tiny, heavy body in my arms, I can't stand the fact that this isn't my son that I'm holding.

We have only a Mini Cooper, but it runs like an antelope. And since I don't have any filming scheduled during the next two weeks, we toss a tent and a haversack in the backseat and take off. Normandy, Brittany, England.

From London we race through the night all the way to Land's End. Portsmouth. Plymouth. This is where Chichester embarked for Australia and Cape Horn. And Chay Blyth. Nonstop around the globe, against all winds and currents. And this is where the sailboats embark on the solo race across the Atlantic.

We scurry about for days on end, looking at all the sailboats and their crews, who are making the final preparations. I feel the same pain that a convict must feel when another inmate is released while he himself has to stay behind. The air has the pungent smell of freedom, which hurts so badly but feels so good. The convict presses his face against the bars, staring, staring, staring! Even if it's then harder to endure incarceration.

Today, as the sailboats head for the open sea, I feel as if I'm back in the jet plane rising from the airstrip in Peru, leaving the jungle far below. And again I have to press my fist against my mouth to keep from screaming.

We travel on, all the way to the rugged coast, where the Atlantic booms and surges, lashed by the icy wind. Where the tide grabs at you, hurling the ocean back even more wildly. No human being can be seen anywhere. Only shrubs, ripped out by the wind and dashing like clouds over the slopes. I feel as if we had broken out of the deadly tomb of civilization, with the remnants of torn chains on our metal collars, on our wrists and ankles. For moments at a time I forget the insidious traps that human society lays for anyone who has the insane idea of crossing the boundary.

A uniformed guard eighty-sixes us from the "nature preserve." We have to take down our tent; you're allowed to pitch a tent only on camping grounds. Ghettos. We wait till it's dark again. Then we creep back into the bushes.

At the crack of dawn, so early that no ghetto guard can stink up the place, we return to the cliffs and light a fire.

We have to cook for ourselves because we never manage to get food around here. We keep arriving too late. Sometimes only five minutes. The personnel always gives us dirty, suspicious looks as if we had insulted the entire nation by not showing up punctually for chow. In other words, because we haven't eaten punctually like everyone else. As if this rubbish weren't disgusting enough that we can't eat it without getting stomach cramps. Everything is oversalted and hard or mushy. As if it weren't sick and arrogant enough that they don't serve beer between two and six in the afternoon. Just because some drunken slut of a queen had the sadistic idea that only she can get sloshed! And then that fish and chips!

Driving back through Brittany, I get into an argument with Minhoï because we're reapproaching the ghetto. I feel as if it's not me raging and screaming, as if I'm hearing and seeing myself raging and screaming and spewing out horrible words and insults. Like in dreams, or in a movie special effect, where a person splits in two. Good separating from evil. An astral body emerges from him and sits down next to him. That's what I feel like. I see the horrible scope of what's happening, and I imagine that my body has to be shattered by this terrible, earth-shaking rage. And that my innards have to rip apart. That my soul has to bleed to death in this carnage. But, as I have said, I see it all as an outsider. I feel the pain, but I feel it as someone else's pain.

Minhoï wants me to stop the car. She gets out and runs across a meadow. When I get out of the car to run after her, I feel such a horrible stabbing in my heart that I shriek and roll on the ground. It's like someone piercing my heart nonstop. I've often had shooting pains there, but they've never been this awful.

I don't know how long I've been rolling on the ground when Minhoï returns to the car and hands me some flowers that she's picked. I'm infinitely thankful to her for her sweet love. But the knife stabs in my heart remain.

I agree to do a photo romance in Monte Carlo. It's very well paid, and the poses you're shot in are no more feeble-minded than what those sleazy directors want. A photo romance takes three to five days. I ask whether I can sign up immediately for fifty or a hundred.

Minhoï wants our son. Now. Today. This instant! She begs me, weeping. I promise her. I yearn for our son as much as she does. But first I want to find a place; I'm like an animal that builds a protective nest for its young.

We drop off our tents in Rome and fly to Paris, where Andrzej Zulawski wants me for his movie *L'Important c'est d'aimer (That Most Important Thing: Love)*. At least a Pole for once, I think.

In Paris Minhoï is pregnant. At the crack of dawn she comes running to me in the bathroom, where I'm shaving, and she shows me a tiny round tab that looks like a leaf under a microscope. It's changed color in her urine. That's how she can tell she's pregnant. After showing me the tab, she very carefully puts it on the glass shelf over the sink, as if it were a baby carriage holding our son.

As of that moment, my insides light up and everything around me lights up. Everything is illuminated, everything. I see flowery meadows wherever I look, even though Paris is gray and cold and nasty. All the people I see appear cheerful and friendly. I feel as if I were just being born. Everything is new for me, and everything seems good and uncorrupted. Nanhoï is growing in me just as he is in Minhoï's belly. We are constantly busy with preparations. We run around for baby linen, inspect a lot of cribs and carriages; Minhoï sews bedclothes and baby shirts from floral textiles in the colors of spring. I have shirts made for me from the same material so that they'll match my son's. We purchase baby bottles and diapers and everything we need, so that our darling baby boy will feel fine and lack for nothing.

I now hate making films as I've never hated it before. All I want to do is prepare for the arrival of my son, whom I love more than anything else in the world. But I have no choice, I have to make movies, because we constantly need money. Now more than ever.

The production company for which Zulawski is filming can't sign a contract with me because the German distributor, who's cofinancing the project, doesn't want me. The reason is that the miserable maggot who's negotiating with the French company wants to get back at me. Years and years ago, he had the hots for Erika when I was fucking her. But Erika wanted to screw only with me. That's why this maggot hated me.

Zulawski says he won't make the movie without me. I don't give a shit about the film. I need bread.

I fly to Munich, where Sabine also lives. Not only is she fucking Herr von S., who heads the distributor's Munich branch, but she's also fucking the American millionaire who owns the whole kit and caboodle, especially in the United States. So I call her up and we make a date. When she opens the door, she's wearing her dressing gown, which is made in such a way that I'd rather fuck right through it standing up. With one leg on a chair. Between her tits. In her mouth. From behind her, up her ass. She's a fabulous slut. That mouth must have slurped a lot of dick in its time. Her eyes are fuck-feverish, set deep in their sockets. She's very, very seductive, very sweet, and very, very cunning. She starts right off by asking me not to tell her guy in America (who, incidentally, is married and has furnished her entire kitschy apartment) anything about Herr von S., who is likewise married and will be showing up in a couple of minutes. At the same time this serves as an excuse: Unfortunately, I can't poke her today. Which means: there's always tomorrow. But at least I can personally tell Herr von S. the whole scandalous skinny.

Just as I'm nibbling on some of the candy that she's offered me, the doorbell rings and Herr von S. is here. I tell him my story, adding that the shithead who refuses to let me appear in the movie is merely Herr von S.'s employee but has gone over his head in making such crucial decisions. Herr von S. hits the ceiling. He promises me on a stack of Bibles (with Sabine as my witness) that he'll take care of the whole matter first thing in the morning. I split, after telling Sabine at the apartment door that Zulawski will give her a role in the flick if she makes sure that it all works out right. So everything's okay.

Meanwhile I've been offered another flick in Paris, *Nuit d'Or* ("Golden Night"). So I'll make this dilettantish junk immediately. Then the Zulawski film.

Now everyone wants to play Kean, the greatest British actor of the nineteenth century. Jean-Paul Sartre has done a stage adaptation of Alexandre Dumas's novel. It's to be mounted at the Théâtre de la Ville. But I can't come to terms about my wages with that fussy queer of a director! What odd conceptions of salaries they have here! Finally he agrees to a figure. He bitches that it's twice what Ingrid Bergman got, and *she* was paid top dollar.

None of that interests me. All I'm interested in is getting more money. That's all! I finally sign the lousy contract.

At our first meeting Sartre is very nice, delighted that I'll be playing Kean. He chows down and guzzles and smokes like a chimney. No wonder he's sick, and almost blind despite his thick, polished glasses. I've skimmed his adaptation and I don't bother cudgeling my brain about the pseudo-socialist bullshit in this outrageously awful play. We've got a whole year to go until the premiere.

I still haven't recovered from Zulawski's intellectual jerking off when I dig out *Kean*, for I have a sneaking suspicion that I won't be able to rescue Sartre's clunker. While reading, I cross out almost every page and try to splice in more and more soliloquies from the Shakespeare plays that Kean performed in. Like cuts in a film— flashes, flashbacks, closeups. But it's no panacea. By the time I'm done, there's almost nothing but soliloquies: Hamlet, Romeo, Richard III, Othello, Macbeth, Mark Antony, King Lear. I go to the fidgety director and tell him to give Sartre my corrections. Maybe he can rewrite the whole crap. Sartre's advisers reply that he refuses to let anyone alter even one comma in his text. Has Sartre forgotten that he plagiarized it all from Dumas's novel? And plagiarized badly at that! He's botched it!

After the publication of my first book, I was compared to Céline and I was asked whether I'd like to play him in a movie. That was the first time I'd heard his name, and I still haven't read a word of his writings. Meanwhile I've learned what he said about Sartre: "That runty, nearsighted shit worm, that Sartre—where was he when the blood flowed? Crawling around in the innards of the damned like the tiny ball of shit that he is! That tiny, phony pinworm, that worm from other people's shit!"

We find a studio apartment in the Marais, the Jewish section of Paris.

The studio is a single, huge, high, bright room with windows all around. There's a balcony and an open kitchen. And the bathtub's in the middle of the living room, right in front of the fireplace. A stairway leads to an open bedroom loft, from where you can step out to a large terrace. You can't hear any traffic from the street. On one side the windows of the gigantic living room face the courtyard of a school. Whenever it's recess, we hear the cheerful and relaxed laughing and screaming of the children, who storm out of the stuffy building and play ball in the courtyard or just frolic about.

Minhoï's belly grows bigger, and she becomes more and more beautiful. Every moment that Nanhoï grows in her is a festival. And sometimes Minhoï takes my hand and puts it on her belly so that I can feel Nanhoï moving. I can also see him kicking in her womb. And when I place my ear on her belly I can hear his heart beating. I have no words for how much I love Minhoï.

Minhoï and Nanhoï are one. And Nanhoï and I are one. And I am growing in Nanhoï. I will be born through Nanhoï. And Nanhoï will be born through me and Minhoï.

The closer Minhoï gets to the birth, the more I feel the grace of life, the more I sense that I'm part of the universe.

An American woman in Chicago once asked me why half of every French flick is devoted to eating. I can't answer her question. She's right: eating and talking about eating. They film every chowdown, starting with breakfast. Dinner is the hardest meal to endure. In bistros, restaurants, and especially in private homes, when friends or several married couples are invited. It's unbearable. Then the dialogue! Which is especially written by dialogue writers (yes, yes, there's such a thing as a dialogue writer). For example, the eaters pass the sauce boat or the salt shaker after saying, "Please pass the sauce," or "Please pass the salt." Then they say "Thank you" and "You're welcome" and "Thank you" again, and so on and on, even though all they have to do is get off their asses and reach for the stuff. (Naturally all this is because the so-called dialogue writers can't hit on anything to write about except eating.) And every other kind of chowing down is filmed as well. Chowing, chowing. So long as it has something to do with chowing and guzzling. As though the characters hadn't chowed or guzzled for a long time and there were nothing more important in the world than chowing and guzzling.

Nuit d'Or is an exception: there's no eating or drinking. This movie has an addiction that's a lot worse than food and booze, and it's spreading faster and faster across the entire planet like an epidemic: the addiction to the sick and the macabre, the addiction to rot and decay, which those garbage-picking movie directors pilfer from the refuse dumps of human brains. Yes, they're also kleptomaniacs. They simply rip off stuff from the trash cans of other movies—as many as possible. Real garbagemen. It's disgusting.

December 23, Minhoï's birthday. I have to shoot until six P.M.; then I dash over to Cartier, where I've picked out a diamond for her.

When I bring Minhoï the diamond, she's not delighted. She does smile gratefully, but I know the diamond means nothing to her. Once again I've done the wrong thing. I know that the diamond can't make up for what I've done to her—but what in God's name *have* I done to her? What worse thing can you do to a person than not love them? But I love Minhoï so much that I would sacrifice my life for her at any time. My only crime is being condemned to carry on this eternal fight with myself. And my fight, the deadly struggle between the opposite forces in me, keeps getting crueler and crueler.

Minhoï has done everything she can out of love for me. She simply can't stand me anymore. The decision isn't hers. It's beyond her. I know it, and yet it won't sink in—or rather, I refuse to understand that I am incapable of making her happy. But I cannot and will not drag around this shitty guilt feeling like a disgusting cross that makes me rage if I refuse to lose my mind altogether. What have I done?

Minhoï threatens me more and more often, saying I'll lose her completely if I don't change. But in what way should I change? Should I violate myself even more and totally cripple my nature?

Can you learn how to become different? I don't mean behave differently—that's no great feat. I mean: Can you become an entirely different person? How is it possible to change your very soul without damaging yourself? And what would become of your thoughts and feelings? I've racked my brain millions of times, wondering why I'm not different and how I could manage to become different. All in vain. I believe that you can't determine your character, I believe that a person's character depends on how strong the magnetism of the universe is and which forces shine upon you. And I believe that no one can influence magnetism or vibrations. Especially when such antithetical forces collide. Can you calm the ocean off Cape Horn? If anyone knows better, then say so now!

To someone who's hard of hearing, these words may sound apologetic. But I apologize for nothing that I have done—and who should I apologize to anyway? Who would my apology help? No. I'm desperately looking for a solution. I've tried everything, too. Nobody helps me. I count the days, the hours, the minutes until the birth of my son, like a convict carving the days, the hours, minutes, and seconds into the walls of his cell. My son will be my redeemer. His love will liberate me from the chains of torment. I know it, I feel it. I can't show it, can't prove it. But I'm filled with the vision of his birth, and it gives me strength even now. Just as a fettered but growing tree smashes the iron rings that threaten to grow into its bark and flesh, as they do into my soul, my son is my strength, pushing to the outside from my innermost depths.

Aguirre finally reaches Paris in a hair-raising English dubbing—after five years! Herzog, talentless as a director, talentless as a producer, pathetic at marketing the flick, has sold it off to some French storefront distributor for a pittance. The even worse German soundtrack, with subtitles, doesn't have my voice because for years I refused to talk to Herzog. I'm allergic to so much as hearing his name or seeing it written. The so-called "press kit" consists of nothing but swaggering puff pieces and brazenly wretched lies about Herzog. The responsible party is a slimy faggot of a "press attaché," who's resolved to devote the rest of his life to kissing Herzog's disgusting ass. The press kit also introduces Herzog's illiterate claim that he forced me in front of the camera at gunpoint.

Gazettes, radio, and TV jerk off their pukey articles about me. They get themselves turned on calling me a genius. They don't know that the film, as it is, exists only because I ordered Herzog to keep his trap shut in order to salvage anything that could be salvaged. At least in hundreds of interviews I finally have a chance to spit at Herzog and call him what he is: a miserable asshole! Nonetheless he insolently grabs up all the conceivable prizes and awards that a feebleminded "kulchur" can produce.

L'Important c'est d'aimer premieres simultaneously in Paris. Here, too, the newspapers and the TV anchormen blabber all sorts of vapid and narrowminded junk about the alleged collaboration between me and Zulawski. The truth is that I put up with this arrogant, recalcitrant, and complacent director—without punching his stupid face—only because that maggot of a distributor in Munich tried to prevent me from filming this rotten and depressing crap.

The totally stupid and draining interviews, which run as long as ten hours or even several days, are all the more grotesque because most of these castrati understand absolutely nothing and they twist and distort it all so that nothing I say makes any sense.

I've now let the word out that I'll be interviewed only by female journalists. Not that they're smarter or more talented, but at least I can nurture some hope of getting a good fuck. If a newspaper, a radio station, or a TV network calls up my agency, I have them find out whether the woman's pretty and how old she is. If she claims she's pretty, then for safety's sake I agree to meet her at the agency. I can always split. One of them writes in her article that I didn't answer a single question, I just kept trying to reach into her crotch and drag her off to my hotel.

None of these cretins will believe that I've turned down Ken Russell, Federico Fellini, Luchino Visconti, Pier Paolo Pasolini, Liliana Cavani, Arthur Penn, Claude Lelouch, and all the other so-called world-famous directors and that I do flicks only to make money. It's really strenuous constantly rejecting the old fast-food rubbish that they keep trying to cram down my throat.

Minhoï takes my hand more and more often and puts it on her belly so that I can feel Nanhoï kicking. His kicks are really hard, and they get stronger and stronger, thrusting out like kung fu kicks. When I manage to make out a tiny foot before it kicks, because I absolutely have to kiss it, and when I quickly try to press my lips to it—it kicks me in the mouth. I'm sure he knows this and is laughing in the womb. From now on, whenever I place my hand on an area where I think there's a little foot, he kicks.

Everywhere in the parks Minhoï talks to mothers with babies, asking them where they bought their baby carriage or where she can find this or that. I'd love Nanhoï to have a huge English pram, the kind I got for Nastassja. Then he'll think he's riding a coach. He can drive me along, shouting "Giddyap!" and whipping me. Then I'll be his pony, pulling him along to wherever he wants to go, walking, trotting, or galloping. But Minhoï doesn't want a big pram because it won't fit into a car if we want to drive our boy to the park or the country. We also ask the mothers about cribs, playpens, and baskets, and where you can find a nursery table, and a bureau for baby things in Nanhoï's nursery. Eventually we get to know all the baby stores with the largest selections of cribs, playpens, and baby carriages. And we also track down the shops offering the cutest little shoes and outfits, and I know where to find all the toys that I want to buy for Nanhoï.

During these reconnoitering and shopping trips, we always start arguing. We get jealous whenever one of us picks out something for Nanhoï. I try hard as I can to keep my mouth shut so as not to get Minhoï agitated, but I'm so overflowing with exuberance about making everything as beautiful as possible for my son that, unable to control myself, I keep spontaneously exclaiming, crying out, shouting whatever I think, wish, yearn for. In short, Minhoï and I are completely intoxicated with our baby boy.

All we talk about is Nanhoï's birth, and all we do is prepare for it. The suspense is unbearable. I feel as if my own body were about to give birth to Nanhoï. As if I'd be bearing our child together with Minhoï. The three of us are a single body: Minhoï, Nanhoï, and I.

Five P.M. Minhoï's contractions are suddenly so powerful that I drive her to the hospital at once. She's taken to the delivery room promptly. But the moment hasn't come yet. All evening long, until deep into the night, the contractions keep increasing and decreasing, increasing and decreasing. I never leave Minhoï's side, and I keep kissing and caressing her and my son in her womb. More and more distinctly I feel my innermost core shaken by a force of nature—the imminent birth that announces itself like an earthquake. But Minhoï and I are not afraid. All I can feel and see is my son, who is coming toward me from far away. My sensations are too vast, too overwhelming to be put into words. I've loaded a Polaroid camera to photograph the birth. Minhoï wants me to. I think it must be the most wonderful thing imaginable to keep looking at those pictures. What mother wouldn't be happy to see herself giving birth to her child?

Four A.M. The birth is beginning. Minhoï lies on her back, her legs wide apart, the backs of her knees in metal stirrups, and she holds tight to the bars as she slightly pushes her abdomen up. Her entire body seems to be opening; she is all birth. I'll have to shoot the photos in a wild hurry so as not to miss a single phase of birth.

I'd like to kneel down. It's the most poignant, most powerful, most dramatic, most joyous, most sensual, and most sacred experience I've ever had. Minhoï must be in pain, but she doesn't seem to notice—for she's laughing! These are the pains of a storm, a roiling sea. . . . The first thing to emerge is the top of Nanhoï's skull. . . . A membrane connected to a stethoscope is placed by the midwife on that tiny head. Then she hands Minhoï and me the stethoscope so that we can hear Nanhoï's heartbeat. And while I listen to the sweetest heartbeat in the world as it pours through me, uniting with my own heartbeat, becoming a cry of sheer joy, Nanhoï's little head comes to light—his face upward, toward heaven. . . . Minhoï gasps and moans, but her breathing is deep and regular as she squeezes Nanhoï out of her belly. . . . The next thing to appear is Nanhoï's little right arm . . . then his little left arm, and both arms dangle, exhausted from the strain of being born. Now the birth has to proceed quickly. Any delay might cut off Nanhoï's air because his tender chest, which is still inside Minhoï, has no room to breathe in. With a tremendous exertion of energy, Minhoï opens her entire body like a flower. . . . Now she no longer seems to be straining . . . and just as the ocean detaches a part of the mainland to make an island, Nanhoï's body slides out of Minhoï's. When the midwife holds Nanhoï out to her, the first thing Minhoï kisses are his little feet. The doctor wants to take Nanhoï next door to wash him, but I wouldn't leave my son alone, not for anything in the world, so I accompany him every step of the way. With a jet of water the doctor washes the rest of the blood off the baby's head, face, and body, and while he holds him upside down by his feet, Nanhoï lets out his first scream, and I kiss his divinely adorable and wrinkled face.

Since Nanhoï's birth everything seems liberated—everything is immense and boundless and one with the universe, as if there are no more barriers, no laws, no religions, no passing of time, and no death. Nothing but love. What do all my pains and sufferings signify next to the light spread by Nanhoï's birth, which illuminates me and gives me unspeakable strength and makes my future radiant, no matter how difficult and arduous it may be?

Anything I have to do during these days I take care of quickly and effortlessly so that I can immediately return to the hospital. In Minhoï's room, Nanhoï lies kicking in a transparent crib. It's by his mommy's bed so she can watch him without having to sit up. I can't wait to see Nanhoï again! Bend down to his little bed, take him in my arms, kiss him, lick him, gobble him up. Kiss his gigantic, heavenly little eyes, which are dark stars like Minhoï's eyes. Kiss his budlike mouth. His teensy feet and strong, teensy hands, which clench into square fists like mine, but are just so tiny.

Minhoï sends me out to buy more baby shirts, baby jackets, rubber panties, diapers, skin cream, baby oil and powder, rompers, and anything else she wants. Sometimes I'm so excited that I get the wrong thing; then I have to go back and exchange it. I ask Minhoï whether I should buy a folding stroller. She says, "No. Not for another six or eight months. Nanhoï shouldn't be sitting yet! Don't make him sit! Babies aren't allowed to sit because of their soft spines!"

Finally the festive day comes when I take Minhoï and Nanhoï home.

At night we spell one another to bottle-feed Nanhoï. I set the alarm clock every three hours to make sure I don't oversleep in case my eyes close in exhaustion. But my little darling cries at exactly the right time. I'm so happy to be holding my baby boy in my arm and feeding him. Feeling his small, robust body getting heavier with every drop as he leans his little head on my shoulder so that he can burp, squeezing out the air he sucked in while drinking. Then he falls asleep again on my shoulder, and I don't stir and I don't dare breathe—I don't want to disturb his baby sleep.

For now, I do all the shopping in stores and at the market because Minhoï is still very weak, and the five-story climb to our apartment is too strenuous. But she is so delirious with happiness and so proud of our son that she soon goes shopping herself, showing Nanhoï off everywhere. This always takes a long time for the Jewish mamas in the Marais can't get enough of him.

Now we take Nanhoï out in his carriage. But wheeling him through the streets is a living hell. You don't know where to turn. The streets are filled with exhaust fumes, gutters, bestial stinks and infernal din, and above all: danger! Plus, dog shit wherever you go. It's like playing hopscotch: if you want to avoid stepping on a turd, you have to hop from one of the few nonshitty spots to another of the few nonshitty spots. Never have I been so anxious to get out of Paris as fast as possible.

When Nanhoï is asleep, I check on him every moment to make sure he's lying correctly. To make sure he's covered properly, getting enough air, not sleeping in a draft. To make sure the room or the terrace isn't too warm. Or too cold. To make sure no mosquito, no wasp, no bee, no fly has wandered in despite the net. The baby fragrance he emanates in sleep is so intoxicating that I'd love to climb right into his crib. But it would probably collapse. I also make sure he's not tossing and turning because of a nightmare. Sometimes he laughs aloud in a dream. Sometimes, when I come up close, he reaches for my finger in his sleep. He has to use his entire little hand to clutch my finger tight. I'd like to let him have my finger forever. But if I have to leave, or if Minhoï is getting impatient because she

wants to be alone with Nanhoï, I withdraw my finger very, very carefully from his little fist.

Minhoï wants me to move out of our apartment. She herself wants to
rent an apartment on the Île Saint-Louis. At first I don't understand
what she means. It's true that years ago she was already talking about
our splitting up after Nanhoï's birth. But I never realized how serious
she was, and I've been so happy that I've forgotten what she said.
She wants me to move out and find my own place, separate from her
and Nanhoï. That is, I would no longer be seeing Nanhoï all the time,
twenty-four hours a day. I wouldn't be playing with him and making
faces for him, which he loves. I wouldn't be getting up in the middle
of the night to make sure he's covered. I wouldn't be giving him his
bottle or washing his diapers or dressing him in fresh little shirts, little jackets, little panties. I wouldn't be washing his baby things anymore. I wouldn't be kissing him day and night and carrying him in
my arms and wheeling him through the park and watching the pup-
pet show and putting him on the merry-go-round and standing next
to him as we whirl around because he's too little and can't hold
on. . . .

It won't sink in. My mind's a blank. Minhoï says that this was our
agreement. She says I promised to leave her alone with our son after
his birth. She says that I've known for a long time that we can't live together. That no one can live with me. I'm paralyzed. Maybe this is all a
bad dream? Maybe I'm imagining it because I'm so exhausted. Maybe
Minhoï will regret it once I'm gone and she wants me back. How can
she think that I'll abandon my son? Never, I'll never do that! My son
needs me! And I can't live without him! Maybe I can patch things up
with Minhoï. She can't just push me away from Nanhoï, that would be
too horrible. Maybe everything will work out, maybe . . .

The thought of looking for my own apartment, away from Minhoï and away from my baby boy, whom I love more than anything in the world, is so fatally sad that I feel dead inside. Dead like a chopped-off branch. I'd have to be pushed, brutally shoved to look at an apartment. But then I'd only stare into space. I just can't manage to work up any interest.

I rent some pad or other that's advertised in *Le Figaro*. The building is 33 Avenue Foch, the most expensive street in Paris. It's an apartment house, heartless and in ghastly taste. A morgue. It was built by a Rothschild, and I'm subletting the apartment from the shah of Iran. The lease for the one-room pad with a kitchenette and a windowless bathroom is personally signed by the shah himself and comes straight from his palace in Tehran.

This guy is a regular landlord. His shitrag of a contract has all kinds of no-nos about small kids and flowers on the balcony! He's probably grabbed up a huge number of such holes, which he calls "luxury studios." Maybe he's even a pawnbroker—who knows? The concierge at 33 Avenue Foch is haughty and arrogant because, as he tells me, the building's underground garage contains the most Rolls-Royces and Bentleys in the whole of Paris—not to mention an Excalibur, plus Maseratis and Ferraris.

I let Minhoï keep our Mini Cooper. I usually walk everywhere—if possible, only at twilight or at night. I can't stand people gaping at me and discovering the lethal torment in my face, which kills and kills and kills and kills. I can't hide it from anyone. I can't stifle the shriek that rages in my face. Everything in me shrieks, shrieks, shrieks! I'm scared of being seen by people. I take the most ridiculous detours because I'm scared of running into them. It would be downright indecent for others to find out what I have to suffer. I feel like a leper in the Middle Ages, or like the Elephant Man, who covers himself so that people won't be disgusted. Sometimes I burst into loud sobs in the middle of the street. I walk faster, I run. I act as if I'm in a hurry, as if I have absolutely no time. I'm completely incapable of doing anything—I can't even eat, and I can't even think of sleeping. All I can think about is my beloved boy, my only beloved, my Nanhoï, whom I can have only every one or two weeks and then for only twenty-hours at most. Worst of all, I never know when. I call Minhoï up daily and ask her whether I can see my son. I plead with her, I beg her. Sometimes she simply says that I can't see him. Or she just hangs up.

If I run past a hooker on Avenue Foch, I smile and glance at my watch as if saying, "Maybe some other time. But now I'm running late, I haven't got a free moment." That's a lie, of course, for I have nothing to do.

Today Minhoï comes and shows me stores where I can buy food, since there are no stores on Avenue Foch. She explains what I have to buy. When she brings Nanhoï to me for a day or for a day and a night, I wait on the concrete balcony facing Avenue Foch. I station myself there hours in advance, trying to see whether every distant Mini Cooper is hers. I keep staring at it in case it's the right one, even though she never comes early. In fact, she's usually late. And if she's even one minute late, and if I don't see her Mini Cooper from far away, then I bang my head against the walls and fall to my knees and tearfully beg Nanhoï to come to me. For whenever Minhoï promises to bring me my baby boy, even if it's a week ahead of time, I live exclusively for the moment when I can see my darling, hold his solid little body in my arms, sniff at him, inhale his roselike fragrance, and squeeze him so tight that he gasps for air. I feel each time as if I've been risen from the dead. Before Nanhoï's arrival I'm nothing but a bruised, trodden clump of soul. That's how it always goes.

If the telephone doesn't ring for days on end, I jump. If it rings, I likewise jump. For hours, days, nights, I pace up and down this luxury cell. I shove my fists into my ears until they hurt, to keep from hearing the infernal traffic din on Avenue Foch. The murderous pandemonium of the traffic doesn't stop even at night. So I lie awake, stuffing my fists into my ears.

When my Nanhoï is with me, we stay inside only if it's raining heavily. I even feed him in the park. We head down Avenue Foch to the Bois de Boulogne, and I push his carriage double-time, which Nanhoï really loves. In the park I can toss him a lot higher than in the room. Higher, ever higher, I toss him aloft, ten times, twenty times, fifty times, a hundred times. Nanhoï never gets enough. I also have to play "pilot" with him, holding him on one arm and whirling around on one leg . . . faster and faster, faster and faster . . . until I get dizzy, and the earth is spinning around us. We go over to the ducks swimming on the pond and we feed them bread. He turns his little head in all directions, discovering and seeing everything.

The most sensational things for my baby boy are the merry-go-rounds. He often rides for hours, until he's so exhausted that he falls asleep, and I have to lift him off the carousel. I very carefully push him home in his little carriage and then put my sleeping boy to bed. After the merry-go-round comes the swing. Then licking ice cream. The most fun of all is a whole day of ice cream, swings, and merry-go-round. But the supreme pleasure for him is licking ice cream. His tiny hands can barely hold the cone, and I'm worried that the scoop of ice cream, which is almost the size of his little head, may tumble off the cone at any moment. Then the ice cream starts to melt before his tiny tongue can lick it up. It's exciting to sit and try to keep his movements and the condition of the ice cream under control.

It's an insult that I have to do the movie *Madame Claude,* and here in Paris to boot. The salary is also wretched. But we need money. The girls who play Madame Claude's prostitutes in the movie fuck like professionals. Especially the very young ones, but also the married ones, whom I can fuck only if their husbands are briefly out of town. A very young extra has a tiny, almost naked cunt, like a mouth, very tiny ass cheeks, and very tiny tits. I always have to telephone her horny mom before I can fuck the daughter.

They call those idiotic and mind-numbing TV programs "talk shows." They're nothing but force-feeding for the public. Now and then someone pukes the garbage back into a pig's face—and that someone is me. I'm sure people will ask why I even bothered going. The first time I didn't really know what I was getting into. I went for the same reason that I always go to such garbage dumps—because some jerk of a publisher or producer keeps nagging me until I finally let myself be trucked over in exchange for something I want from him.

The French moron who, to crown it all, calls himself a talk master (master!) was, I believe, named Philippe Bouvard. That mangy worm squeezing its way out of a stiffly startched collar is the most nauseating thing I've ever met on such an occasion. I sit in that whorehouse of a TV studio and have to wait until midnight, when it's finally my turn. In my presence, this dog-shit worm asks a young woman who's participating in the same program: What was the name of the first john she went to a hotel with as a prostitute?

The young woman is very embarrassed and bewildered and can't answer. She's written a best-seller called *Denial.* This is the dramatic and exciting story of a whore—the young woman herself—who managed to escape the torture of pimps and brothels. Her book describes Rue Saint-Denis, the most infamous red-light street in Paris, where hundreds upon hundreds of very young hookers stand in the doorways of brothels, often with no panties, and with (or without) skirts so short that the men can see their asses and twats. The young author—her name is the Claudette—was forced by her pimps to fuck as many as seventy johns a night. I don't give a shit how many men she fucked. For me she's a woman. No one has the right to sling crap at her just because men treated her like crap!

Claudette blushes at the talk show host's nasty question. In a whisper I tell her to ignore anything this sewer jellyfish asks, and we make a date for the next day.

I want to film *Denial* and I ask Claudette if she'd give me the rights. Not only does she agree, but she stipulates that her book can be filmed only if I make the film. . . . She kisses me the way a loving woman kisses her man—long and passionately. She bites my lips, licks my ears, sucks my nipples. Licks my hands, sucks my fingers and my cock. She's desperate for a fuck. She digs her fiery fingers into my flesh, trembling and moaning, and her moan intensifies into a long shriek. She doesn't spare herself. There's nothing whorish about her. She devotes herself completely, spends herself, gives herself up. Exactly like a woman in love. She perspires. Her belly swells. So do her arteries. The tiny blue veins in her temples. Her abdomen works greedily. She returns my brutal thrusts more and more wildly. . . . Then she's completely exhausted, with deep, dark rings under her eyes. But soon she wants it again and again. . . . I sleep with her.

She's just furnishing a small, modest apartment in the Seventh Arrondissement. She shows me the two small, still-uncompleted rooms. She's doing a lot of the painting herself. She's already got a little furni-

ture. We fuck and sleep on a mattress on the parquet floor; the bedstead is still leaning against the wall. A table, a chair, a floor lamp, and
some other necessary basics. The kitchen is only half equipped, but
still she cooks for me, and she's shopped for us.

I fuck her again. On my knees from behind. On my back. She
rides me. And again on her back, her legs wide apart and high up. She
wants me to move in. But she knows it's impossible.

She keeps wanting to kiss me and she keeps wanting me to give
her my seed.

Entebbe (Operational Thunderbolt). Menahem Golan rings me up
from Israel and tries to talk me into making the flick. The money is so
insulting that I ought to punch him in the mouth. Furthermore, I
haven't the foggiest idea what he's talking about. Anyone I tell that I'm
going to be doing *Entebbe* instantly knows what it is. I'm the only one
who's out of it because I never read the papers, listen to the radio, or
watch the news on TV—I switch it off as soon as the news comes on.
But when I hear the story, I'm so enthusiastic that I agree to the outrageous pittance that Golan offers me.

But first I have to finish shooting *Madame Claude.*

I meet with the producer Raymond Danon to discuss the filming
of *Denial.* I want Maria Schneider to play the lead. She has an un-
canny resemblance to Claudette. Maria visits me on Avenue Foch.
There's no trace of drugs. Only her tiring blabber that the prostitute
in *Camille* was actually fourteen years old and had syphilis. She says
she got it from Zeffirelli. He wanted to do a movie with her. You can
imagine the faggoty shit that would have come of it. In any case, Maria
seems okay, aside from some facial pimples. But Danon doesn't trust
the project because Maria has a reputation as an addict. He'll guarantee the financing of the movie if I can guarantee that Maria won't fall

on her face during the shooting as she did with Antonioni, or behave the way she did with Buñuel. I tell him that I guarantee it.

Until tonight. For tonight she's high again, babbling like a moron. No one wants to risk it, and so I don't make *Denial.*

I've talked Minhoï into coming along to Israel. I'm overjoyed and I ring up Menahem Golan in Tel Aviv, asking him to reserve a four-room suite at the Hilton, with a crib and two bathrooms. Minhoï wants to bring along a girlfriend to baby-sit.

I think about the gorgeous young Jewish girls I fucked the first time I was in Israel. About the smell of musk in the bazaars of Haifa and Jerusalem. And about a certain young mother: I had to climb through her window every night and then back out at dawn so our fucking wouldn't be discovered by the neighbors, and especially her husband. . . . The wife of the New York diamond dealer at the Tel Aviv Hilton: I fucked her for such a long time in her taffeta gown that she missed her flight to New York, and her husband divorced her. . . . The makeup woman, the costume mistress, the dresser . . . and I think about racing to all the others in one and the same night.

First I fly alone to Tel Aviv for the costume tryouts. This time, right after my arrival, I screw Sabine in her hotel room, crouching be-hind her as I shoot into her. She's still clutching her makeup case. . . . Next, the Arab girl with the husky voice; she sings like a guy, and her hole is so tight I feel as if my dick were wedged in a vise. . . . The wait-resses at the Hilton restaurant; the cooks; none of whom must know about the others. . . . Then I fly back to Paris. Shooting is to start in four weeks.

Sometimes Minhoï lets me spend the night in her apartment on Île Saint-Louis. Then I kneel by Nanhoï's crib in the nursery and let him clutch my forefinger or my thumb until he drifts off. When he wakes up at night, I carry him around the room and sing lullabies until I believe that he's sunk into a deep sleep and I can lay him down very gently in his crib. Occasionally, when I'm about to tiptoe out of his room, he wakes up again, crying, because he no longer feels my presence. Then I kneel down again by his crib and let him grab my index finger or my entire hand, and I stroke his sweet little head until he drops off again. Or else I again carry him around the room until he calms down, and I sing Brahms' lullaby or some other, until he starts dreaming.

I'm so happy with Nanhoï that I always forget how unhappy I am without him. As soon as Minhoï is nice to me or serves me some food, which I regard as love, I feel as if nothing had happened earlier. Sometimes she asks me to leave, and I'm always scared to death, and we end up arguing. But I'm so completely dependent on Nanhoï that I'm ready to put up with any kind of abuse or humiliation so long as I can be near him. And near Minhoï.

The shooting in Tel Aviv is sheer torture. Plus the swill we have to eat! We shoot fourteen, sixteen, eighteen, twenty hours at a stretch. Sometimes in the cockpit of a plane with no air-conditioning and no hot coffee until four A.M. We don't even have a moment to piss.

I spend most of my time on location. In the evening, if it's not too late, I buy Minhoï flowers or try to surprise her with something.

I don't give up trying to reunite our little family. Minhoï is bored in Tel Aviv and she's dying to get to the Red Sea, where Golan owns a hotel. I've got three days off, but I can't join her. I have to fly to Paris to complete *Madame Claude*.

Boulevard Saint-Germain, eleven A.M. A girl with glasses blocks my way and asks if she may touch me. I say, "Come over here with your beak and try." She forces her tongue, which is as big and hard as a dick, into my mouth. With our arms around each other, we head toward a fuck hotel.

As we enter the windowless room, I kick the door shut and push the girl, as is, up against the door panel. I don't even take off her glasses; I reach under her dress and rip up her soaked panties. She shrieks, pulls her legs apart, opens her ass cheeks, and bends her knees slightly without resisting. My cock has gone haywire, and it takes four hands to shove it into her. The glasses have flown off her face and she looks blind. I don't know whether she can see me without glasses. She merely smiles and feels up my face.

I can't remember the name of the chick with the blond curls, but I meet her on Boulevard Saint-Michel, right by the corner of Saint-Germain, where the girl with the glasses spoke to me. This one has a moronically huge guitar under her arm and she yells, "Kinski!" which sounds like "Fuck me." I don't know her, but I kiss her on the mouth. She says she has no time now because she's supposedly going to a guitar lesson—though I'm convinced that she can't play the guitar and will never learn how. But she absolutely wants to get together with me. Midnight. She doesn't want me calling her. Midnight, and that's that. She gives me the street and the house number and tells me to wait in front of the building. Twelve midnight on the dot. Then she lugs her moronically huge guitar over to a cab, where she turns around and her fingers signal the number 12 in the air. Five fingers. Another five. Then thumb and index.

She'll probably be sneaking out of the bed she shares with her guy—her boyfriend, her husband, or whoever. I wouldn't care if she had ten husbands. All that interests me is that I absolutely have to fuck that blond hole.

I've been standing outside her house, 5 Rue de l'Université, since eleven P.M., banging my half-frozen feet against one another. I think about how hot her body is now and maybe she's being poked by a dick that's just shooting now. I'm fed up with freezing my ass off and

I'm not gonna do it for another hour. I walk to the next building and back, in both directions, so I keep turning around on the off chance that she'll come down earlier and not recognize me from behind in the darkness. I don't cross the street because her guy may be at the window and get suspicious.

Midnight has already struck, and I hate the sweet blond slut for not showing up. I'm frozen stiff, and my cock is rigid. Just as I'm about to dash off and look for a taxi I hear the heavy entrance door creak, and an almost unrecognizable shadow comes flitting out. This time with no guitar, thank God. She's recognized me instantly. Slipping her arm through mine, she leads me down the street, then along a narrow alley to Boulevard Saint-Germain. After crossing it, we head into Rue Monsieur le-Prince, take the second left, then right, then left again. I believe it's the Rue des Quatre-Vents or something similar, but I'm not sure. I'm too numbed by the aroma of the blond slut, who smells as strongly of fucking as if she'd come to me directly from another guy's bed. She seems to be a steady customer at the fuck hotel. The chummy female night pimp hands her a key as if it were the same room each time. I don't have to pay.

After she bolts the door on the inside, I go to the toilet in order to empty my bladder completely before fucking. She follows me, asking if she can hold my dick. I say yes. She takes it in her bowllike open hand as if weighing it on a scale, cautiously half-closing her fingers as if measuring the caliber that she'll soon be feeling deep in her pussy. But experienced as she is, she leaves enough room for my cock to grow in her hand. And, as expected, it promptly gets thicker and heavier at the touch of her fingers. She hastily gives it back, as if scared that it may get too thick and heavy for her little hand, and probably because she can't stand not having it in her hole. She hurries back into the room and gets to work on the bed. By the time I emerge from the toilet, she's hurled away the covers, the cases, the pillows, the woolen blankets, and she's already lying on the mattress in a fuck position. Her back and her skull are against the headboard, which consists of a decrepit mirror. After splaying her legs against her shoulders like a contortionist, she shoves out her hips, pulls her labia apart with both hands, and opens her pussy like a secret door. Her entire lower body catapults up as if from a trampoline—and my dick feels like it's charged with heavy current. . . . She's all fuck and wants nothing but to get fucked, nonstop, ruthlessly and endlessly. . . .

Sometimes I manage to talk Minhoï into trying to live with me again, and I scurry around hunting for a large, bright apartment with enough room for both of us—and especially enough space and light for Nanhoï. This is very difficult because it has to be located right near the Bois de Boulogne so that Nanhoï can play and we don't have to drive through the poisonous and dangerous Paris traffic. Now and again we check a few possibilities together. But then something happens, and we blow it. Still, no matter how much Minhoï assures me that we'll never live together anymore, I keep telling myself that it's because I haven't found the ideal apartment yet, and so I don't stop looking at apartments and town houses. I'm obsessed with the juvenile idea that I can save our little family if I really rent one of these places.

I can't see her face from behind; she's window-shopping at a boutique in Montparnasse. All I can see is her high butt, which hypnotizes me all the way from the other side of the street. The sight of an ass like that, which you normally see only on black women, goes right to my nuts. The first black woman I savored was an American student in Paris, even before I met Jasmin. Her creamy goo—white lava gushing over my face and tongue—tasted sharp and exotically sweet, like wild honey. She smelled so bewilderingly like a beast woman that I couldn't tell whether it was her aroma or the countless orgasms that made me dizzy.

I yearn for the smell of a black woman. I cross the street and move so close to her that my boner almost grazes her ass cheeks. Her ravenous animal face is mirrored in the shop window. She turns toward me. Face to face with this black woman who was born to fuck, I stutter and stammer so disgustingly that she smiles and places two fingers of her wet hand on my lips as if saying, "Save your breath for fucking."

During the first few days she comes to my apartment regularly, but she stays for only a couple of fucks. She's shacked up with a guy who's keeping her, and she's also very busy running around, telephoning and meeting embassy and government officials to help release her father, a former member of the Ethiopian cabinet. He's been in prison in Addis Ababa ever since the negus got toppled.

The hookers on Avenue Foch are as famous as the ones in Pigalle, on Rue Saint-Denis, and at the Bois de Boulogne. On Avenue Foch they work both sidewalks, the entire length of the street. Naturally they get as far as Number 33. The whores of Avenue Foch and its surroundings are individually very distinct. Even in fucking. And I mean the way they move and behave, and especially the way they're dressed. The ones on Avenue Foch usually wear tight, short skirts, like women who've pulled up their skirts to take a leak. Their undies are barely large enough to cover their righteous pussies.

Toward the end of the night they usually have no panties on, or no skirts. They wear only a coat, under which they're either stark naked or wear just a bra and garters.

The other kind, who hang out more on the Champs-Élysées and the streets approaching the Arc de Triomphe, wear normal, middle-class stuff, very bourgeois, so as not to arouse suspicions that they're streetwalkers. Maybe these are the same clothes they wear all over and all the time. They don't look the least bit like hookers. Or fucked out or wiped out, except that some of them have slightly bluish shadows under their eyes, but they make cunning use of powder. They don't smoke or drink—at least not when they're hooking, and they probably sleep their fill after the strains of fucking. I'm convinced that some of them even work out in order to stay fit. If you don't take a closer look they seem uninteresting, even boring. In short, they melt completely into the crowd of pedestrians, and no one would give them a second glance, much less try to hit on them, if they're weren't standing on a corner or pacing to and fro, or hanging out at bus stops without ever stepping into a bus. But they do that, too, with a feminine instinct: the way they move and act as if they weren't interested in the glances of a male passerby, the way they check their watches from time to time, peering in different directions as if they were waiting for someone special, a close friend—in other words, they pretend they have a date, maybe with a boyfriend or a husband. They never address anyone or challenge anyone with their eyes or return the glances of an unknown man. You have to catch them, know them, discover them, and get right down to the nitty-gritty. And they don't always stand at the same crossing or walk the same beat. Nor do they work every day, for that matter. Or maybe they work different neighborhoods each day. One thing is clear: They live in some very distant arrondissement, so that no one around here knows them. These are perfectly normal home-makers, wives and mothers, university or even high school students earning money on the side. At the same time, of course, they're horny as all get-out—or at least they get that way once they've licked blood. Sex is like a drug, and they become hopelessly addicted.

I merely pull their skirts up and their panties a little down, expos-ing the asshole, the butt, and the twat and some of their thigh flesh. Then I fuck them from behind as they bend over—or like a bug, on my back. Sometimes I have them lie on their backs on the table, holding their knees apart as I shoot. A concentrated load. No more. Although women like this fuck very sweetly, they're anything but cunning or kinky. They're not even trained, though I can imagine that they must have had their share of dicks. They're even nervous and embarrassed, and in a touchingly bashful way they offer the fuck position that they may be used to taking with their husbands. Or else it's the position in which they have the most powerful orgasms. Or in which a big cock hurts the least, and so forth. They do it, as I've said, cunningly, through passive resistance, avoiding any other position and slipping back into their favorite way of fucking. But I never let them get that far—I fuck them ruthlessly and thoroughly. Many women—and this is quite natural—want to be taken violently, and they spurt more strongly when they're raped. They turn out to be super-horny fuckers.

One of them, on towering high heels, does a spontaneous belly landing over the back of my only chair—she's like a sacrificial lamb on an altar. But, contrary to what you'd expect, she doesn't pull in the small of her back or open up her ass so that her pussy squeezes out. Instead she bends her spine like a drawn bow and tightly squeezes her ass cheeks together, turning them down. Dripping wet, she goes totally ballistic, yammering and whimpering as she grabs for my nuts and comes long and hard. So do I. Then she says good night with lowered eyes, as if she's committed a sin that she secretly but obviously enjoys. A week later I see her standing at a different street corner.

A Paris lawyer writes me that Minhoï has hired him to start divorce proceedings. He'd like to meet with me to discuss the possibility of an agreement between me and Minhoï. But I don't want to meet with him. I don't want to talk to anyone about a divorce. I don't even want to think about it. I burn the letter.

Today, as always, I sprint along, wheeling my Nanhoï from Avenue Foch to the Bois de Boulogne. He smiles and looks at me as if he knew how ineffably sad I am. I take him out of the carriage and toss him in the air, which he loves. He keeps calling, "Again! Again!" Then his diapers come off and fly in all directions, and he howls with laughter, whirling his arms like two propellers, the way humming-birds do. Oh, God! Don't let my baby boy notice anything about the unbridgeable gulf that's opened up between me and Minhoï! No, I don't want to think about the divorce. Not now. Not when I'm with my son. I want to be merry for him, exuberant. The more exuberant and boisterous I am, the happier it makes him. I want to make faces, grimaces that'll make him burst into roaring laughter as they always have since his birth. I don't want to be a sad clown à la Pagliacci, the kind who really screams in pain when he laughs. My Nanhoï would notice; he feels everything. I want to be a merry clown, a silly prankster, doing the most ridiculous and nonsensical things. I also want to be in form for my son and teach him all the tricks and ploys that I learned when I was a little street urchin. I want to teach him all the games a boy can play. I also have to tell him about all the potential dangers that constantly lurk everywhere. I never try to force anything on him, except when he has to be protected. I never say "Do this" or "Do that," or utter nonsense like "You should be able to do that by now" or "You're old enough now," and so forth. What does "old enough" mean? What does "old" mean, or "enough"? Does it mean that a small child has been small long enough? I wish my child would never have any age at all. No child should ever have an age!

I'm incapable of enjoying anything without my Nanhoï. Anything at all. I live solely for my son, whom I love beyond all earthly and heavenly things. I live for him alone.

Without Nanhoï the nights on Avenue Foch are worse than anything I've ever endured. Worse than prison. Worse than a nuthouse.

The instant I'm done fucking or getting a blow job, I want the chick to leave. Sometimes a girl keeps sucking me all over until I finally let her sleep with me, but if she tries to cuddle I kick her away.

It's only when Nanhoï spends the night in my arms that I can forget the damnation I'm living in. Then, to avoid waking my baby boy, I don't stir all night long. Even if I drift off, I don't move in my sleep. Only my lips very cautiously and carefully breathe a kiss on his little head. And when he wakes up in the morning, I press big, wild, thick kisses on his head. Then my baby boy climbs on top of me, sits on my face, and reels off long tirades in divine baby language, which only babies understand. And he emphatically waves his little arms as if giving a speech to all the other babies in the world.

Then that same bleakness when Minhoï picks him up. The emptiness, in which I think no thoughts and feel no feelings, and then the sudden, horrible awareness of my loneliness without him and my torturous despair, from which I see no way out.

Then the telephoning starts. First every day, then several times a day, then every hour, I beg and beg Minhoï to bring me my son. The arguing. The screaming. Threats. Hangups. Redialing. And hanging up again and redialing again. Until Minhoï refuses to pick up, and I, half-crazy, go running through Paris. If it's still light out—that is, not truly dark—I have to use out-of-the-way back streets to avoid being seen. I don't want to talk; I don't want to hear or see anything. Especially not that doorman with the butcher face. I'm convinced he'd volunteer to hang someone. Then those whorish aristocrats and those trash millionaires, who size you up with shameless, vulgar eyes, treating you according to the car you drive. I have no car and no money, not even a face that I can show. And I live in a torture chamber.

If it's light out, perhaps even sunny, I have to spend the whole day in this mass grave of cement. From left to right. From right to left. In a circle. From right to left. From left to right. Two steps to windowless bath and toilet. And out again. To the flowerless concrete balcony. Look up. Look down. Look left. Look right. At all the other flowerless balconies. I mustn't lean too far over the railing, because the doorman may be talking to a Rolls-Royce chauffeur, twisting and turning his fat head like a TV camera, with his eyes constantly sweeping across the façade of 33 Avenue Foch. The din from the street crashes in on me from all sides, numbing my mind, sending my legs reeling back. When I then shove the heavy steel frame and shut the large glass door to escape the deadly stream of traffic and the pneumatic hammers, and the lock snaps in like that of a steel cell door—then I struggle with madness and death. It is purely owing to Nanhoï's love and my love for him that I have eluded death so far and not fallen prey to madness.

Once it's dark out, I run like a driven quarry through dimmer back streets. But this gets harder and harder the closer I get to the business district, which I have to cross, but which is ablaze with glaring neon lights. Then there's the barrage of streetlights and headlights. Avenue George-V and the Champs-Élysées become an all-out gauntlet, but I'm forced to run it—even if I do it farther down on the quais, which would be a detour. Either way, I reach the Seine, where I hurry along down by the water as much as I can. In the evening, especially when it's raining, there's no one there aside from tramps. You can't see all the dog shit in the dark, and you stumble over garbage and rubbish, banging your bones. But that wouldn't matter if it weren't for the bridges, where I have to return to the busy and garishly illuminated streets. Nevertheless this route is the one where I have the least chance of being seen. And it's also the fastest. After dashing the six miles, I vanish inside the driveway of 82 Rue St.-Louis-en-l'Île and breathlessly sneak up the five flights to Minhoï's apartment. I use the steps even though this ancient building has the only elevator on the entire island. The ramshackle elevator makes such a deafening noise that it sounds like cattle cars when their steel bumpers smash into one another. Besides, someone upstairs may have pressed the button, making the brutal and senile elevator stop at a different floor on its way up. Then I'd have to face one of the tenants. They all know me, and perhaps they make fun of my situation. Also, the space is so cramped that there's no room for two passengers unless they squeeze together. Maybe someone on the fifth floor has rung for the elevator. Maybe it's even Minhoï. Or maybe she's in the kitchen, which is next to the apartment door. Or in the hallway or the dining room or the living room. But even in her bedroom or Nanhoï's nursery, which is at the other end of the apartment, she'd hear the unbearable din made by that horror of an elevator. When it jerks to a stop, the noise is so devastating that it leaves cracks in the walls of the staircase. She'd automatically prick up her ears to find out if someone's getting in or out, if the person's looking for her and is about to press her buzzer, or if it's one of her neighbors coming home. If so, then right after the elevator's arrival she'd hear the jangling of keys, the opening and slamming of an apartment door. Any other passenger would be looking for a neighbor or an acquaintance. In that case, he would buzz the appropriate apartment. If Minhoï didn't hear this logical sequence of familiar sounds, she might get suspicious. On no account can I risk her suddenly opening the door. She must never have so much as an inkling that I often come here without letting her know in advance and getting her permission. I feel like someone who's committed a misdeed and has to hide. Is it criminal of me to love my boy so much that I can't live without him? How I envy every other father—when he comes home, he can take his son in his arms and kiss him and kiss him and keep kissing him as often as he likes. He can sit down on the floor where his son is playing. He can give him a piggyback ride. Lean over his boy's bed, lift him up, feel the sturdy little arms wrapped around his neck. Cuddle him, squeeze him, roughhouse with him until both are exhausted from playing and they laugh and joyfully collapse and fall asleep mouth to mouth. . . . Feed his boy on his lap even though he can long since hold the spoon and eat by himself. Press his lips to the back of the boy's warm, fragrant head . . . Then take him to beddy-bye—wait till he's asleep after telling him a story and singing him a lullaby . . .

I picture what it would be like if I now took two or three steps at a time after calling out Nanhoï's name from the bottom of the stairs . . . and then, wildly impatient, banged both fists and both feet on the door until Minhoï or my son opened up because none of us could wait to hold one another tight and cover one another with kisses . . . Instead, I have to steal up soundlessly. Hold my breath. Not stir. Cower. Hug the wall halfway up a flight. Hit the floor, my face in the dirt, if anyone else is using the stairs because the elevator is too slow or is out of order. Than I have to race all the way down and hide behind the garbage cans until the person's left the building. Then I skulk back up the five flights. On every landing I have to be prepared in case a tenant suddenly opens an apartment door that I'm slinking past. I can never tell whether anyone's watching me through the peephole.

On the fifth floor I first listen for any noise from the two neighboring doors. If I do hear anything, I try to interpret it and picture what the person may be doing. What they're about to do. Whether the sounds indicate that they're on the verge of opening the door. If nothing stirs, I still shouldn't be fooled, I have to listen closely anyway.

Minhoï's apartment is only two feet from the stairs. After tiptoeing one step I wait for a long time because the worm-eaten floorboards creak and I have to make certain that no one's standing behind the door, watching every move I make. Then I tiptoe the second step— that is, I very quietly pull my other foot over the floor and then distribute my weight over both feet as I carefully lower my heels. Now I'm standing fully on both soles again. This also takes a long time because even shifting my body weight from my toes to my soles makes the boards creak. Now I'm so close to the door that I can almost graze it with my mouth, and I run my fingertips across it like a blind man or a deaf-mute, someone who goes by vibrations, picking up sounds and even spoken words. I listen with my entire body . . . for Nanhoï's voice or even his laugh. . . . The scurrying of his feet . . . the wheels of his small wooden tricycle on the stone floor of the hallway . . . his ball bouncing against the door . . . the clattering of his spoon or plate if he's sitting at his little table. . . . Building blocks . . . tops . . . a rubber animal that squeaks when he steps on it or squeezes it with his fists . . . breathing . . .

But I don't want to be pushy. I'm happy and thankful just to hear Nanhoï standing on the kitchen garbage can, where Minhoï puts him so he can watch her cook. Just to hear the sounds she makes, any sound, so I know they're both here! The lid on a pot. The faucet. The toilet flushing. A window. A drawer. Broom noises. Laundry being washed. Anything at all. Just to know they're nearby. Then everything's fine. My God! I believe Nanhoï is standing right behind the door. He often stays there for a long time, peering at a tiny part of something he's found, tinier than the head of a pin. I cautiously kneel down . . . right where my fingertips feel that his wet, half-open mouth must be—and I press my mouth on the wood with its gray coat of paint. The stench of turpentine jabs into my nose, irritating my mucous membranes. But only a fraction of an inch of wood separates my lips from the lips of my baby boy, who presses his mouth against the wood on the other side. . . . I hear little words bubbling in French; I don't understand them. . . . And then two syllables that slash into my soul and make me so ineffably happy: "Papa . . ."

The shock of hearing the elevator is like the blade of a guillotine, as if I'd been kneeling for my execution. The instant I hear the iron grille open, I dash down all five flights on tiptoe. Was it all my imagination? I'll never know. And what if Minhoï and Nanhoï were coming home in the elevator? Normally I'd have heard his little voice all the way up the staircase. But often he's so worn out from playing that he falls asleep in Minhoï's arms or mine, and we carry him straight to his little bed. I hear a door being unlocked, but from down here I can't tell which of the three doors it is on the top story.

Before dashing the six miles back to Avenue Foch, I run across the bridge linking the Île Saint-Louis to Notre-Dame and then along the street to the small park of the cathedral, where even the flower beds are behind bars. And where a policeman blows his shrill whistle the instant a little child kicks a ball. And the policeman drives the mother and her children out of the park the moment the belfry clock strikes closing time, and then, like a prison guard, he locks the iron gates of the park of this infamous Cathedral of Notre-Dame. Inside this park, which is entirely surrounded by bars and which is not much bigger than an acre, there's a small sandbox, where Nanhoï often plays. Most important, this is where the swings are. Not like those in Luna Park, which have a minimum age requirement because they can turn you upside down. The swings here are for little kids, but they fly fairly high, so that every child has to be tied in. Nanhoï is utterly intoxicated by these swings, and that's the first place he pulls me to when we enter the park.

I often come here secretly, hoping to spot Nanhoï on a swing or in the sandbox and at least to watch him, if only from far away. Then I have to hide behind parked cars or other pedestrians, or duck behind baby carriages, to keep Nanhoï from noticing me. Or else I sneak through the bushes surrounding the cathedral and creep as close as possible to the sandbox so I can watch my son through the branches. I'd love to whisper, "Psssst!" and beckon him over. But Minhoï would notice, for no mother lets her child out of sight here for even an instant. I know it's silly looking for Nanhoï in the park at this time of day. The gate is already chained and padlocked. Nevertheless my eyes wander about, and I peer every which way, hoping to glimpse Minhoï and Nanhoï. Even when a tourist boat passes under the bridge, I try to make out Minhoï and Nanhoï among the numerous passengers staring up at the bridges. I'd then wave at them from the bridge. And once they vanished under the bridge, I'd dash over to the opposite balustrade and watch them emerging on the other side. And I'd run along the quais as fast as humanly possible, keeping up with the boat and waving until it disappeared around a bend in the river.

I don't believe they're on a boat, but I cling to anything—no matter how absurd—that occurs to me in my desperate plight.

I don't find them anywhere. I usually don't. I don't know where to turn; I run along the quais as far as Avenue George-V and then zigzag grotesquely through the darkest and most deserted back streets until I reach Avenue Foch. When I see Number 33 in the distance, I shy away like a horse, refusing to go any farther. I feel as if I'm voluntarily climbing into my grave. What should I do? Where should I go? Those questions hammer in my brain as I crawl into a thicket in the Bois de Boulogne and, exhausted and despairing, fall asleep.

More French flicks. I don't know how many—ten or twelve, perhaps more. I don't ask about the titles or the directors. All that's important is getting money. I buy a four-wheel Range Rover. At last there's room for Nanhoï and his toys.

Whenever I see Nanhoï now, he tells me that he's going to Egypt with Mommy. With a concentrated effort, he keeps forming and re-forming the two difficult syllables, as if rehearsing difficult notes on a flute—and triumphantly succeeding: "E-gg-y-pt."

During the last few days before they leave, I'm allowed to stay in their apartment, and also for the three weeks they'll be away. Three weeks! That's the first time I'll be separated from Minhoï and Nanhoï for such a long period. I can't even manage to picture it.

But at least until their departure, I can see my baby boy all day long. Play with him. Roughhouse with him.

When I take Minhoï and Nanhoï to the airport, I still don't fully realize what I'm in for. It's only as I'm heading back to Paris that a horrible emptiness suddenly emerges from the earth, when I picture Minhoï and Nanhoï, now over thirty thousand feet in the air and moving farther and farther away from me. I'm haunted by that thought. If only I could hit on something. My thoughts are like a teeming mass of worms.

There's that frizzy-haired girl who spoke to me after the screening of my Japanese flick at Claude Lelouch's Club 13. Her tight black curls twist and writhe like a brood of snakes. Eyes set in deep slits, the brows above them linking up like black wire. The ski nose opens its nostrils, greedily pulling up the upper lip. The bared canines are rounded, probably because she sucked her thumb for too many years. Ideal for sucking dick now . . .

I call for her at her grandparents' place. On the way back we pass the Bois de Boulogne. I park in the first convenient spot, just beyond the entrance, because neither of us can wait. When I rip off her clothes in the backseat, a man's face appears at the side window. I have just enough time to see her body: bony . . . childlike torso and tits . . . hot, raw, taut skin . . . wide pelvis; firm, small, oval ass cheeks . . . The man presses his lecherous face against the glass. I know that a lot of men do this. They loiter in these areas merely to watch other people fucking and to jerk off. Okay. I climb into the driver's seat without my pants—while the chick remains naked, covering herself with her panties. Pretending to lose my bearings, I keep driving in a circle, unable to decide where to go—almost paralyzed by horniness, like a cat in mating season. I drive across the sidewalk to a bridle path and stop.

Her body is hairy. The hair isn't dense, but it's all over. Hard black hair creeps all the way up to her belly. From her armpits. Over her arms, legs. On the back of her neck, her vertebrae, all the way down to her butt crack . . . Once again men are sneaking around the car, vanishing into the shadows of the darkness setting in. They must have followed us. Or maybe not—the park is filled with them. We have no choice but to take a stab at it somewhere else. So to the speed-way. No matter where to. I have to spurt my come into the girl right away. When I think we've shaken our pursuers, I veer into the first right-hand exit and head toward an area with as few lights as possible.

Her little pussy is firm and almost round, like a field mouse. There! Another face? This time at the rear window. I can't stand it any longer—I dig my borer vertically into her cunt. Grossly twisting her face, shutting her slanting eyes, she shrieks and shrieks. . . . She doesn't notice the man at the rear window watching us fuck. Propped on her shoulder blades and cervical vertebra, she sinks deep into the backseat, her legs splaying high above her head, shoves up her free-floating torso, and screams and spurts and screams and spurts and spurts. Then we head over to Minhoï's apartment and fuck all night long.

In the morning, for no reason at all, she starts blabbering about Communism, so I kick her out.

I haven't heard from Minhoï and Nanhoï since they flew to Egypt, and they're incommunicado. I have no address, phone number, or hotel—I don't even know what part of Egypt they're in. Minhoï wanted to travel way down south and cruise the Nile in a felucca. And suddenly I feel as if I've spoken, heard, or read the word

"Egypt" several times during the past few days. Wherever you look, headlines about airplane accidents. Railroad accidents. Hijackers. I never read newspapers. But the headlines insidiously try to invade you, like deadly, contagious diseases, as if waiting for someone like me, someone whose tense and irritable condition teeters on paranoia and whose nerves are shot. Which makes him especially vulnerable.

Even in the apartment I catch only fragments of TV newscasts, which I switch on accidentally, never on purpose. I don't know my way around the buttons and I often press the wrong ones. I never understand what the anchormen are talking about and I can't make head or tail of the commercials. This time I feel as I've caught the word "Egypt"—or did I see it in a front-page headline? I'm not quite sure. I buy all the newspapers and listen to the nauseating TV news. Those voices! But there's nothing about Egypt in the papers or on TV. Yet I could have sworn that I've repeatedly heard or read the word "Egypt." Maybe it was days ago. In my condition I have no control over time and logic.

It takes sixteen days for Minhoï's and Nanhoï's picture postcard to get from the Pyrénées to Paris. Who knows where my darlings may be now?

It's late in the evening when the telegram guy buzzes and hands me a wire from Minhoï, who says they're coming back. I want to race out to the airport right now, this very instant, three days ahead of time, and spend the nights there waiting for them.

I get to the airport two hours early. I don't understand a word of the banging and bleating that pour out of the loudspeakers, announcing each landing and takeoff. Nor do I rely on the monitors indicating the airlines, flight numbers, arrivals, and delays. I scurry nonstop from exit to exit, checking out every passenger, no matter what line he's flown in on.

I was right. Minhoï plane arrives much earlier than it is expected. She's quickly pushing Nanhoï in his stroller, almost running toward the stairs leading to the baggage claim. At first all I see of Nanhoï is his teensy head. When they left, he looked much bigger because his full, long hair hung way over his shoulders. Now his hair's been cut short, almost shorn—he's like a little lamb. I pick him up from the stroller, and we kiss each other, and I don't let him out of my arms until we reach Minhoï's apartment, where I put him to bed.

Minhoï says that my place on Avenue Foch is a waste of money since I spend most of my time in her apartment. But neither of us has any illusions. The longer I live with her, the more we fight. And the more we fight, the more we lunge away at one another, and the more monstrous and violent and terrible our arguments and fistfights. We're not like married couples who live together out of sheer habit and hate each other because they're no longer interested in each other. Oh, no! Quite the contrary! We're driven by passion. By jealousy. Suspicion. Love. Despair. Which generate accusations and revenge that turn into fury.

If we go at it full force in Nanhoï's presence because we're both more explosive than nitroglycerin, or if he hears us shouting, he comes dashing into the room and throws himself between us to pry us apart. He grabs each of us with a little fist and braces his feet against our shoes to hold us apart. He's ready to kick us if we dare go at it again.

If Nanhoï sees us kissing or hugging or just caressing, then he envelops our legs, pulling us together in a single body, as if refusing to ever let us separate again.

Minhoï can no longer endure the mental anguish I inflict upon her, the "violent ebbs and flows," as she puts it. She says I suffocate her. She accuses me of having made all decisions for her from the very start. Her clothes, her makeup, her hair, her nail polish, her underwear—everything. I've never seen it that way. I never meant to "decide" anything for her. I didn't want to *patronize* or *stifle* her. I never wanted to curtail her freedom—after all, I can't live without freedom myself! Today I understand that jealousy spells slavery for all of us. Patronizing and violating are nothing but the unceasing process of creation: formation, destruction, reshaping, changing— everything, constantly, incessantly. But that doesn't mean that I ignore, much less exclude, Minhoï's imagination, her ideas, gifts, wishes, decisions. Picasso painted with his fingers even in the sand on a beach. It is the creative process going forward. I can't help it, it simply happens.

Minhoï says, "Everything about you is too much!" Those are her words; I've been hearing them for years and I can't hear them anymore. When I was a child people were already telling me that I had "no self-control."

Minhoï says I have "too much" love. "Too much" passion. My yearnings, my desires are "too immense." I'm "too sensitive." "Too sentimental." "Too wild." "Too exuberant." "Too cheerful." "Too silly." "Too sad." "Too noisy." "Too quiet." "Too nasty." "Too good." "Too softhearted." "Too ruthless." "Too tender." "Too brutal." "Too," "too," "too," "too," "too," "too," "too," "too," "too" . . .

I follow Minhoï like a fool when she heads to the market. Then I can carry my baby boy in my arms, push him in a stroller. In order to be with Nanhoï, I put up with any humiliation. I let Minhoï boss me around, cut me off. But the more I put up with, the worse we fight. Once again Minhoï sends me packing to Avenue Foch and refuses to let me visit her and Nanhoï in their apartment.

Minhoï's been given a date in divorce court, and I'm subpoenaed. I'm reluctant to set foot in the building. But I have no choice because I can't afford an attorney for now.

Upon entering the building with its sticky shade, I feel as if I'm walking into a slaughterhouse on its day off. I reach the top floor, and when I arrive in the room were Minhoï and I are to be divorced, the insanity of all mankind sticks to me like cold sweat. The judge blabbers about some flick he saw me in. I holler at him and dash out of the room—lemme outa here! Minhoï's lawyer brings me back in from the corridor, saying that the judge will lock me up if I ever yell at him again and run away. Minhoï is very embarrassed. Finally the judge says we ought to take another stab at it, especially for the sake of our little boy. The divorce is put off for six months.

Whenever I see flowers, I want to take them to Minhoï. She usually doesn't want my flowers, or she doesn't even care. But when I see flowers, I forget that and I bring her some as often as I can. This morning I once again brought her some—a huge bouquet of cheerful, colorful blossoms. Then I had to go on location, outside Paris.

In the evening, I'm back in my goddamn cage on Avenue Foch. There's a huge bouquet of cheerful, colorful flowers on the table. My heart melts when I see the bouquet—especially because of the letter lying next to it: I recognize Minhoï's handwriting. I assume that she's sent me the flowers. And even though they look just like the ones I brought her this morning, I don't understand that they're the same ones. And why are they here on Avenue Foch and not in Minhoï's apartment on the Île Saint-Louis? Even when I read and reread the letter, it won't sink in. . . . I don't understand what Minhoï means

when she says "going away" and "for a long time." . . . I don't understand why the flowers are here and not in her apartment . . . or why
she and Nanhoï are no longer here . . . or why she brings me flowers
when she's inflicting a mortal wound on me . . . or why the flowers are
the same ones I gave her this morning. . . . Reality takes effect like a
very slow poison. . . .

   She doesn't say where she's gone to. Or for how long. She only
writes, "for a long time," saying she can't stand it anymore. Once
again no address. No phone number. Nothing.

After weeks of hunting Minhoï and Nanhoï through the whole of Europe, I've found them on the Spanish island of Ibiza.

Herzog rings me up at Avenue Foch at one A.M., asking if I want to
play the title roles in *Nosferatu* and *Woyzeck*. I yell at him for calling
me up at one A.M., but I agree. I've totally forgotten that ten years ago I
refused to play Woyzeck onstage because it's suicide, and I tossed the
script into a garbage can. I don't know why I've said yes this time. It's
all destiny, no doubt. It's not me who decides, it's my destiny that
agrees or rejects for me. A greater power. And there must be some sig-
nificance (even though I don't give a fuck) in the fact that I play parts
involving what I have to experience myself but can barely endure. Or
do I have to experience it personally after playing the part? Is it a
warning or a repetition? Is it a chain reaction? Does one detonate the
other? Or do both happen simultaneously—my life, and the part I
have to play? Do I transfer other people's hells to my own life, or do I
transfer my own life to the character I have to play? Does the event in
question occur in my own life through mystical force, so that I may
suffer more deeply when I have to play the part? No one can answer

these questions. In any case, it's part of the curse of being—as they put it—"the ultimate actor." Which, however, has nothing to do with this hammy bullshit.

Minhoï insists on the divorce. The judge grants her petition. I dash out of the deadly room, down the stairs, through the hall—where a hand-cuffed man is led past me and a buckling, crying woman presses her handkerchief to her mouth. I dash out of the court, into the street. I feel as if people are uncamouflaged—like in Hieronymus Bosch's paintings, but a lot more disgusting. I have to see Nanhoï! I race along the quais. I keep turned away from the pedestrians and vehicles. I feel as if everyone were gaping at me, even the cars, even from far off—the way people push and shove, trying to watch an execution, or drive slower past an accident scene to gawk at the victims. They stare at me. A monster. An Elephant Man. Too disfigured not to be discovered. It is *my shriek* that dashes through the streets, not belonging anywhere.

At the Notre-Dame sandbox, I grab Nanhoï into my arms, and my tears drop down to the sand behind him.

A girl's been watching him during the divorce proceedings, and I tell her she can leave. I want to be alone with my son and far, far away.

When I bring Nanhoï to Minhoï's apartment for lunch, she blocks my way in the staircase, refusing to let me pass.

Nosferatu for Twentieth Century Fox. In Holland and Czecho-slovakia and all the way to the Tatra Mountains on the Czech-Polish border.

The departure point is Munich. Four weeks before shooting starts, I have to fly there for costuming. And this is where I shave my skull for the first time. I feel exposed, vulnerable, defenseless. Not just physically (my bare head becomes as hypersensitive as an open wound) but chiefly in my emotions and my nerves. I feel as if I have no scalp, as if my protective envelope has been removed and my soul can't live without it. As if my soul had been flayed.

At first I go outdoors only when it's dark (I've been through that with *The Idiot,* but this is much, much worse). Besides, I wear a wool cap all the time even though it's spring. You may think, "So what? Some guys are bald." But the two have absolutely nothing to do with one another. What I mean is the simultaneous metamorphosis into a vampire. That nonhuman, nonanimal being. That undead thing. That unspeakable creature, which suffers in full awareness of its existence.

Currently I leave home only to go to my costume tryouts.

When we fly to Holland, Minhoï and Nanhoï follow. And even though I have to shoot most of the time, often all through the night, I can at least see my baby boy asleep or at breakfast before they pick me up for the day's work.

Herzog has put up the entire gang in a ramshackle house, where they camp on the floor like pigs, in groups of three or more. The chow is inedible.

When we move from Holland to Czechoslovakia, Minhoï and Nanhoï fly back to Paris.

I demand a trailer that I pick myself so I can live in it, sleep in it, cook, and do my laundry. I don't want to be billeted in some shitty Czech hotel, where you run into the whole motley crew after shooting.

Nosferatu is finally done. And then without a break and in the same dump: *Woyzeck.* The worst fate I've ever suffered in a movie. I've already said that the story of Woyzek is suicide. Self-laceration. Every shooting day, every scene, every angle, every photogram.

At night in my trailer, which they've stationed in a deserted park, I bang my head against the wall. I truly believe that I've gone crazy.

But I won't let madness off the hook. I'll fight. I weep, shriek, get feverish, run through the pitch-black park, get plastered on piss-warm beer because there's no ice. I bring back girls and usually kick them out before I even bother to fuck them.

In deathly panic, I keep pushing the shooting along as if I had to get it over with before madness gets the upper hand. I don't have to "rehearse" or listen to the crap spewed out by Herzog's brain. I tell Herzog, I warn him, to keep his trap shut and leave me be. This time he appears to catch my drift—at least, he keeps his trap shut. Today, after sixteen days of filming, there's only one scene left. The scene in which Woyzeck stabs his wife and then, holding her corpse in his hands, succumbs to madness. It's three A.M. I tell Herzog I'm gonna shoot the scene only once. There's no such thing as repeating death and insanity!

After the take, I'm running through the pitch-black park when I hear a vehement sobbing. It's Eva Mattes, who plays my wife in the movie and whom I murdered in the scene we just shot. She's trembling from head to foot, shrieking, on a crying jag. I take her in my arms, bring her to her hotel, and wash the blood off me. I'm supposed to be driven across the border to Vienna; from there I'm to fly to Paris. But everyone's vanished. The entire company. All of them. As if they were fleeing the madness triggered by the film.

At my hotel in Vienna, I can't take off my shoes and stockings without rolling on the floor.

During the opening credits, Woyzeck is drilled in the barracks courtyard. He's tortured with rifle exercises, push-ups, squats until he collapses. And whenever he collapses, a booted sergeant kicks him in the back of the neck. That's what I wanted, it was my idea, and I had told the actor playing the sergeant to keep kicking until I really couldn't take it anymore. Which is what happened. When I tried to straighten up one last time and with my last ounce of strength, I really collapsed. For days on end I couldn't walk without help from other people.

It's gonna take me a long time to recover. But the damage done to my soul is a lot worse.

On a street in Paris, a dog eyes me, and I can't help crying. What did I do to the dog? Or rather, what did it do to me, compelling me to cry? I also have to cry when I see people, objects. I'm pained by the sight of anything I look at. By anything I hear, by anything I think, feel.

I want to see my baby boy! But I find a letter from Minhoï telling me she's flown to Mexico with him. This time she doesn't say for how long.

Nastassja's doing a flick with Roman Polanski in northern France: *Tess.* I visit her, and we spend nearly a week together. Polanski shows me the first few dailies. Nastassja is overwhelming. But deeply as I miss her, I can't feel good so long as I don't know where Minhoï and Nanhoï are, how they are. My anxieties about them and my longing for them are like thorns growing through my heart. Day and night, every moment. So I can't fall asleep at night or get any rest, even though Nastassja's there. I return to Paris and wait for Minhoï to call me from Mexico.

I can't say how many weeks it's been since she flew to Mexico with Nanhoï. I can't even think in terms of time.

In the middle of the night the phone rings: Minhoï is calling from Mexico. When she tells me to come, all I can think of is flying to her and Nanhoï at the crack of dawn, on the very first plane to Mexico City.

When the taxi in Mexico City brings me to the hotel where they're waiting for me, my heart pounds so intensely that it hurts. This time it's pounding with joy. Suddenly I'm afraid to make the slightest sound as I dash up the staircase, so I halt. . . . I'm terrified that Minhoï and Nanhoï might run away when they hear me coming, and I tiptoe to the room indicated by the desk clerk.

My heart overflows when I hear Nanhoï squealing and splashing in the bathroom. He pulls me fully dressed into the bathtub and hugs me, and Minhoï hugs me too and kisses me. And all pains become sweet as if I'd been put under.

The night with Minhoï and Nanhoï is filled with peace and bliss.

The very next morning, we fly to Miami, planning to visit the Bahamas, where I want to buy an island.

In Nassau we hop a one-engine seaplane for the Exuma group and check out the island. It has a small jungle, a snow-white beach that extends far into the ocean at the ebb tide, and a cliff on which sea eagles nest. There is also a bewitching underwater garden. From a rowboat your naked eye can see a hundred yards under the surface and you can watch the strange, iridescent fish and the magical structures of radiant coral.

I buy the island, and that same day we fly back to Nassau, where we've rented a house.

But we've fooled ourselves. Or rather, we so deeply needed the caressing hand of peace that we were actually able to live together for an instant. Then suddenly, as if starting from a profound dream, we realize that it will never be possible again. The tension becomes so unendurable that we can't even go out to a restaurant and eat at the same table. We leave.

In Paris I give up the torture chamber on Avenue Foch. While hunting for an apartment, I stay at L'Hôtel, where Oscar Wilde once resided. It's across from the Route Mandarine, the first Vietnamese restaurant Minhoï ever took me to. L'Hôtel was also the first Paris hotel that I stayed at with Minhoï. Now it's a nightmare. But I'm at a loss where else to go.

I'm starved for pussy, so like a satyr I drag any cunt to bed with me and fuck and fuck and fuck. Salesgirls. Waitresses. Chambermaids. Married women. Mothers. Black women from Haiti, Mozambique, Jamaica. Frenchwomen. American tourists. Students from Russia, China, Japan, Sweden, Chile, India, Cuba. A Bedouin. Schoolgirls from Africa. The naked black women from the Paradis Latin. The sweet asses from the Crazy Horse. The seven black models from Yves Saint-Laurent, all seven of whom devour me with the fleshy sponges of their wet, heavy lips. The wife of the gas station owner. The girl from the reception desk. The toilet cleaner at the Route Mandarine. The wife and mother with the big scar on her face. And all the girls in the cafés who smile at me as I pass or whom I run into on the way to the toilet.

The chambermaids at the hotel can't come to my room at night. Besides, some of them are married and at night they have to get fucked by their husbands. I fuck them when they come to clean up my room, or I call them with some flimsy excuse when they're making the beds next door or vacuuming the stairs. I fuck them on the bed, on the floor, on the toilet, on the bidet, on their backs, on my knees, on their bellies, standing, bending, squatting. . . . We mustn't take too long, otherwise they'd be missed. If necessary, they keep the vacuum on. Some of them show up a bit later for the next fuck.

I still haven't recovered from *Woyzeck*. Sometimes I stuff my fist into my mouth to avoid shrieking. Or I bore my fists into my ears or my eyes, or I strike my head to shake off the malevolent creatures of my visions. They lurk everywhere, digging their claws into me. I wonder how long I can stand this.

I've found an apartment on Quai de Bourbon on the Île Saint-Louis, almost on the other side of the block where Minhoï and Nanhoï live. Now I only have to go around two corners and I'm with my babyboy. Sometimes Minhoï brings him to me and visits awhile. But not often, and even when she stays it's not for long because we always start fighting.

I don't want to own anything. I've got almost no clothes, because every few months I check through them, dumping out anything I don't need. I don't have any books except for a couple of Jack London novels and accounts of solo sailing trips around the globe. I burn scripts, letters, pictures, just as I do with every book after reading it. During such a raid on useless ballast, I stumble upon my handwritten manuscript about Paganini, *The Devil's Violinist*. I'm about to burn it, because so much of my past is involved, but something keeps me from tossing it into the fire.

Nastassja visits us whenever she can, even for a few minutes. She's crazy about Nanhoï and constantly hugs and kisses him, rolling on the floor with him and shrieking for joy.

Today, as we drive to the Banque Rothschild , where Nastassja has opened an account, she bursts into tears, and I can't calm her down. She clings to me for help as if afraid of being swept away by a raging torrent and losing me forever once she lets go. Her entire body is so profoundly shaken by shocklike convulsions that she can't breathe, and her words come like shrieks torn from her choking throat.

"You . . . don't . . . love . . . m-me. . . ."

I'm dumbstruck, I can't speak. That makes me even more suspect, and she's about to shove open the car door and jump out. I forcibly hold her back and hug her very tight and kiss her for a long time.

Now it dawns on me! We've been separated since she was seven—that is, during all these years, we've met only sporadically and for brief periods. But her love and yearning have been growing and growing. The truth is that I wasn't with her when she needed me. Now she sees how I love Nanhoï and she believes that I can't love her as much as I love my son. That I've never loved her like this. I try to make her realize that she's distorting everything in her pain and not seeing the truth. That I've painfully missed her since our separation and that I've never stopped loving her. But even though she gradually calms down, I have a feeling she doesn't believe me.

I tell her about Paganini and that I absolutely have to have her for my movie. She is to play the young woman Paganini longs for with such wild passion. Nastassja is happy.

The German government writes me that it has awarded me the supreme distinction for an actor: the Gold Film Ribbon. What gall! Who gave those shitheads the right to award me anything? Did it never occur to them that there might be somebody who doesn't want their shit? What filthy arrogance to award me—me, of all people!—a prize! What does this prize mean, anyway? Is it a reward? For what? For my pains, sufferings, despair, tears? A prize for every hell, every dying, every resurrection? Prizes for death and life? Prizes for passion, for hate and love? And how did you shitheads intend to hand me the prize? As a gift? As a favor, like those tasteless hosts that the pope distributes like fast food? I'll kick you! Or do I come submissive, whimpering? I'll kick you again! And there's not even a check. It's outrageous!

Then they send me the piece of shit in Paris. Nanhoï doesn't even want this disgusting trinket to play with. He kicks it away. So I toss the Gold Ribbon in the garbage can.

The premiere of *Nosferatu* takes place at the Paris Cinémathèque. When Nosferatu first appears on screen—shorn bald, chalky white, with fangs, a reptile with long claws like spider legs—Nanhoï's little, joyfully quivering voice calls through the dark silence:

"Papa!"

Then the carnival of the Cannes Film Festival begins. I've never before known what it really is. Now everyone blabs away at me, saying I have to go to Cannes because of *Woyzeck.*

Minhoï has dashed off to India with Nanhoï. Today the first picture postcard arrives. I'm gonna hop a plane—today if possible—and look for them in India. But I can't decipher the name of the village in the postmark. I buy a magnifying glass, but the print is so blurred and broken that I can barely piece a name together. I buy a huge map of India, and with the magnifying glass I scour the whole country, hunting for a place that sounds like that name. But there are too many. How can I track Minhoï and Nanhoï down among a billion people in that huge land? I feel helpless and ridiculous. Why is Minhoï doing this? She must know that I can't live without my son! Why does she make things worse all the time? Why?

And while I keep asking myself the same senseless questions day after day, trying to decipher the name of the Indian village on the postcard, my flight to Cannes keeps drawing closer and closer. I'm determined to forget about the festival if Minhoï and Nanhoï don't return in time to come with me.

One day before the start of the festival, Minhoï and Nanhoï return from India, and she doesn't even bother to unpack. Together with a nanny, we fly to Cannes. Minhoï can lie on the beach and recover from her strenuous trip across India while Nanhoï splashes in the swimming pool at the Hotel Majestic. He stays there all day long. I drudge like a horse, prattling and prattling for TV, radio, newspapers. . . . And always the same old questions: How? And why? And what's the next project? And all the other dumb, sterile crap. I refuse to believe that the public cares one way or another. On the contrary: People hate being bamboozled by these programmed reporter robots!

And then the hysteria over these crummy prizes! And it's only a gang of twelve lousy jurors who actually imagine they're sitting in judgment (their supreme wish!). If they had their druthers, they'd be weighing the life and death of a human being. There's so much gossip about my getting (yet another) prize. It's like the cattle market, where the bulls get prizes for their dicks and the cows for their udders. After yet another TV interview, I'm just heading off to take a piss when I jump back into the media room and shout into the mike that no one should dare try to mock me by giving me such a prize.

Menahem Golan, whom we know from Israel because of *Entebbe,* sits down at my table and asks if I want to star in his first Hollywood flick. I ask him if he's got a checkbook handy. He shows me his checkbook, which is wedged under his shirt because it's hot out and he's not wearing a jacket. That is, he holds the checkbook halfway out at the level of his fat gut. This reminds me of the Moroccan who kept pointing to the cigarette pack in his hand, to his fly, and to the bushes, wanting to fuck me up the ass in that public park, in broad daylight. Instead of cigarettes, Menahem tears a scrap from a newspaper and scribbles on the blank margins with his ballpoint: the sum, the date, and the title of the movie. Meanwhile he again pulls the checkbook halfway out of his sweaty shirt at the level of his fat belly and points alternately to the shred of newsprint and to his half-visible check pad.

"Can't you wait until tomorrow?" I ask him. "Then we can type up the most important stipulations."

"Tomorrow you're getting the Cannes prize. Then you'll be twice as expensive."

"Tomorrow I'll be twice as expensive even without this stupid prize," I say.

That's how all of them are—these cattle dealers. As if a person were different just because he's been awarded a "prize"!

I put off the dealing until tomorrow so that he won't take advantage of me. And yet I'm tempted to take a check for half the salary, or at least a third, right now, right here at the table, without doing a thing for it. A pile of money right in my hand after signing a scrap of newsprint for a movie that I'm supposed to start in six months and that may never be shot.

The street kid in me says, "Grab the money and run—who cares who it's from! Don't think about whatever you have to do for it or when you have to do it!"

After Cannes I go to Hollywood to make the mindless flick for Golan. I've gotten my entire salary in advance, and so I have to swallow the repulsive pill—like it or not. There's also some other American crap, with Ornella Muti as my wife, and directed by James Toback. But at least Jimmy gets me girls.

I've also promised Twentieth Century Fox to go on a PR tour for *Nosferatu* in the United States and Canada and to participate in the New York Film Festival. After hustling for *Nosferatu* in seven European countries, I now have to keep my promise. Minhoï, Nanhoï, and I spend four weeks traveling the length and breadth of the United States and Canada. Four hundred and eighty newspaper interviews, God knows how many TV shows, and more than six thousand radio stations! Every day from seven A.M. until midnight, nothing but bullshit.

It's important for me to have Nanhoï close by. And even though I now mostly see him asleep or at breakfast, I can at least look at him and touch him and kiss him and hug him tight.

Not only is the interview whoring a horrible grind, but I never get a chance to choke down a bite of food. Even when I'm having lunch with up to thirty journalists, I have to keep answering their sterile, superfluous questions while they themselves slurp down their soup, not missing the opportunity to stuff their guts. At least they listen—which is quite extraordinary for so-called journalists. They're thrilled by my openness and they write down whatever I say.

At the Beverly Wilshire Hotel, where I'm staying, the first girl I get into bed is Hawaiian. She has a broad, dancing ass like a hula performer's, and a dark twat with thick lips.

Sabbath is one of the managers of the Beverly Wilshire, a black-haired Mediterranean devil. All it takes is a single glance of her huge black eyes to open your fly. Whenever I complain to her, she insists on personally showing me another room, even though she knows it's not another room that I want. I pull off her panties and put her belly down on the bed, no matter how much her beeper may be beeping. The more I fuck her, the more she wants me to fuck her. Day and night I've got so many complaints about something in the Beverly Wilshire Hotel that Sabbath and I could do nothing but fuck. Except that Marlayna, my driver, gropes my crotch during the drive to the shooting site. Marlayna isn't as big as the giant hooker in Pakistan, but she's still so big and powerful that she makes all the other studio chauffeurs look like dwarves, and they are very respectful of her.

Unlike the Pakistani giant, who, in proportion to her body, had huge, fleshy pussy lips, Marlayna has a tiny, chubby piggy-cunt that vacuum-pumps my cock head like a pouting mouth.

Sometimes I crash in Sabbath's pad. Then we can finally fuck long and hard, and I fuck her not only from behind, like in the hotel, but also from in front, on her back, and on her side. Or else she rides my dick. I eat her pussy, and she slurps my balls, my asshole, and my cock. In short, she fucks shamelessly, like a good slut.

I fuck Marlayna only once because I always have a date with some other chick after the shooting. Marlayna is horny, but she works a lot of overtime, so she hardly ever gets to stuff a righteous piece of dick into her twat.

Catherine Burkett plays my daughter in the Golan flick. When I fuck her in my hotel room, I really think I'm fucking my daughter. Scenes from the movie emerge in me: I see my daughter naked in the shower and I can't take my eyes off her, can't stop thinking how excitingly slutty she looked in "my wife's" clothes. Now those images blend with the present, when she's lying on my bed, half undressed, her skirt hiked way up. And she childishly kicks around as I pull down her stained panties. Her piggish ass cheeks, her small belly, her trembling thighs, her mini-cunt, seemingly unfucked and offered for devirginizing (though she lives with some old guy, who probably fucks the shit out of her), her curious asshole that keeps closing and opening—all her apertures shriek: "I wanna be your little wife!"

Twentieth Century Fox has made me a present of a license plate that says NANHOI—I wanted it so badly. I buy a Jeep so that I can get the license plate. Then I ship the Jeep to Le Havre in northern France to show the plate to my baby boy in Paris.

I squeeze my Nanhoï so wildly and for such a long time that I knock the breath out of him. Then, together with Veronica D., I take the train to Le Havre in order to pick up the Jeep.

As she calls up her husband, who's in Marseilles, Veronica squats with my dick inside her from behind. He doesn't even realize that she's in Le Havre instead of Paris.

Today, at the crack of dawn, Veronica and I drive back to Paris in the Jeep. I show it to Nanhoï and then unscrew the plate, which belongs to me forever now. And then I sell the Jeep.

I've come only to hug Nanhoï and show him the Jeep with the license plate. Then I have to fly back to Hollywood.

Herzog suddenly pops up in Lalaland and goes all over, begging for money to shoot *Fitzcarraldo*. But nobody in America wants to lend him all the cash it would take. Finally, that garbage producer Roger Corman screws him over like a real rag dealer. He pays him—I think—$300,000 for the American rights. That's laughable. And Herzog, who's been raking in prizes since *Aguirre*—there's hardly any country where *Aguirre, Nosferatu,* or *Woyzeck* hasn't gotten some kind of award—now boasts about Corman, thereby risking his reputation.

When we were shooting *Nosferatu,* I brought him a pair of white slacks from Yves Saint-Laurent in Paris because I could no longer stand seeing him in the same old fart-soaked, unwashed, shit-colored pants. Always the same sweat-stained, unwashed, shit-colored sweater, and always the same sticky, unwashed, shit-colored shirt. It all looked like a prison or nuthouse uniform. Who knows what he did with the Yves Saint-Laurent trousers? In any case, he's still sporting those unwashed, sweat-stained, fart-soaked rags—and he's just as unwashed as ever. And his teeth are as rotten as ever. And he's just as recalcitrant and he still stuffs his face like the garbage can he is—without ever picking up the check.

Golan keeps asking me about *Paganini*. But I don't trust him. I'm convinced he doesn't know shit about what I'm saying when I tell him about my script. The first thing he shows me at his office on Sunset Boulevard is his Oscar nomination for *Entebbe (Operation Thunderbolt)* It reminds me yet again of the swill I had to choke down during that drudgery in Israel. I wonder why these award perverts don't hang their nominations in the toilet. That way they could jerk off in front of them, undisturbed, at any time.

Back to Paris for *La Femme Enfant* ("The Child-Woman").

I don't think there's a nastier and more suicide-inducing region in France than the area this director bitch has chosen for the flick. It's near Belgium. Brutal and insidious, and now, in November and December, it's gray and bleak, with a freezing slush. Fog, snow, and icy roads.

The hotel is an imitation of a small seventeenth-century château; construction's going on day and night, and we're filming during the day. Drills, hammers, saws, tractors, yells, poisonous dust, and the stench of whitewash—day and night. The so-called deluxe "Turkish" baths, with their huge, round plastic tubs where you could easily drown, function as follows: If you flush the toilet, shit and piss well up from the bathtub drain. If you turn on the cold-water faucet, out comes boiling water that stinks of shit. And so on. It's a Laurel and Hardy flick. This so-called luxury château is used by Parisian men and their whores as a weekend brothel. I could go bananas in this cesspool, but that's not the only reason to commute from Paris. I drive the 120 miles back and forth every day in case Minhoï suddenly lets Nanhoï spend the evening with me at my apartment.

The shooting is one long battle against the aggressive obstinacy of the "directress" bitch and her clod of a cameraman—and the two of them stick solidly together in their obduracy.

Minhoï flies to friends in California, and Nanhoï and I go on our first vacation for just the two of us.

We fly to an island in the Bahamas. We splash all week long in emerald and turquoise water, over which the turquoise and pale-violet sky shifts from rosy lilac to hot red every evening and morning. We dig in the snow-white sand and build castles, we cook on an open campfire, roast crabs and shrimps and the tastiest fish—and sleep on the beach under millions of stars that are right within grasp. And we cover ourselves with the galaxies that hang deep down on us. Nanhoï asks me if the earth is round and if it really turns. He's three and a half.

Steven Spielberg offers me a part in *Raiders of the Lost Ark*. Someone brings me the script from Hollywood to Paris. But much as I'd like to do a movie with Spielberg, the script is as moronically shitty as so many other flicks of this ilk. At the same time, Claude Lelouch is nagging me to do his film *Les Uns et les Autres* (*Bolero*). I'd be willing to do this project, but not for the shabby pittance that this rat offers me. Besides, the American movie *Venom* is still in the running—all three at once. I pick *Venom* because the salary is very high, even though I hate London, where the flick's to be shot.

First I have to go to Tokyo. *Fruits of Passion* is a Japanese film set in Japan and China. The girls, the women, the boys, the men, the director, the cameraman, and the rest of the crew are all Japanese. There are also two Frenchwomen. I'm supposed to fuck both of them in front of the camera. In Paris I immediately drag one of them to my pad on the Quai Bourbon and fuck her on the floor right inside the apartment entrance. The other Frenchwoman is hysterical and is still resisting long after I've stuck my dick into her pussy and shot. She's

married, and during the fuck she babbles about "rape . . . adultery . . .
scoundrel . . ." Yet her bodacious butt sticks out so hornily that she
can't want anything but adultery.

Minhoï and Nanhoï come along to Japan.

The Japanese flick has a lot of fucking. Real fucking. In all positions,
even in the mouth. It's the story of a man who puts his girlfriend in a
brothel in Shanghai because it turns him on. The girl does it out of
love for the man, but her torments are horrible. The flick is set chiefly
in a whorehouse in Tokyo—or rather, fifty miles outside of Tokyo, in
Japan's oldest and most primitive silent-film studio. There's no air-
conditioning, the mercury hits 106 in the shade, we work twenty-four
hours a day nonstop, and all we get to eat is watery soup. The Japanese never complain, for the simple reason that they like to work. We're
practically out of oxygen, you could cut the air to pieces with a knife,
every breath you take is a struggle. And we're all sweating buckets, the
water is literally streaming down our ass cracks and out of our pants.
We can barely open our eyes; the salty sweat running down from our
soaked hair burns our lids like fire.

I've had the same experiences with other movies. But this is a different situation. According to the script, we have to fuck—for real!
Right in front of the camera, in every possible position. During the
fucking our sex organs, especially our boners, have to be seen clearly,
plain as pikestaffs. But every dick in the place is hanging slack, even
though the producer and the director, Shuji Terayama, signed a contract stipulating at least six sexual acts—meaning that I have to fuck
five girls in front of the lens. One of the Japanese girls I have to
screw—and who I bang in the hotel after the shooting is done—takes

care of the other Mr. Softies. She pulls each guy into a dark corner of the studio and keeps sucking his dick until it finally stands at something like attention. She has to know exactly when to stop sucking. The cock mustn't start spurting—until it's in front of the camera.

The instant one of these soft dicks gets hard, the girl dashes over to Terayama and signals that filming can begin. Now, a dick may rigidify in the girl's hot, greedy mouth, which has milked it for all it's worth. But the unbearably heavy and muggy tropical heat weighs on your nuts like sandbags, and without the milkmaid the blood pressure in your dick promptly heads south. Your hard-on collapses before the camera starts rolling.

From time to time, what I do is reach into the cunt's panties and draw in the pungent aroma. Or I suck the briny sweat out of the long hair in her armpits. It hits my blood like a vaccine, and my fiddle bow is instantly restrung.

Of course, in this murderous heat I've got little staying power, and the first take has to be enough.

The girl I'm supposed to place in a brothel has a delicious cheese. During one scene, she truly has a nervous breakdown when a mechanical dick on a kind of fuck machine is inserted into her hole. She throws herself on the cold, slimy sand floor of the studio and rolls and wallows in the filth, shrieking her lungs out. No one can get near her. I lovingly calm her down and take her to my dressing room. There I bend her over the makeup table in front of the mirror and give her a rough and thorough fuck from behind. Then she's fine again.

Nastassja is in Tokyo for the premiere of *Tess*. I instantly ring up the Hotel Imperial, but she furiously screams at me for not calling her in Hollywood. I didn't even know we were there at the same time. I'd combed the world for her because she never tells me where she is.

Minhoï and Nanhoï fly from Japan directly to California, then drive to Marin County, where the two of them live in a tiny cottage, a doll-house, in the middle of a forest. It's all like a fairy tale: woods and hills and dales and meadows and ravines and flower-covered rocks and al-batrosses and eagles and does and stags and elks and big wildcats and pumas from far away—and the sea, where sharks swim and whales glide past. The deer pause right in front of me and stare at me. They know I won't hurt them. The woods are still undamaged, as virginal as in the days of the Indians. Here the Pacific coast is free of the ven-omous claws of the consumer plague, thanks to an unusual man named Gary Giacomini, the administrator of Marin County. Gary be-comes my best friend.

I rent a small room, and Nanhoï jumps up and down on my mat-tress like on a trampoline until he can't anymore, and, hugging, we lapse into a sweet sleep.

Every day some Hollywood moron calls me up trying to talk me into doing a flick in Australia and New Zealand. I don't want to make a movie in Australia. Not now. Not for all the bucks in the world. I'm exhausted and disgusted. But my chief reason is I can spend two whole months with my Nanhoï for the first time. Just the two of us, all alone, day and night. We'll be able to do whatever we like, eat what we want to, play at anything and for as long as we like.

This is because Minhoï wants to spend those two months in Guatemala. It's sheer madness, because the country's teeming with murder. But I can't dissuade her.

Before she leaves I have to go to L.A. to check out houses to rent while I'm shooting in Hollywood. Most of the houses are like tombs, stuffed with ghastly furniture like coffins. Everything is decaying. Decayed human souls and brains. Bars everywhere, electric fences, electric entranceways, TV cameras, intercoms, "No Trespassing" signs, "Patrolled by Armed Guards" notices, cable TV, washing machines, dishwashers, garbage disposals hooked up to sinks, fireplaces with cement wood and gas-fueled flames, gardeners, poolmen, barbecues, leaf blowers, lawn mowers—and the house that I eventually lease even has an asshole-washer on the toilet. The house is in Bel Air. Everything is white—the walls, the carpeting, the furniture. The walls are made largely of glass, and you can see the distant mountains from the bed. Otherwise nothing but trees, plants, flowers, and sky.

It's Christmas again, and I'm alone with my little boy in the dollhouse in the middle of the forest. I've brought back a small fir tree from the woods and trimmed it very colorfully. Now I'm in the tiny kitchenette, cooking for my baby boy. I've just done our laundry in the bathtub, and it's hanging on a line above the stove, where a wood fire is crackling. And there are two bunk beds, like in a youth hostel. We sleep in the top bunk, which is so high that I practically have to do chin-ups to get there after helping Nanhoï up. And the bunk is so narrow that we wouldn't have any room if we didn't squeeze together. I lie on the outer edge so my baby boy won't fall out, while he rolls into the corner the sloping roof makes with the inner edge of the bunk. Maybe I'll always be able to tell Nanhoï that each Christmas "is the most beautiful Christmas I've ever had." But so far this is indeed the most wonderful Christmas imaginable!

My agent gets me a young Japanese housekeeper named Niko for my house in Bel Air. She is a fantastic cook, Japanese and Chinese, and she washes, irons, keeps the house spotless, washes our car, does the shopping, answers the phone, cleans the swimming pool, waters the flowers, and waters the lawn. And she does everything quickly and quietly, smiling all the while. Besides paying her, I have to fuck her.

Morning, noon, evening, night. Whether she's cooking, cleaning, or standing at the washing machine, or even hosing the car. Whenever I pull down her panties and fuck her, that hot, naked pussy snaps for my boner like a growling puppy that bares its teeth if you try to take away its reward.

That piece of Hollywood shit with Billy Wilder [*Buddy Buddy*] is over, thank God. No outsider can imagine the stupidity, blustering, hysteria, authoritarianism, and paralyzing boredom of shooting a flick for Billy Wilder. The so-called "actors" are simply trained poodles who sit up on their hind legs and jump through hoops. I thought the insanity would never stop. But I got a shitload of money.

"From now on you'll do serious movies with Herzog and comical ones with me." That's what Billy Wilder told me when we first met at the La Scala restaurant. But I think the reverse is true. For a long time now Billy Wilder's so-called comedies have been uptight and anything but funny, and your laughter freezes in the corners of your mouth. And Herzog's so-called serious flicks would be unintentionally funny if I did what he wanted me to do.

Those hack parasites track me down even here—bedbugs sucking their fill of my blood. They all want to write about me: biographies, filmographies, videographies, cover stories, comic strips, talk shows, and God only knows what other garbage spewed from human brains. After trying to cash in on me for doctoral dissertations, they now use me for high school essays—as warnings to young girls?

Jack Lang, the French minister of culture, sends me an award—Commander of the Order of Art and Literature—through the French consulate in Lalaland. What's this all about? "For what you have done for France and the rest of the world." Once again, there's no check attached! Who's the lunatic here? Where does that guy get off "awarding" me such garbage? They must all have a screw loose! I tell my agent to send back all this bloody crap!

Months ago I told Herzog that he could go fuck himself, and I hung up on him. So he began *Fitzcarraldo* without me, using someone from New York, plus Mick Jagger as Fitzcarraldo's best friend. Now Herzog fucking shows up in L.A. and begs me to star in the movie.

After some four weeks of shooting with the guy from New York, Herzog, even with his moronic brain, must have realized that the result was all garbage and that he had to start all over again from scratch. For the fourth time this blowhard has proved that without me he's a nonentity. Nevertheless he tries to rip me off in L.A. Every single word in the contract has to be retyped—until Herzog finally throws in the towel: At midnight he runs out of the office of the Beverly Hills lawyer and lets me write anything I like.

Minhoï and Nanhoï are in Marin County. I fly to my baby boy to hug and kiss him one last time before taking off for South America, where I'll be for such a long time.

Nanhoï makes me promise to give up smoking forever. I promise him.

The five months in the Peruvian jungle are just like the months we spent filming *Aguirre* ten years ago. Once again our lives are constantly put at risk because of Herzog's total ignorance, narrowmindedness, arrogance, and inconsideration, which threaten to bring about the collapse of the shooting and the financing. Once again the crew feeds on inedible chow cooked in lard. Once again we lack the barest necessities to keep up our strength and ward off dangerous diseases. Once again we lack fruit, vegetables, and especially drinking water. Mine is the only contract to stipulate a daily ration of lemons, papayas, and mineral water.

And I'm the only one to avoid eating that swill Herzog supplies. Whenever possible, I catch fish in the river or shoot wildfowl and roast them on a wood fire.

The instant Herzog smells the roast, he sticks to me like a fly to dung and tries to eat up my food. No matter how much I curse, insult, and even threaten him, the moment he wants something from me, he's here, like malaria, like the stench billowing out from a pile of shit.

He's the same decaying garbage heap that he was ten years ago— only more moronic, more mindless, more murderous.

Day and night he keeps a notebook in the leather kit on his belt and he jots down his distortions about the shooting. He's also hired Les Blank, a so-called documentary filmmaker, who thinks of nothing but food. He's supposed to shoot a flick about Herzog, but this chow hound is so lazy that he sleeps through everything. If ever, by some chance, he happens to be in the right place at the right time, he dawdles and dawdles until his camera is finally attached to its tripod—and by then it's too late. He never uses a hand-held camera. He's probably too shaky, but the main reason is no doubt the camera itself: It's too heavy and uncomfortable.

Once again Herzog and his cameraman go for weeks without washing. Once again their clothes are stiff with filth. Not soil, not mud, not clay. No. Filth! Their own filth. For hygienic reasons the thin leather over the rubber edge of the viewfinder normally ought to be changed daily. But it's not changed for weeks—no, months—so it's covered with a kind of blackish-gray slime. And it stinks so unbearably that I can't get near the camera. Furthermore, they're all disgustingly lazy and voracious—they're still asleep at eight or nine A.M., whereas the jungle day dawns at three, and its wondrous and enchanting light reveals creation in all its mysterious power and purity.

Before my very eyes the jungle arises from the colorful morning fog, just as a body is born from a mother's womb. Everything is new, young, and untouched. No human beings have ever seen this on a movie screen.

Today the morning fog is rosy, almost violet. Using a machete I hack a path through the plant walls until I can look across the river. On the steeply sloping opposite bank, the 350-ton ship is hanging from a single steel hawser—as if it were sailing straight up to the rosy and violet clouds in the heavens. It's four A.M. I plunge through the jungle, return to the camp, and kick Herzog out of his sleep. When he sees with his own eyes what I've been yelling into his ears, he finally hauls ass and runs along the river. Five A.M. The fog will be shredded in twenty minutes, and nothing is repeated in nature, nothing resembles the past. There's barely time to shoot the image I want.

That's how it goes, day in, day out, several times a day. Over and over again I refuse to stick to Herzog's hair-raisingly crappy script or take his amateurish "direction." I have to force him to accept every camera angle I want. I have to show that dimwit of a cameraman where the camera belongs, and I have to get the lens and the distance. I never "rehearse" a single scene. I say, "Roll 'em!" and I shoot only once.

The movie is practically finished. A few more weeks, and I'll be rid of the vermin. The final scene, which is moved up, is shot on the boat sailing along the Amazon. I have to smoke a gigantic cigar. I stand on deck, right in the wind, which hurls the black billows from the smokestack right into my face and lungs. It's the smoke of rubber tires burning in the engine room—for the vessel, which is supposed to look like a steamship, is actually driven by a diesel engine. I feel like puking my guts out by the time the scene's been shot with different lenses. I'm so ill that I nearly blank out—then Herzog comes over and says he wants to do another take. This creep must be totally crazy! He wants me to go through that same hell again? What for? The take was fine, I know it! That'll do!

I knock Herzog to the ground with a kung fu lunge and kick him in the face. Then I go belowdecks to avoid having to see him.

"Did you have to?" that creep asks when he comes sidling over to me.

"We'll see," I say. "You can get more if you like."

"Are you ready to continue shooting?" that worm whimpers.

"Of course, you bastard," I say. "That's why I'm here."

In Iquitos I receive a letter from my baby boy, the very first letter he's ever written.

> *Please watch out for snakes.*
>
> *I love you*
> *Nanhoï*

I can't help crying. I can't help laughing. I have to cry as I laugh. I have to laugh as I cry. Oh, my dearest darling! You're the only person I can't forget in the wilderness. Your words are the sweetest.

The shooting has to be interrupted. The blowhard has refused to listen to the Indians. The level of the river have sunk so low that the ship is stuck in the mud bottom. We won't come back until two and a half months from now to complete the filming.

Herzog gives one of those pukey "going-away parties" that producers throw after beating the crew bloody. Then they all get drunk on cheap rotgut and stuff their bellies at the self-service buffet. I don't attend.

This afternoon, shortly before my plane is to take off, Herzog shows up at the airport. He hugs me and thanks me. I'm gonna toss my cookies.

I give up my Paris apartment and have my Range Rover shipped to L.A. I hop a plane from Paris to San Francisco via New York. I want to get back to Marin County, where I was alone with my baby boy for the first time—for two months!—in that dollhouse in the magic forest.

I've found a parcel of land for sale: over forty acres of woods. All day long buzzards circle in the sky, gliding so low over my head that I can feel the breeze in their wings. The does hop around me or stand in front of me, staring at me. I can even creep up to within ten feet of the wildcats. The partridges walk when they see me. The butterflies let me touch them. I peer right into the eyes of the mice. The weather changes nonstop. Fog billows in from the sea, rolling six feet high across the hills in broad daylight, as if these dense patches had an appointment in the hollows of the small valleys. The sun breaks through the wildly racing clouds. Or else there's an icy hailstorm. Or both at once. Rainbows. Lulls, like in the Peruvian jungle—and storms like ocean tempests. Here the nights are packed in profound darkness that erupts from the black sky—and here the nocturnal dome of the sky is flooded with shiny white stars like diamonds, all the way to the outermost edge of the horizon.

I buy the land. Nanhoï will be free here, as free as the birds in the sky.

I fly to L.A. and buy a Mercedes station wagon for Minhoï and Nanhoï and a Mercedes limousine for Nanhoï and me. In L.A. I drive from one dog breeder to another. I want to buy a young Alsatian. All the young dogs are adorable, but for Nanhoï I want a huge, strong dog that'll grow with him and protect him. I name him Stronger.

After buying the land, I go to Marin County as much as I can, often only overnight, to supervise the construction of the house. It's a simple wooden house in the midst of a forest. A single great room with a sleeping loft and a huge fireplace that can heat the entire house. We've got enough fuel—trees, that is—for millions of years, and we pump our own water from the ground. There's also a huge vegetable garden, which we can cultivate all year round, and we have all sorts of fruit trees: cherry, apple, apricot, almond, and plum. I'd like to bake our bread myself. I want to be free, independent. Free of all coercion. Free of any need to rely on other people. I have no credit cards, nor do I want any. I toss the cash on a table. I leave others in peace and I want to be left in peace. I spend my nights sleeping on the ground in the forest. I embrace trees as I have done all my life. I smell their bark and kiss it. I lay my face on the moss and breathe in the spicy aroma of fruitfulness as if I were lying on a woman's belly.

It's been six months since Minhoï and Nanhoï left on a trip around the world. So far I've received only one postcard from Nanhoï in Nepal and one telegram from Minhoï in Australia. Her wire says they're coming back.

Once again I arrive at the airport hours in advance, clutching the telegram, which I reread endlessly to make sure I'm not fantasizing. And I keep asking the information girl about the Qantas plane. Date, time, flight number. I feel like a wolf who's been chased into the city. I stare at the monitors to get the data on the Qantas plane, but I'm too agitated. I don't understand the signs. I get dizzy. I start sweating. I halt exactly where the passengers come streaming through an automatic double door that keeps opening and closing.

My Nanhoï is so tiny that my eyes fill up with tears when I see him. He's wearing a little knapsack and he takes long strides as if hiking through the world.

A few days later Minhoï goes to Marin County; she wants to find a house for herself and Nanhoï. I'll follow her in the Range Rover with Nanhoï and Stronger.

Herzog and his cohorts keep bombarding me with phone calls, yammering and begging me to attend the Cannes Film Festival. I say, "Fuck off!" But they're like vermin, they keep coming back. Eventually, I think, Okay. I have to visit my dentist in Paris anyway, and they can pay for my trip.

In Cannes, that same old garbage heap. That same riffraff. Again press conferences, together with that totally moronic Herzog.

Tonight is the so-called gala premiere of *Fitzcarraldo*. I'm already wearing a repulsive tux, which feels like a straitjacket in a nuthouse. This is the last time. Tomorrow morning I'm gonna dump it in the trash.

I don't know what time it is; I don't have a watch. But it's already dark, and I probably should have been called for long ago. But no one comes to drive me to the gala premiere. Herzog and his cohorts went there alone! Without me! Without Fitzcarraldo! That would be reason enough to beat the shit out of them. But I don't care. All I care about is having Lola. I first saw her late this afternoon outside the Hotel Carlton. She asked me for my autograph, and when she spoke, her rosy-red strawberry mouth swelled as if it were her pussy with my dick inside. I told her to come to my room.

Under the pretext of having her try on my tux, I strip off her clothes. Even her panties. First I pull the tux trousers over her naked ass. Then over her curiously peeping twat. Then I draw the suspenders over her heavy young udders, I zip the zipper over the pumpkin of her small schoolgirl belly, and I button the black jacket over the white flesh of this horny fruit. Then I drag her out on the balcony and seat her on my lap, claiming that I want to watch the people way below on the beach promenade, which is ablaze with spotlights. How simple is the brain of a tomcat in heat! But when her ass touches my painfully rigid dick, which leaps between her gaping cheeks, I have to stuff one of her udders into my mouth to keep from shrieking in my horniness. With her tit so deep in my throat that I'm practically choking, I carry Lola to the bed.

Once more New York. To dub *Venom*. Arthur Penn wants me for a film. I turn him down. I've turned down Fellini and Visconti and Pasolini as well as Ken Russell and Liliana Cavani—usually because of the money. And I'd have turned down Eisenstein and Kurosawa for the same reason. By now I've made over 250 movies and turned down over a thousand.

This year I have to fly around the world three more times. From now on I won't accept any project during Nanhoï's vacation. Not for all the money in the world. I will spend time with Nanhoï. I will play with him endlessly. In the evening, before we go to bed, I tell him stories. Stories that I've personally experienced. Stories from the jungle or the desert, from the Himalayas and the ocean. Nanhoï asks me for details over and over, even days and weeks later.

We go to the beach and fly kites that I've brought back from China and Japan. They float so high that they fray and tatter in the wind. Nanhoï tussles with a kite like a lion cub with an eagle. His face is defiant, almost angry, and he struggles hard. Soon he manages to get two-string kites to rise and plunge and shoot back up from right above the ground.

Stronger is almost a year old. We've built him a gigantic dog-house right near the cottage. But he never sets foot in it, not once. He doesn't even go near it, as if it were an outrage and beneath his dignity. He sleeps directly under our loft window, which faces the woods, and he lets out a brief, raw bark whenever he catches any sound. He owns the woods and the hills, which go all the way to the Pacific Ocean, as far as the eye can see. Tens of thousands of acres of forest with its rank and impenetrable thickets, towering tree giants, enchanted paths, which mysteriously open and close as in a fairy tale. Wilderness, jungle . . .

Stronger leaves in the morning and returns in the evening. He runs and runs, ten or fifteen miles a day. And the longer he's here, the more his face reveals the landscapes of the time when his forebears were wolves. He's free. No collars, no dog tag.

I have to race around the world over and over again. Nanhoï is with Minhoï, and no one's with Stronger. I ask Tony, the son of an old farmer from the Azores, who lives a mile from our house, to bring Stronger his food when I'm gone. At first it works nicely, but Stronger stays away for longer and longer stretches because Nanhoï and I aren't waiting for him in the evening. And Stronger can't understand why there's no one here when he comes home. Stronger doesn't come back.

Back in Marin County I harvest the first plums in my life. This is the first time I eat plums that I haven't bought or stolen. I make preserves, using honey instead of sugar. This is the most delicious jam I've ever eaten. Four twelve-inch jars. The jam's meant for the winter, but in no more than two weeks my baby boy and I have emptied all four jars.

How often, as a small boy, I pressed my face against the gates of bakery cellars, inhaling the exciting smell of bread, as warm and protective as a womb. I have to learn how to bake my own bread. I have to learn it for the great trip. Lola gave me one of her mother's recipes. She also gave me a recipe for *napfkuchen.* Sometimes I bake a good one. Sometimes it's only an ordinary lump, but I eat it all the same.

Our garden is so big that we could live off it. Nanhoï planted the first seeds: sunflowers, radishes, beans, corn, and potatoes. But we have to plant a lot more veggies, especially tomatoes. We need more apple, pear, peach, and apricot trees. We've got whole jungles of huckleberries, raspberries, mountain cranberries. Chanterelles and other mushrooms spring up after each rain. And there are blueberries and wild strawberries galore. We're going to add gooseberries and rhubarb. Then we can have rhubarb pudding and rhubarb compote in the hot summer months. We're going to plant all the herbs that the Indians did.

We could live without electricity and without a phone. If only I didn't have to go to stores anymore. Or to restaurants. Or post offices or gas stations.

Beauty and the Beast for ABC in Hollywood. I think of Cocteau's magical film. I can't think of anything else, not even when I read the hair-raising script, which degrades the most beautiful of all fairy tales to banal Hollywood trash.

They promised to get Jessica Lange to costar. Instead they want to force some New York actress on me. They do give me the right to translate Cocteau's words verbatim, from French into English—but all the other characters speak the unimaginative, proletarian, idiotic dialogue of the American TV version. The shooting is indescribable.

I do the flick in five days. In the middle of the close-up of the death scene, the prince who's been transformed into a beast is saying, "A poor animal that's lost its love can only creep away and die." Then some creep yells through the loudspeakers: "Quitting time!"

It's about six in the afternoon. The working day set by the union is over!

My agent calls. George Roy Hill wants me for *The Little Drummer Girl.* Producer: Warner Bros. Shooting time: five months. Locations: Germany, England, Greece, Israel. They're messengering the script over to me. Shit!

At night I grope my way through the woods, my forehead touching the starry sky, or else I sail a surging ocean, or I lie on moss in the daytime, clouds drifting overhead and buzzards soaring in circles. At such times I know that I'm far away and that I'll never go back to the vile traps of human beings and their ghettos, where madness lurks and roams. Nanhoï's love will redeem me from my hell on earth.

All my life I've stuttered whenever I try to express what's inside me, what I feel, what I suffer, and what makes me happy.

People call me an "actor." What's that?

In any case, it has nothing to do with the shit that people have always blabbered about it. It's neither a vocation nor a profession— although it's how I earn my living. But then so does the two-headed freak at the carnival. It's something you have to try and live with— until you learn how to free yourself. It has nothing to do with nonsense like "talent," and it's nothing to be conceited about or proud of.

Eleonora Duse, the greatest actress in Italy, said at the end of her life: "I did everything wrong. I should have devoted myself totally to my child. The theater has never given me the fulfillment that I had when I was with my child."

When I was a little boy I sometimes put on my mother's clothes because I had nothing else to play with. I was fascinated by my image in the mirror: My reflection was like a multitude of pictures copied atop one another, one of which pushed through—while my clothing kept changing nonstop. My mother's clothes kept changing under the duress of my fantasies, which conjure up my previous lives. Or my future lives. It is the incarnation that dictates the costume. Without it clothes have no meaning. They remain anonymous, like a disguise at Mardi Gras, when anyone can put on any costume whatsoever.

I once owned a Japanese wooden mask. One of those white, silent, neutral masks that seem totally expressionless. I bet some friends that as soon as I had the mask on my face I could will it to take on any expression. That is, the mask would express whatever I felt. It would suck up my expression and be imbued with it, become impregnated by it and give birth to it anew. I put on the mask, which covered up my face. Then I alternately smiled and wept. And the mask likewise smiled and wept.

The same thing happened to me as had happened when I was a little boy putting on my mother's clothes. But this time it was unconscious. Later I triggered the rebirth more and more often and fully consciously, in precise terms and whenever I wanted it. Today I can no longer resist it, even if I'm on the alert day and night, even in my sleep, even in my dreams—I'm like a wolfhound, who perks up his ears even when he's fast asleep. The danger that I can no longer discard the incarnations that I evoke becomes greater and greater. They spawn other incarnations, which in turn spawn others, and so on.

They're unruly plants pushing up, no matter what, from the

bottom of my soul, leaving nothing but devastation behind. Soul plants, chaotically shooting upward and in all directions. They hide out in the finest ramifications of my dreams. They poison my sleep. Strangle me. Try to drive me insane. A ruthless struggle begins and never seems to end.

A producer tells me the plot of a movie. At one point, I scream and refuse to let him continue. I can't stand the fate of my character, whom I am already living during the producer's description. The incarnation does not take place deliberately here; I can't force it. I'm at its mercy. Unshielded. Wide open and ready to receive—from the very moment that I allowed the producer to start narrating the plot of his film.

It's especially when I'm worn out and feeble that I'm ambushed by the demons. They come in packs, surrounding and harassing me. No matter whether I'm dreaming or waking, in the dark of night or in broad daylight. If I collapsed, they would pounce on me.

In Vienna I stand at a shop window where violins are displayed. In one corner I see a twelve-inch portrait of an unusual-looking man. His face is wild and devastated by passion. "The black tails of my crumpled tuxedo, which I haven't changed in thirty years . . . My raven curls fluttering down my shoulders . . . My grotesquely contorted body is wooden . . . like a crazed animal. . . . My long arms and gigantic hands seem extended by the bow in one and the violin in the other. . . . My ugly head with the toothless, cynically twisted mouth . . . My dreadful face engraved with indelible signs of profound anxiety, genius, and hell . . . No wife hesitates for even an instant to deceive her husband with me—when I place my violin under my chin and start to play."

I must have been standing at this window for a very long time;

twilight is already setting in. I step into the violin shop and ask the proprietor who the violinist is. He says, "Paganini." I dash from the store. I know that I was Paganini.

"Acting schools!" I could never understand what they're all about. Someone told Eleonora Duse that she ought to open an acting school in the United States—a so-called actors studio. It would be a sure hit because so many people would apply. Duse answered: "I'm the most unsuitable person for that role because on the very first day, I would tell the students not to come back."

How can anyone believe that you can "learn" how to feel and learn how to express it? How can anyone teach another person how to laugh and how to cry? How to be cheerful and how to be sad? Teach them what pain is, and despair, and desire, and passion? Hate and love? How can anyone waste their own and somebody else's time with that idiocy?

But far worse than the morons who think they can learn these things are the people who claim they can teach them. In the end, they teach bad manners. If one of their trained poodles sits down in public, he doesn't sit, he slouches—which is supposed to mean that his behavior is "natural." He or she scratches his or her head and picks his or her nose, which is supposed to mean that he or she has no complexes and acts very spontaneously. So this is what a New York talk show looks like.

In Paris the TV interviews are even worse. Your clothes have to be grimy and at least arouse a suspicion of Communism. You're unshaved and a bit sweaty, your hair is stringy and unkempt, and naturally you're wearing an ancient leather jacket that looks as if you'd bought it at the flea market. You chew on your dirty fingernails, scratch your belly and your legs, stick your fingers in your ears and up your nose, and of course, whether you're male or female, you scratch your head.

All these things are the results of those actors studios. I experience them personally when I'm shooting in Hollywood. Everywhere in the world you concentrate before each take (to the extent that you understand that you have to be quiet, as silent as possible, on the set). Or at least you shouldn't disturb whoever's in front of the camera. If you're not part of this take, you keep your mouth shut, don't make a sound, and don't stir once the bell has rung. But this time, instead of shutting up, some creeps who've just gotten their degrees from one of those idiotic "acting schools" start hopping around—as if in the throes of Saint Vitus's dance—making puke noises, grunting like pigs, making ridiculous faces, laughing shrilly and unnaturally, bleating and bawling. I think I'm witnessing the crises of lunatics. I feel harassed by it all.

Many people see the apogee of acting as the ability to "slip into someone else's skin."—How do you do that? Shakespeare wrote Hamlet for a fat player in his troupe—a man he viewed as capable of doing the part. Is every actor now going to fatten up in order to become a fat Hamlet?

People always think of Hamlet as slender, Romeo as handsome, Othello as gigantic. And then they're surprised when they find a gorgeous girl who lets herself be fucked by an ugly and much older man. Or who even loves him.

Naturally, the exterior is a detail in perfecting an incarnation—but that doesn't tell you *which* exterior, and as a mere detail it's subordinate and of varying importance. Nor can you tell whether the incarnation is a *re*incarnation, which only you believe in. It's important to know that everything is *re*incarnation and that the real point is whether the metamorphosis is *perfect*. The kind, the shape, and the color are produced by the metamorphosis itself.

Long ago, and without any difficulty, I could have been a dog or a horse, a bird, a snake, a cat, a fish, a caterpillar, a butterfly, or even a worm. Not through stupid grimaces. But with their organs. With their ocular prisms. With their hearing, their sense of smell. With their sexuality, mating, copulation, pregnancy, bearing. I felt all this as a child, but I couldn't interpret it. The first time I realized it physically was when I played the woman in Jean Cocteau's *La Voix humaine.* At night I went out in full drag: panties, bra, garters, and high heels. Not to flaunt anything, but for my own sake. Dressing like a woman struck me as natural, as a matter of course, because I felt like a woman once the metamorphosis began. I was fully conscious of being a woman.

I find the totality of metamorphosis most terrifying when I'm Woyzeck. Woyzeck, who murders his wife, the person he loves most in the world, and who then goes insane and drowns himself, orphaning their little boy.

Suffering through that had as devastating an impact on me as if I hadn't only always suffered as Woyzeck but continue to do so over and over. Malaria of the soul, recurring again and again. My total being is one large breeding ground for the shocks of the world past, present, and future. All living and dying, all vibrations pass through me. The entire universe pours into me, rages in me, rampages through me and over me. Annihilates me. It comes and goes whenever it likes. It rules me, commands me, envelops me, threatens me, and waits for me everywhere and all the time. It sucks me up, sucks me dry, grows through me. It's in my spinal marrow. In my brain mass. In my blood, in my bones. My muscles. Guts. Genitals. Sperm. Flesh. Eyes. Hearing. Taste. Smell. Balance. Laughter. Tears. In my days and my nights. In my thoughts. In my feelings. In my courage and my fear. In my despair and my hope. In my weakness and my strength. Everywhere and all the time.

I'm torn apart by the most conflicting feelings, the most conflicting thoughts—often at the same time, with no concern as to whether I can endure it.

I don't know how this will end. All I know is Nanhoï's love. My son is my life. I believe in the magic of his love. He is the embodiment of life to me. The embodiment of beauty. Through him I'll find redemption and salvation. Then the wound in my soul—the wound I thought would never scar over—will stop bleeding. I thought I would have to tear it open once it began to heal. Back then, when I didn't know that there is no backing out once you start becoming the incarnation of all existence. Back then, when I felt I couldn't stop being what is called an actor, when I told myself that I was only doing it for the money and that it could be worse. Now, today, I'd rather be poor, but without nightmares and without the torture. If only I could! If only the choice were mine! I don't want to be an actor! I wish I'd never been an actor! I wish I'd never had success! I'd rather have been a streetwalker, selling my body, than selling my tears and my laughter, my grief and my joy.

On the flight from New York to San Francisco, the guy sitting to my right introduces himself as "Professor So-and-So." Who asked him? Then he shakes my hand as if we were old buddies just because he's got the seat next to mine. This is not politeness, mind you! Quite the contrary: It's very impolite to force me to be interested in him. He just wants to prattle and rattle, get to know me, stick his dirty nose into my business, sniff and snoop. He's using me. I'm supposed to divert him, entertain him, help him kill time. Aside from his shameless indiscretion, he wants to have a garbage can for his refuse, which is already piled sky-high in his brain and stinks to high heaven. And why is he yelling? I'm not hard of hearing! The other passengers are already gawking. Then, cunningly and out of a clear blue sky, as if he'd read it in Dostoevsky and were trying to trap me with his sneaky questions like Inspector Porfiri, he says, "What did you say your profession was?" And then, "I didn't quite catch your name." I didn't give him my name. I didn't say anything, not even "Hi!" Nor do I plan to say anything. I can't tell whether he even notices that I'm not replying—that I don't want to reply! In any case, he grinds away, unbidden; he says he was in New York acting as an expert witness in some kind of trial—and he brazenly takes it for granted that I've been gobbling up all the TV and newspaper garbage and that I'm informed about the case. In short, he's an authority on all questions of pregnancy complications and he's called upon for all kinds of litigation. His son-in-law is also a professor, also a specialist, but not in pregnancy matters. The guy is practically shouting by now. And even though the pilots are letting the Boeing 747 engines run full throttle, this fucking asshole of a professor is outshouting the jet racket: ". . . womb . . . ovaries!" he hollers triumphantly, pointing unabashedly and stupidly at the nearby stewardess, who's flirting with a passenger. I stand up and sit down in a window seat in an empty row, determined not to look around until the wheels of the plane touch down in San Francisco.

During the hollering about "wombs" and "ovaries," I recall Viva from Istanbul. I simply have to ring her up. Her solid, massive body weighs on my memory as if she were lying on me full-force. She's a Jewish girl from Morocco whom I met in Tel Aviv when we were shooting *The Little Drummer Girl*, and I fucked her up the ass. Her husband had left Israel earlier for business reasons. But he had told the hostess in the restaurant to keep an eye on his wife—that is, watch her. That's what I was told by the hostess, whom I've known for years. She could see that I was horny for the Moroccan girl and that the girl herself was in heat.

Viva came promptly to my room that night, about to shed her

vast, pajamalike pants right at the threshold. I could feel her oval ass cheeks and thick-lipped pussy right through the loose silk. She showed me that all I had to do was pull on a string to make her pants fall. She willingly knelt down and offered me her butt as I guided her toward the mattress with her face, tits, and belly. I just had to fuck her from behind no matter what! No matter what! She had the widest pelvis I've ever seen on a woman. Wider than on the giant whore in Pakistan! And when her wonderful butt cheeks opened wide, her pelvis grew even wider, so that I could barely envelop it—like the pelvis of a full-grown cow. "It'd be better if you fucked me in the asshole," she panted. "I've just gotten pregnant again, even though I wear an IUD. Besides, ass-fucking is great. . . . Please, please, fuck me in the asshole, please!" So, I fucked her in the ass. She squealed and grunted and rattled.

A guy comes from Munich to San Francisco in order to talk me into doing a film. I don't even listen to him. All I know is that he's also signed up a certain actress. And I have to have her! I don't know her and I've never seen any of her movies. I don't even realize that she's Germany's biggest female movie star. All I know is that I got a boner when I saw a photo of her face in a newspaper.

I tell the guy that I'll do his fucking movie if I can fuck the star. He's to phone her. This instant. Now. She's to hop a plane today and come. For one night. She comes. The three of us have dinner at the Hilton. Then we send the guy away and she comes to my room.

She has the longest vaginal lips I've ever licked and stuck my horny cock into. Then I ram into her from behind. Her face is on its side on the mattress so that I can see her swollen mouth, which shamelessly twists in dreadful passion. After I shoot my second load in her, she has to fly back.

I'm supposed to make a movie based on a novel by Alberto Moravia. So I have lunch with Rossana, my agent in Italy, and the producer, a woman.

"Where's Moravia?" I ask.

"Moravia didn't want to go out," says Rossana. He's not feeling well, but he's invited us over for coffee this afternoon.

After lunch we go to his place. Moravia's wife, Carmen, opens the door. She laughs, opening up her mouth as if she had to suck my dick. She kisses Rossana and the producer ogles me, leaving me no choice but to think, "Just wait a little." In the parlor she sits opposite us on the sofa, crossing her legs under her ass, stretching and kicking with outspread thighs, like a corrupt little girl who wants to show her covered pussy.

Moravia is a lucid and therefore simple man, who, impatient and almost irritated, waves other people's chatter away like bothersome flies. We say what we have to and quickly come to terms. After the coffee, we decide to drive to the production office so they can show me photos of possible costars.

At the production office Carmen deliberately enters a side room to lure me over. I follow her, talking loudly to avoid arousing suspicion while I grab her pussy, reach sideways into her wet panties, and massage her hole with my index and my middle finger. This takes only a few seconds, during which I talk even louder because she is moaning. My hand gets so wet that I have a hard time drying it quickly on her clothes. Like it or not, we have to pull ourselves together and wait till she can visit me in my hotel.

It all sounds like the Borgias. Rossana had told me that Moravia didn't want to come to lunch since he was feeling under the weather. Rossana in turn told Moravia that I, Kinski, didn't want him to join us. And Moravia told Carmen that he, Moravia, was invited, but that she wasn't. Whereupon Carmen had a fit and threatened to leave Moravia if he tried to prevent her from meeting me.

When Moravia drives me to the hotel with the three other women, I get out of his car and lean toward Carmen, over her right shoulder, so that she has to turn her head to the right and Moravia can't see me stuffing my tongue into her mouth. Moravia evidently feels the good-byes are taking too long, so he steps on the gas and zooms off—even though the producer is still climbing out from behind the driver's seat. Her right foot is on the asphalt but her right ass cheek is still in the car. I run alongside the car, which Moravia steers wildly through the pedestrians, who leap aside. I keep yelling at him—he's hard of hearing—until he finally catches on and stops the car. The producer, who's scared to death and shaking like a leaf, dashes off to safety.

That night, Carmen shows up at the Hotel Nazionale to get fucked. I rip her pants off from behind. I can sense whether a woman wants to be fucked from the front or the back. I fuck Carmen from behind.

She'd be coming for a fuck every day and every night—any time she can get rid of Moravia. But then Cloé, Idi Amin Dada's friend, bends over the reception desk at the Hotel Nazionale, sticking out her magical black butt, which orders me to fuck her before I even see her face. I kiss her sticky lips. Her tits, her belly, her hips, her thighs, and her ruthless ass are a trap for men, and you may see the trap but you can't escape it.

Cloé visits me I don't know how often. She wants me to beg her on the phone and say that I can't stand it anymore, that I'm getting blue balls—this is how she tries to make me think that fucking is not only unimportant but downright degrading. Yet her skirt smells more pungent the more often she visits. I know her kind. The man wants to fuck her no matter what, and she wants to get fucked no matter what, but she keeps teasing his cock until he ends up raping her. For her this period of his torment and hers is a sweet intensification of her randiness, which triggers an orgasm whenever she needs one.

Each time Cloé does visit, she stays a bit longer. She wears silk underwear in unbelievably beautiful colors. She truly looks like the daughter of a cannibal king. Her pussy smell, which clings to her entire body, even her hair, has a magical effect on me. Even when I'm so drained that I'm in pain from my skull down to my dick, the itching in my cock is stronger.

In L.A. she lives with me at the Château Marmont. After a meal at Le Dôme, I kiss Morgan Fairchild and her sister outside the restaurant. Cloé, seething with hatred, hisses: "You leave me—a princess!—standing in the street just to kiss that slut!"

"Why is Morgan a slut?" I ask. "Just because she's so erotic? She hasn't done anything to you. Besides, you're getting on my nerves with your princess crap. I fuck you because you're a super-cunt and not because you daydream!"

I kick her out of the hotel. That evening she comes back. We fuck all night. I rage all over her and lunge and lunge—and when she takes a leak I even go to the toilet with her.

More and more films. We plan a flick about Céline's final years. Movies in Alaska, Japan, Africa. A movie high up in the Himalayas, the Karakorum Range, where the Americans tried to storm the peak of K2. We plan a flick in the Sahara and one at sea. Movies in South

Africa, Brazil, and Alaska. Who knows which movie we're shooting? Which movies are worth drudging for? I'm more and more scared of making movies because they keep me away from my baby boy.

I'm very lonely. I'm not with my son.

I will tell you everything, Nanhoï, in case something should happen to me. People will say that I am dead. Don't believe them!

(Klaus Kinski passed away on November 23, 1991, in his cabin in Lagunitas, California. He was sixty-five. The cause of death was a massive heart attack.)

EPILOGUE

I came into this world in the form of a human, but the sun, the stars, the winds, fire, deserts, forests, mountains, skies, oceans, and clouds were trapped inside me. Do not be sad, Nanhoï. The truth is, I can never die.

For I will be in everything and see you in everything and watch over you. I am your reflection in the water of a mountain lake. I am your shadow and I am the light that creates your shadow. I am your fairy tale. Your dream. Your wishes and desires, and I am their fulfillment. I am your thirst and your hunger and your food and your drink. . . . I am your tenderness and the strength and hardness of your fists and feet. I am the gentle puff of air that caresses your eyes. And I am the icy wind that reddens your cheeks. I am the turning of the puma's head when it stares at you for a long time. I am the dandelion, whose tiny floating parachutes delight you so. I am the falling star that blazes and fades. I am the sweet flesh of the mango, which your teeth bite into. And the berry whose juice you suck. I am the leaves on which you step, and the moss on which you press your lips. I am the cobweb in the morning dew—the web that, spun across the path, clings to you and embraces you. I am the clouds that drift through your eyes. I am the fire that warms you, and the coolness that refreshes you. I am the snowflakes that kiss you with tiny mouths. And the heavy raindrops that cover you with their swollen lips. I am your instinct. Your touch. Your smell. Your taste. Your hearing. Your voice. Your will and your deed.

We can never be separated. For we have become one: light, air, fire, water, sky, wind.

INDEX